AF556194

The Rights of the Child

The Rights of the Child

Bharti Satsangi

RANDOM PUBLICATIONS
NEW DELHI (INDIA)

The Rights of the Child

ISBN 978-93-5111-510-6
© Reserved

All Rights Reserved. No Part of this book may be reproduced in any manner without written permission.

Published in 2015 in India by

RANDOM PUBLICATIONS

4376-A/4B, Gali Murari Lal, Ansari Road
New Delhi-110 002
Phone : +9111-43580356, 011-23289044, 011-43142548
e-mail: sales@randompublications.com,
info@randompublications.com, randomexports@gmail.com

Reprinted 2025

Type Setting by : Friends Media, Delhi-110089

Digitally Printed at : Replika Press Pvt. Ltd.

Preface

Children's rights are regularly violated around the world. They are suffering because their human rights are not being protected. Crimes against the innocent, the vulnerable, and the forgotten, occur everyday, in every country.

Millions of children around the world are exploited, abused, and discriminated against. They need special protection to promote their physical, mental, spiritual, moral, and social development. These children include child labourers, children affected by armed conflict, sexually exploited children, children in conflict with the law or in the care of the state, as well as children living on the streets, coping with disabilities, or suffering from discrimination because of their religious or ethnic-minority status.

It is because of the unique vulnerability of children that their rights are of priority concern of the international civil society. In 1989, the United Nations adopted the Convention on the Rights of the Child, which is the most widely and rapidly ratified of the core international human rights treaties. The Convention, together with its two optional protocols, provides a solid foundation for the protection of children's rights worldwide.

Children's rights have earned increased attention across the United Nations spectrum. Resolutions on the rights of the child have been adopted at both the Human Rights Council, and its predecessor the UN Commission on Human Rights, and the UN General Assembly. The UN has designated November 20 as Universal Children's Day, marking the day on which the Assembly adopted the Convention on the Rights of the Child in 1989.

Apart from the normal style, this book contains some thematic discussion on the rights of the child. Each and every chapter of this book gives a different outlook on the problem to the readers. The book will be highly useful to academic people, anthropologists, policy makers, NGOs, research students, development agencies and others, interested in studying the growing problems of children.

Author

Contents

1

Understanding Children's Rights

Children's rights are the human rights of children with particular attention to the rights of special protection and care afforded to the young, including their right to association with both biological parents, human identity as well as the basic needs for food, universal state-paid education, health care and criminal laws appropriate for the age and development of the child. Interpretations of children's rights range from allowing children the capacity for autonomous action to the enforcement of children being physically, mentally and emotionally free from abuse, though what constitutes "abuse" is a matter of debate. Other definitions include the rights to care and nurturing.

"A child is any human being below the age of eighteen years, unless under the law applicable to the child, majority is attained earlier." According to Cornell University, a child is a person, not a subperson, and the parent has absolute interest and possession of the child, but this is very much an American view. The term "child" does not necessarily mean minor but can include adult children as well as adult nondependent children. There are no definitions of other terms used to describe young people such as "adolescents", "teenagers," or "youth" in international law, but the children's rights movement is considered distinct from the youth rights movement.

The field of children's rights spans the fields of law, politics, religion, and morality.

As minors by law children do not have autonomy or the right to make decisions on their own for themselves in any known jurisdiction of the world. Instead their adult caregivers, including parents, social workers, teachers, youth workers, and others, are vested with that authority, depending on the circumstances. Some believe that this state of affairs gives children insufficient control over their own lives and causes them to be vulnerable. Louis Althusser has gone so far as describe this legal machinery, as it applies to children, as "repressive state apparatuses".

Structures such as government policy have been held by some commentators to mask the ways adults abuse and exploit children, resulting in child poverty, lack of educational opportunities, and child labor. On this view, children are to be regarded as a minority group towards whom society needs to reconsider the way it behaves.

Researchers have identified children as needing to be recognized as participants in society whose rights and responsibilities need to be recognized at all ages.

Definition of Children's Rights

Consensus on defining children's rights has become clearer in the last fifty years. A 1973 publication by Hillary Clinton (then an attorney) stated that children's rights were a "slogan in need of a definition". According to some researchers, the notion of children's rights is still not well defined, with at least one proposing that there is no singularly accepted definition or theory of the rights held by children.

Children's rights law is defined as the point where the law intersects with a child's life. That includes juvenile delinquency, due process for children involved in the criminal justice system, appropriate representation, and effective rehabilitative services; care and protection for children in state care; ensuring education for all children regardless of their origin, race, gender, disabilities, or abilities, and; health care and advocacy.

Types of Children's Rights

Children's rights are defined in numerous ways, including a wide spectrum of civil, cultural, economic, social and political rights. Rights tend to be of two general types: those advocating for children as autonomous persons under the law and those placing a claim on society for protection from harms perpetrated on children because of their dependency. These have been labeled as the right of empowerment and as the right to protection. One Canadian organization categorizes children's rights into three categories:

1. *Provision:* Children have the right to an adequate standard of living, health care, education and services, and to play and recreation. These include a balanced diet, a warm bed to sleep in, and access to schooling.
2. *Protection:* Children have the right to protection from abuse, neglect, exploitation and discrimination. This includes the right to safe places for children to play; constructive child rearing behavior, and acknowledgment of the evolving capacities of children.
3. *Participation:* Children have the right to participate in communities and have programs and services for themselves. This includes children's involvement in libraries and community programs, youth voice activities, and involving children as decision-makers.

In a similar fashion, the Child Rights Information Network, or CRIN for short, categorizes rights into two groups:

1. *Economic, social and cultural rights,* related to the conditions necessary to meet basic human needs such as food, shelter, education, health care, and gainful employment. Included are rights to education, adequate housing, food, water, the highest attainable standard of health, the right to work and rights at work, as well as the cultural rights of minorities and indigenous peoples.
2. *Environmental, cultural and developmental rights*, which are sometimes called "third generation rights," and including the right to live in safe and healthy environments and that groups of people have the right to cultural, political, and economic development.

Amnesty International openly advocates four particular children's rights, including the end to juvenile incarceration without parole, an end to the recruitment of military use of children, ending the death penalty for people under 21, and raising awareness of human rights in the classroom. Human Rights Watch, an international advocacy organization, includes child labor, juvenile justice, orphans and abandoned children, refugees, street children and corporal punishment.

Scholarly study generally focuses children's rights by identifying individual rights. The following rights "allow children to grow up healthy and free":

- Freedom of speech
- Freedom of thought
- Freedom from fear
- Freedom of choice and the right to make decisions
- Ownership over one's body

Other issues affecting children's rights include the military use of children, sale of children, child prostitution and child pornography.

Children's Rights vs. Youth Rights

In the majority of jurisdictions, for instance, children are not allowed to vote, to marry, to buy alcohol, to have sex, or to engage in paid employment." Within the youth rights movement, it is believed that the key difference between children's rights and youth rights is that children's rights supporters generally advocate the establishment and enforcement of protection for children and youths, while youth rights (a far smaller movement) generally advocates the expansion of freedom for children and/or youths and of rights such as suffrage.

Parental Rights

Parents affect the lives of children in a unique way, and as such their role in children's rights has to be distinguished in a particular way. Particular issues in the child-parent relationship include child neglect, child abuse, freedom of choice, corporal punishment and child custody. There have been theories offered that provide parents with rights-based practices that resolve the tension between "commonsense parenting" and children's rights. The issue is particularly relevant in legal proceedings that affect the potential emancipation of minors, and in cases where children sue their parents.

A child's rights to a relationship with both their parents is increasingly recognized as an important factor for determining the best interests of the child in divorce and child custody proceedings. Some governments have enacted laws creating a rebuttable presumption that shared parenting is in the best interests of children.

Children's Rights Movement

The Children's Rights Movement is a historical and modern movement committed to the acknowledgment, expansion, and/or regression of the rights of children around the world. While the historical definition of child has varied, the United Nations Convention on the Rights of the Child asserts that "A child is any human being below the age of eighteen years, unless under the law applicable to the child, majority is attained earlier." There are no definitions of other terms used to describe young people such as "adolescents", "teenagers" or "youth" in international law.

Thomas Spence's The Rights of Infants (1796) is an early English-language assertion of the natural rights of children.

In the USA, the Children's Rights Movement was born in the 19th century with the orphan train. In the big cities, when a child's parents died or were extremely poor, the child frequently had to go to work to support himself and/or his family. Boys generally became factory or coal workers, and girls became prostitutes or saloon girls, or else went to work in a sweat shop. All of these jobs paid only starvation wages.

In 1852, Massachusetts required children to attend school. In 1853, Charles Brace founded the Children's Aid Society, which worked hard to take street children in. The following year, the children were placed on a train headed for the West, where they were adopted, and often given work. By 1929, the orphan train stopped running altogether, but its principles lived on.

The National Child Labor Committee, an organization dedicated to the abolition of all child labor, was formed in the 1890s. It managed to pass one law, which was struck down by the Supreme Court two years later for violating a child's right to contract his work. In 1924, Congress attempted to pass a constitutional amendment that would authorize a national child labor law. This measure was blocked, and the bill was eventually dropped. It took the Great Depression to end child labor nationwide; adults had become so desperate for jobs that they would work for the same wage as children. In 1938, President Franklin D. Roosevelt signed the Fair Labor Standards Act which, amongst other things, placed limits on many forms of child labor.

Now that child labor had been effectively eradicated in parts of the world, the movement turned to other things, but it again stalled when World War II broke out and children and women began to enter the work force once more. With millions of adults at war, the children were needed to help keep the country running. In Europe, children served as couriers, intelligence collectors, and other underground resistance workers in opposition to Hitler's regime.

In the early 20th century, moves began to promote the idea of children's rights as distinct from those of adults and as requiring explicit recognition. The Polish educationalist Janusz Korczak wrote of the rights of children in his book How to Love a Child ; a later book was entitled The Child's Right to Respect. In 1917, following the Russian Revolution, the Moscow branch of the organization Proletkult produced a Declaration of Children's Rights. However, the first effective attempt to promote children's rights was the Declaration of the Rights of the Child, drafted by Eglantyne Jebb in 1923 and adopted by the League of Nations in 1924. This was accepted by the United Nations on its formation and updated in 1959, and replaced with a more extensive UN Convention on the Rights of the Child in 1989.

From the formation of the United Nations in the 1940s and extending to present day, the Children's Rights Movement has become global in focus. While the situation of children in the United States has become grave, children around the world have increasingly become engaged in illegal, forced child labor, genital mutilation, military service, and sex trafficking. Several international organizations have rallied to the assistance of children. They include Save the Children, Free the Children, and the Children's Defense Fund.

The Child Rights Information Network, or CRIN, formed in 1983, is the group of 1,600 non-governmental organizations from around the world which advocate for the implementation of the Convention on the Rights of the Child. Organization's report on their countries' progress towards implementation, as do governments that have ratified the Convention. Every 5 years reporting to the United Nations Committee on the Rights of the Child is required for governments.

While there is a long history of children's rights in the U.S., scholars contend that there is no "golden age". Many children's rights advocates in the U.S. today advocate for a smaller agenda than their international peers. Groups predominately focus on child abuse and neglect, child fatalities, foster care, youth aging out of foster care, preventing foster care placement, and adoption. A longstanding movement promoting youth rights in the United States has made substantial gains in the past.

Anti-Children's Rights propagandists often raise the spectre of Rights without Responsibilities. The Children's Rights Movement assert that it is rather the case that children have rights which adults, states and government have a responsibility to uphold. The UK maintains a position that UNCRC is not legally enforceable and is hence 'aspirational' only - albeit a 2003 ECHR ruling states: "The human rights of children and the standards to which all governments must aspire in realizing these rights for all children are set out in the Convention on the Rights of the Child.". 18 years after ratification, the four Children's Commissioners in the devolved administrations have united in calling for adoption of the Convention into domestic legislation, making children's rights legally enforceable.

Many countries have created an institute of children's rights commissioner or ombudsman, the first being Norway in 1981. Others include Finland, Sweden, and Ukraine, which was the first country worldwide to install a child in that post in 2005.

The United Nations Convention on the Rights of the Child has outlined a standard premise for the children's rights movement and has been accepted by all but two states - the United States and Somalia. Somalia's inability to sign the Convention is attributed to its lack of governmental structure. The US administration under Bush opposed ratifying the Convention, stating that there were "serious political and legal concerns that it conflicts with US policies on the central role of parents, sovereignty, and state and local law."

The Convention is supplemented by the Optional Protocol on the Involvement of Children in Armed Conflict (against military use of children) and the Optional Protocol on the Sale of Children, Child Prostitution and Child Pornography (against sale of children, child prostitution and child pornography).

The opposition to children's rights far outdates any current trend in society, with recorded statements against the rights of children dating to the 13th century and earlier. Opponents to children's rights believe that young people need to be protected from the adultcentric world, including the decisions and responsibilities of that world. In the dominate adult society, childhood is idealized as a time of innocence, a time free of responsibility and conflict, and a time dominated by play. The majority of opposition stems from concerns related to national sovereignty, states' rights, the parent-child relationship. Financial constraints and the "undercurrent of traditional values in opposition to children's rights" are cited, as well. The concept of children's rights has received little attention in the United States.

International law to Protect Child Rights

The Universal Declaration of Human Rights is seen as a basis for all international legal standards for children's rights today. There are several conventions and laws that address children's rights around the world. A number of current and historical documents affect those rights, including the 1923 Declaration of the Rights of the Child, drafted by Eglantyne Jebb and her sister Dorothy Buxton in London, England in 1919, endorsed by the League of Nations and adopted by the United Nations in 1946. It later served as the basis for the Convention on the Rights of the Child.

Convention on the Rights of the Child

The United Nations' 1989 Convention on the Rights of the Child, or CRC, is the first legally binding international instrument to incorporate the full range of human rights—civil, cultural, economic, political and social rights. Its implementation is monitored by the Committee on the Rights of the Child. National governments that ratify it commit themselves to protecting and ensuring children's rights, and agree to hold themselves accountable for this commitment before the international community. The CRC is the most widely ratified human rights treaty with 190 ratifications. Somalia and the USA are the only two countries which have not ratified the CRC. The CRC is based on four core principles, namely the principle of non discrimination, the best interests of the child, the right to life, survival and development, and considering the views of the child in decisions which affect them (according to their age and maturity). The CRC, along with international criminal accountability mechanisms such as the International Criminal Court, the Yugoslavia and Rwanda Tribunals, and the Special Court for Sierra Leone, is said to have significantly increased the profile of children's rights worldwide.

Vienna Declaration and Programme of Action

Vienna Declaration and Programme of Action urges at Section II para 47, all nations to undertake measures to the maximum extent of their available resources, with the support of international cooperation, to achieve the goals in the World Summit Plan of Action. And calls on States to integrate the Convention on the Rights of the Child into their national action plans. By means of these national action plans and through international efforts, particular priority should be placed on reducing infant and maternal mortality rates, reducing malnutrition and illiteracy rates and providing access to safe drinking water and basic education. Whenever so called for, national plans of action should be devised to combat devastating emergencies resulting from natural disasters and armed conflicts and the equally grave problem of children in extreme poverty. Further para 48 urges all states, with the support of international cooperation, to address the acute problem of children under especially difficult circumstances. Exploitation and abuse of children should be actively combated, including by addressing their root causes. Effective measures are required against female infanticide, harmful child labour, sale of children and organs, child prostitution, child pornography, as well as other forms of sexual abuse. This gave an influence to adoptions of Optional Protocol on the Involvement of Children in Armed Conflict and Optional Protocol on the Sale of Children, Child Prostitution and Child Pornography.

Enforcement

A variety of enforcement organizations and mechanisms exist to ensure children's rights. They include the Child Rights Caucus for the United Nations General Assembly Special Session on Children. It was set up to promote full implementation and compliance with the Convention on the Rights of the Child, and to ensure that child rights were given priority during the UN General Assembly Special Session on Children and its Preparatory process. The United Nations Human Rights Council was created "with the hope that it could be more objective, credible and efficient in denouncing human rights violations worldwide than the highly politicized Commission on Human Rights." The NGO Group for the Convention on the Rights of the Child is a coalition of international non-governmental organisations originally formed in 1983 to facilitate the implementation of the United Nations Convention on the Rights of the Child.

Many countries around the world have children's rights ombudspeople or children's commissioners whose official, governmental duty is to represent the interests of the public by investigating and addressing complaints reported by individual citizens regarding children's rights. Children's ombudspeople can also work for a corporation, a newspaper, an NGO, or even for the general public.

United States Law

Children are generally afforded the basic rights embodied by the Constitution, as enshrined by the Fourteenth Amendment to the United States Constitution. The Equal Protection Clause of that amendment is to apply to children, born within a marriage or not, but excludes children not yet born. This was reinforced by the landmark US Supreme Court decision of In re Gault. In this trial 15-year-old Gerald Gault of Arizona was taken into custody by local police after being accused of making an obscene telephone call. He was detained and committed to the Arizona State Industrial School until he reached the age of 21 for making an obscene phone call to an adult neighbor. In an 8–1 decision, the Court ruled that in hearings which could result in commitment to an institution, people under the age of 18 have the right to notice and counsel, to question witnesses, and to protection against self-incrimination. The Court found that the procedures used in Gault's hearing met none of these requirements.

There are other concerns in the United States regarding children's rights. The American Academy of Adoption Attorneys is concerned with children's rights to a safe, supportive and stable family structure. Their position on children's rights in adoption cases states that, "children have a constitutionally based liberty interest in the protection of their established families, rights which are at least equal to, and we believe outweigh, the rights of others who would claim a 'possessory' interest in these children." Other issues raised in American children's rights advocacy include children's rights to inheritance in same-sex marriages and particular rights for youth.

German Law

A report filed by the President of the INGO Conference of the Council of Europe, Annelise Oeschger finds that children and their parents are subject to United Nations, European Union and UNICEF human rights violations. Of particular concern is the German (and Austrian) agency, Jugendamt (German: Youth office) that often unfairly allows for unchecked government control of the parent-child relationship, which have resulted in harm including torture, degrading, cruel treatment and has led to children's death. The problem is complicated by the nearly "unlimited power" of the Jugendamt officers, with no processes to review or resolve inappropriate or harmful treatment. By German law, Jugendamt officers are protected against prosecution. Jugendamt (JA) officers span of control is seen in cases that go to family court where experts testimony may be overturned by lesser educated or experienced JA officers; In more than 90% of the cases the JA officer's recommendation is accepted by family court. Officers have also disregarded family court decisions, such as when to return children to their parents, without repercussions. Germany has not recognized related child-welfare decisions made by the European Parliamentary Court that have sought to protect or resolve children and parental rights violations.

References

Ahearn, D., Holzer, B. with Andrews, L. (2000) *Children's Rights Law: A Career Guide.* Harvard Law School. Retrieved 2/23/08.

Covell, K. and Howe, R.B. (2001) *The Challenge of Children's Rights for Canada.* Wilfrid Laurier University Press. p 158.

Franklin, B. (2001) *The new handbook of children's rights: comparative policy and practice.* Routledge. p 19.

Starr, RH (1975) *Children's Rights: Countering the Opposition.* Paper presented at the 83rd Annual Meeting of the American Psychological Association in Chicago, Illinois, Aug. 30-Sept.

2

Abuses of Children's Rights

Child abuse is the physical, sexual or emotional mistreatment or neglect of a child or children. In the United States, the Centers for Disease Control and Prevention (CDC) and the Department for Children And Families (DCF) define child maltreatment as any act or series of acts of commission or omission by a parent or other caregiver that results in harm, potential for harm, or threat of harm to a child. Child abuse can occur in a child's home, or in the organizations, schools or communities the child interacts with. There are four major categories of child abuse: neglect, physical abuse, psychological or emotional abuse, and sexual abuse.

Different jurisdictions have developed their own definitions of what constitutes child abuse for the purposes of removing a child from his/her family and/or prosecuting a criminal charge. According to the Journal of Child Abuse and Neglect, child abuse is "any recent act or failure to act on the part of a parent or caretaker which results in death, serious physical or emotional harm, sexual abuse or exploitation, an act or failure to act which presents an imminent risk of serious harm".

Child abuse is an international phenomenon. Poverty and substance abuse are common widespread international issues, and no matter the location, show a similar trend in the correlation to child abuse.

Although these issues can likely contribute to child maltreatment, differences in cultural perspectives play a significant role in the treatment of children. In certain nations, the battle for equality within the sexes plays a large part in a child's upbringing. During the Soviet period, there were conflicts regarding the traditional housewife versus the emphasis on equality within the sexes. Some women felt a considerable amount of pressure to carry out their motherly duties, obtaining an "authoritarian" parenting style, acting dominating and emotionally distant towards her children while overly involved in her own career. Many were encouraged to use more firm and direct disciplinary methods, as well as be overbearing and overprotective of their children.

Now that this Communist Era has ended, there are many positive changes being put into play. While there is a new openness and acceptance regarding parenting styles and close relationships with children, child abuse still remains a serious concern. Although it is now more publically recognized, it has certainly not cease to exist. While controlling parenting may be less of a concern, financial difficulty, unemployment, and substance abuse still remain to be dominating factors in child abuse throughout Eastern Europe.

A study conducted by members from several Baltic and Eastern European countries, together with specialists from the United States, examined the causes of child abuse in the countries of Latvia, Lithuania, Macedonia and Moldova. In these countries, respectively, 33%, 42%, 18% and 43% of children reported at least one type of child abuse. According to their findings, there was a serious of correlations between the potential risk factors of parental employment status, alcohol abuse, and family size within the abuse ratings. In three of the four countries, parental substance abuse was considerably correlated with the presence of child abuse, and although it was a lower percentage, still showed a relationship in the fourth country (Moldova). Each country also showed a connection between the father not working outside of the home and either emotional or physical child abuse.

These cultural differences can be studied from many perspectives. Most importantly, overall parental behavior is genuinely different in various countries. Many may view child abuse, both emotional and physical, as socially acceptable. Each culture has their own "range of acceptability," and what one may view as offensive, others may seem as tolerable. Behaviors that are normal to some may be viewed as abusive to others, all depending on the societal norms of that particular country.

Asian parenting perspectives, specifically, hold different ideals from American culture. Many have described their traditions as including physical and emotional closeness that ensures a lifelong bond between parent and child, as well as establishing parental authority and child obedience through harsh discipline. Balancing disciplinary responsibilities within parenting is common in many Asian cultures, including China, Japan, Singapore, Vietnam and Korea. To some cultures, forceful parenting may be seen as abuse, but in other societies such as these, the use of force is looked at as a reflection of parental devotion.

The differences in these cultural beliefs demonstrate the importance of examining all cross-cultural perspectives when studying the concept of child abuse.

Child abuse can take several forms: The four main types are

1. physical abuse,
2. sexual abuse,
3. psychological abuse, and
4. neglect.

Physical Abuse

Physical abuse involves physical aggression directed at a child by an adult. Most nations with child-abuse laws consider the deliberate infliction of serious injuries, or actions that place the child at obvious risk of serious injury or death, to be illegal. Physical abuse is the intentional or non-accidental production of a physical injury. Bruises, scratches, burns, broken bones, lacerations, as well as repeated "mishaps," and rough treatment that could cause physical injury, are the results of physical abuse. Beyond this, there is considerable variation. The distinction between child discipline and abuse is often poorly defined. Cultural norms about what constitutes abuse vary widely: among professionals as well as the wider public, people do not agree on what behaviors constitute abuse. Some professionals claim that cultural norms that sanction physical punishment are one of the causes of child abuse, and have undertaken campaigns to redefine such norms.

Causes of Physical Abuse

The causes of physical abuse against children are numerous but listed below are some of the common causes according to Mash and Wolfe.

- Many abusive and neglectful parents have had little exposure to positive parental models and supports.

- There is often a greater degree of stress in the family environment.
- Information-processing disturbances may cause maltreating parents to misperceive or mislabel their child's behavior, which leads to inappropriate responses.
- There is often a lack of awareness or understanding of developmentally appropriate expectations.

No one single cause has been identified that explains the occurrence of all cases of physical abuse. The multifactorial nature of physical abuse requires a more comprehensive amalgam of models and conceptual frameworks to account for the heterogeneous set of cases classified as physical abuse.

Circumstances that may give rise to the occurrence of a child's injury via physically abusive actions have been organized into a typology having the following 5 subtypes:

- Caregiver's angry and uncontrolled disciplinary response to actual or perceived misconduct of the child
- Caregiver's psychological impairment, which causes resentment and rejection of the child by the caregiver and a perception of the child as different and provocative
- Child left in care of a babysitter who is abusive
- Caregiver's use of substances that disinhibit behavior
- Caregiver's entanglement in a domestic violence situation

This typology describes commonly observed circumstances that may result in nonaccidental injury to children; however, it does not shed light on why the circumstance leads to a child's injury.

Forms of Physical Abuse

- Striking
- Punching
- Pushing, pulling
- Slapping
- Striking with an object
- Excessive pinching on the body
- Kicking
- Tripping

- Kneeing
- Strangling
- Headbutting
- Drowning
- Sleep deprivation
- Exposure to cold, freezing
- Exposure to heat or radiation, burning
- Exposure to electric shock
- Placing in stress positions (tied or otherwise forced)
- Cutting or otherwise exposing somebody to something sharp
- Exposure to a dangerous animal
- Throwing or shooting a projectile
- Withholding food or medication
- Blinding a person or causing impairment of sight.
- Biting
- Eye poking

Sexual Abuse

Child sexual abuse is a form of child abuse in which an adult or older adolescent uses a child for sexual stimulation. Forms of child sexual abuse include asking or pressuring a child to engage in sexual activities (regardless of the outcome), indecent exposure (of the genitals, female nipples, etc.) to a child with intent to gratify their own sexual desires or to intimidate or groom the child, physical sexual contact with a child, or using a child to produce child pornography.

The effects of child sexual abuse can include depression, post-traumatic stress disorder, anxiety, propensity to further victimization in adulthood, and physical injury to the child, among other problems. Sexual abuse by a family member is a form of incest, and can result in more serious and long-term psychological trauma, especially in the case of parental incest.

The global prevalence of child sexual abuse has been estimated at 19.7% for females and 7.9% for males, according to a 2009 study published in Clinical Psychology Review that examined 65 studies from 22 countries. Using the available data, the highest prevalence rate of child sexual abuse geographically was found in Africa (34.4%), primarily because of high rates in South Africa; Europe showed the lowest prevalence rate (9.2%); America and Asia had prevalence rates between 10.1% and 23.9%. In the past, other research has concluded similarly that in North America, for example, approximately 15% to 25% of women and 5% to 15% of men were sexually abused when they were children. Most sexual abuse offenders are acquainted with their victims; approximately 30% are relatives of the child, most often brothers, fathers, uncles or cousins; around 60% are other acquaintances such as 'friends' of the family, babysitters, or neighbors; strangers are the offenders in approximately 10% of child sexual abuse cases. Most child sexual abuse is committed by men; studies show that women commit 14% to 40% of offenses reported against boys and 6% of offenses reported against girls. Most offenders who sexually abuse prepubescent children are pedophiles, although some offenders do not meet the clinical diagnosis standards for pedophilia.

Under the law, "child sexual abuse" is an umbrella term describing criminal and civil offenses in which an adult engages in sexual activity with a minor or exploits a minor for the purpose of sexual gratification. The American Psychiatric Association states that "children cannot consent to sexual activity with adults", and condemns any such action by an adult: "An adult who engages in sexual activity with a child is performing a criminal and immoral act which never can be considered normal or socially acceptable behavior."

Types

Child sexual abuse includes a variety of sexual offenses, including:

1. *Sexual assault* – a term defining offenses in which an adult touches a minor for the purpose of sexual gratification; for example, rape (including sodomy), and sexual penetration with an object. Most U.S. states include, in their definitions of sexual assault, any penetrative contact of a minor's body, however slight, if the contact is performed for the purpose of sexual gratification.
2. *Sexual exploitation* – a term defining offenses in which an adult victimizes a minor for advancement, sexual gratification, or profit; for example, prostituting a child, and creating or trafficking in child pornography.

3. *Sexual grooming* – defines the social conduct of a potential child sex offender who seeks to make a minor more accepting of their advances, for example in an online chat room.

Incest

Incest between a child or adolescent and a related adult has been identified as the most widespread form of child sexual abuse with a huge capacity for damage to a child. One researcher stated that more than 70% of abusers are immediate family members or someone very close to the family. Another researcher stated that about 30% of all perpetrators of sexual abuse are related to their victim, 60% of the perpetrators are family acquaintances, like a neighbor, babysitter or friend and 10% of the perpetrators in child sexual abuse cases are strangers. A child sexual abuse offense where the perpetrator is related to the child, either by blood or marriage, is a form of incest described as intrafamilial child sexual abuse.

The most-often reported form of incest is father–daughter and stepfather–daughter incest, with most of the remaining reports consisting of mother/stepmother–daughter/son incest. Father–son incest is reported less often; however it is not known if the actual prevalence is less or it is under-reported by a greater margin. Similarly, some argue that sibling incest may be as common, or more common, than other types of incest: Goldman and Goldman reported that 57% of incest involved siblings; Finkelhor reported that over 90% of nuclear family incest involved siblings; while Cawson et al. show that sibling incest was reported twice as often as incest perpetrated by fathers/stepfathers.

Prevalence of parental child sexual abuse is difficult to assess due to secrecy and privacy; some estimates state that 20 million Americans have been victimized by parental incest as children.

Disclosure

Children who received supportive responses following disclosure had less traumatic symptoms and were abused for a shorter period of time than children who did not receive support. In general, studies have found that children need support and stress-reducing resources after disclosure of sexual abuse. Negative social reactions to disclosure have been found to be harmful to the survivor's well being. One study reported that children who received a bad reaction from the first person they told, especially if the person was a close family member, had worse scores as adults on general trauma symptoms, post traumatic stress disorder symptoms, and dissociation. Another study found that in most cases when children did disclose abuse, the person they talked to did not respond effectively, blamed or rejected the child, and took little or no action to stop the abuse. Non-validating and otherwise non-supportive responses to disclosure by the child's primary attachment figure may indicate a relational disturbance predating the sexual abuse that may have been a risk factor for the abuse, and which can remain a risk factor for its psychological consequences.

The American Academy of Child and Adolescent Psychiatry provides guidelines for what to say to the victim and what to do following the disclosure. Asa Don Brown has indicated: "A minimization of the trauma and its effects is commonly injected into the picture by parental caregivers to shelter and calm the child. It has been commonly assumed that focusing on children's issues too long will negatively impact their recovery. Therefore, the parental caregiver teaches the child to mask his or her issues."

Treatment

The initial approach to treating a person who has been a victim of sexual abuse is dependant upon several important factors:

- Age at the time of presentation
- Circumstances of presentation for treatment
- Co-morbid conditions

The goal of treatment is not only to treat current mental health issues, but to prevent future ones.

Children often present for treatment in one of several circumstances, including criminal investigations, custody battles, problematic behaviors, and referrals from child welfare agencies.

The three major modalities for therapy with children and teenagers are family therapy, group therapy, and individual therapy. Which course is used depends on a variety of factors that must be assessed on a case by case basis. For instance, treatment of young children generally requires strong parental involvement, and can benefit from family therapy. Adolescents tend to be more independent, and can benefit from individual or group therapy. The modality also shifts during the course of treatment, for example group therapy is rarely used in the initial stages, as the subject matter is very personal and/or embarrassing.

Major factors that affect both the pathology and response to treatment include the type and severity of the sexual act, its frequency, the age at which it occurred, and the child's family of origin. Roland C. Summit, a medical doctor had defined the different stages the victims of child sexual abuse go through, Child Sexual Abuse Accommodation Syndrome. He suggested that children who are victims of sexual abuse depict a range of symptoms that include secrecy, helplessness, entrapment, accommodation, delayed and conflicted disclosure and recantation.

Offenders

Offenders are more likely to be relatives or acquaintances of their victim than strangers. A 2006–2007 Idaho study of 430 cases found that 82% of juvenile sex offenders were known to the victims (acquaintances 46% or relatives 36%).

More offenders are male than female, though the percentage varies between studies. The percentage of incidents of sexual abuse by female perpetrators that come to the attention of the legal system is usually reported to be between 1% and 4%. Studies of sexual misconduct in US schools with female offenders have shown mixed results with rates between 4% to 43% of female offenders. Maletzky (1993) found that, of his sample of 4,402 convicted pedophilic offenders, 0.4% were female. Another study of a non-clinical population found that, among those in the their sample that had been molested, as much as a third were molested by women.

Typology

Early research in the 1970s and 1980s began to classify offenders based on their motivations and traits. Groth and Birnbaum (1978) categorized child sexual offenders into two groups, "fixated" and "regressed." Fixated were described as having a primary attraction to children, whereas regressed had largely maintained relationships with other adults, and were even married. This study also showed that adult sexual orientation was not related to the sex of the victim targeted, e.g. men who molested boys often had adult relationships with women.

Later work (Holmes and Holmes, 2002) expanded on the types of offenders and their psychological profiles. They are divided thus:

- *Situational* – does not prefer children, but offend under certain conditions.

- *Regressed* – Typically has relationships with adults, but a stressor causes them to seek children as a substitute.
- *Morally Indiscriminate* – All-around sexual deviant, who may commit other sexual offenses unrelated to children.
- *Naive/Inadequate* – Often mentally disabled in some way, finds children less threatening.
- *Preferential* – has true sexual interest in children.
- *Mysoped* – Sadistic and violent, target strangers more often than acquaintances.
- *Fixated* – Little or no activity with own age, described as an "overgrown child."

Causal Factors

Causal factors of child sex offenders are not known conclusively. The experience of sexual abuse as a child was previously thought to be a strong risk factor, but research does not show a causal relationship, as the vast majority of sexually abused children do not grow up to be adult offenders, nor do the majority of adult offenders report childhood sexual abuse. The US Government Accountability Office concluded, "the existence of a cycle of sexual abuse was not established." Prior to 1996, there was greater belief in the theory of a "cycle of violence," because most of the research done was retrospective—abusers were asked if they had experienced past abuse. Even the majority of studies found that most adult sex offenders said they had not been sexually abused during childhood, but studies varied in terms of their estimates of the percentage of such offenders who had been abused, from 0 to 79 percent. More recent prospective longitudinal research—studying children with documented cases of sexual abuse over time to determine what percentage become adult offenders—has demonstrated that the cycle of violence theory is not an adequate explanation for why people molest children.

Offenses may be facilitated by cognitive distortions of the offender, such as minimization of the abuse, victim blaming, and excuses.

Pedophilia

The term "pedophilia" refers to persistent feelings of attraction in an adult or older adolescent toward prepubescent children, whether the attraction is acted upon or not. A person with this attraction is called a "pedophile".According to the Mayo Clinic, approximately 95% of incidents of sexual abuse of children age 12 and younger are committed by offenders who meet the diagnostic criteria for pedophilia; and that such persons make up 65% of child molestation offenders. Pedophilic child molesters commit ten times more sexual acts against children than non-pedophilic child molesters.

In law enforcement, the term "pedophile" is generally used to describe those accused or convicted of child sexual abuse under sociolegal definitions of child (including both prepubescent children and adolescents younger than the local age of consent); however, not all child sexual offenders are pedophiles and not all pedophiles engage in sexual abuse of children. Law enforcement and legal professionals have begun to use the term predatory pedophile, a phrase coined by children's attorney Andrew Vachss, to refer specifically to pedophiles who engage in sexual activity with minors. The term emphasizes that child sexual abuse consists of conduct chosen by the perpetrator.

Recidivism

Recidivism rates for sex offenders are lower than for the general criminal population. Estimated rates among child sex offenders vary. One study found that 42% of offenders re-offended (either a sex crime, violent crime, or both) after they were released. Risk for re-offense was highest in the first 6 years after release, but continued to be significant even 10–31 years later, with 23% offending during this time. A study done in California in 1965 found an 18.2% recidivism rate for offenders targeting the opposite sex and a 34.5% recidivism rate for same-sex offenders after 5 years.

Child and young adolescent offenders

When a prepubescent child is sexually abused by one or more other children or adolescent youths, and no adult is directly involved, it is defined as child-on-child sexual abuse. The definition includes any sexual activity between children that occurs without consent, without equality, or due to coercion, whether the offender uses physical force, threats, trickery or emotional manipulation to compel cooperation. When sexual abuse is perpetrated by one sibling upon another, it is known as "intersibling abuse", a form of incest.

Unlike research on adult offenders, a strong causal relationship has been established between child and adolescent offenders and these offenders' own prior victimization, by either adults or other children.

Prevalence

The prevalence of child sexual abuse in Africa is compounded by the virgin cleansing myth that sexual intercourse with a virgin will cure a man of HIV or AIDS. The myth is prevalent in South Africa, Zimbabwe, Zambia and Nigeria and is being blamed for the high rate of sexual abuse against young children.

South Africa has some of the highest incidences of child and baby rape in the world. A survey by CIET found around 11% of boys and 4% of girls admitted to forcing someone else to have sex with them. In a related survey conducted among 1,500 schoolchildren, a quarter of all the boys interviewed said that "jackrolling", a term for gang rape, was fun. More than 67,000 cases of rape and sexual assaults against children were reported in 2000 in South Africa, compared to 37,500 in 1998. Child welfare groups believe that the number of unreported incidents could be up to 10 times that number. The largest increase in attacks was against children under seven. The virgin cleansing myth is especially common in South Africa, which has the highest number of HIV-positive citizens in the world. Eastern Cape social worker Edith Kriel notes that "child abusers are often relatives of their victims – even their fathers and providers."

A number of high-profile baby rapes appeared since 2001 (including the fact that they required extensive reconstructive surgery to rebuild urinary, genital, abdominal, or tracheal systems). In 2001, a 9-month-old was raped and likely lost consciousness as the pain was too much to bear. In February 2002, an 8-month-old infant was reportedly gang raped by four men. One has been charged. The infant has required extensive reconstructive surgery. The 8-month-old infant's injuries were so extensive, increased attention on prosecution has occurred.

Child rape is on the rise in the war ravaged eastern Democratic Republic of the Congo. Aid workers blame combatants on all sides for a culture of sexual violence, who operate with much impunity.

Child sexual abuse occurs frequently in Western society. The rate of prevalence can be difficult to determine.

In the UK, a 2010 study estimated prevalence at about 5% for boys and 18% for girls (not dissimilar to a 1985 study that estimated about 8% for boys and 12% for girls). More than 23,000 incidents were recorded by the UK police between 2009 and 2010. Girls were six times more likely to be assaulted than boys with 86% of attacks taking place against them. The estimates for the United States vary widely. A literature review of 23 studies found rates of 3% to 37% for males and 8% to 71% for females, which produced an average of 17% for boys and 28% for girls, while a statistical analysis based on 16 cross-sectional studies estimated the rate to be 7.2% for males and 14.5% for females. The US Department of Health and Human Services reported 83,600 substantiated reports of sexually abused children in 2005. Including incidents which were not reported would make the total number even larger. According to Emily M. Douglas and David Finkelhor, "Several national studies have found that black and white children experienced near-equal levels of sexual abuse. Other studies, however, have found that both blacks and Latinos have an increased risk for sexual victimization".

Surveys have shown that one fifth to one third of all women reported some sort of childhood sexual experience with a male adult. A 1992 survey studying father-daughter incest in Finland reported that of the 9,000 15-year old high school girls who filled out the questionnaires, of the girls living with their biological fathers, 0.2% reported father-daughter incest experiences; of the girls living with a stepfather, 3.7% reported sexual experiences with him. The reported counts included only father-daughter incest and did not include prevalence of other forms of child sexual abuse. The survey summary stated, "the feelings of the girls about their incestual experiences are overwhelmingly negative." Others argue that prevalence rates are much higher, and that many cases of child abuse are never reported. One study found that professionals failed to report approximately 40% of the child sexual abuse cases they encountered. A study by Lawson & Chaffin indicated that many children who were sexually abused were "identified solely by a physical complaint that was later diagnosed as a venereal disease...Only 43% of the children who were diagnosed with venereal disease made a verbal disclosure of sexual abuse during the initial interview." It has been found in the epidemiological literature on CSA that there is no identifiable demographic or family characteristic of a child that can be used to bar the prospect that a child has been sexually abused.

In US schools, according to the United States Department of Education, "nearly 9.6% of students are targets of educator sexual misconduct sometime during their school career." In studies of student sex abuse by male and female educators, male students were reported as targets in ranges from 23% to 44%. In U.S. school settings same-sex (female and male) sexual misconduct against students by educators "ranges from 18–28% of reported cases, depending on the study"

Significant underreporting of sexual abuse of boys by both women and men is believed to occur due to sex stereotyping, social denial, the minimization of male victimization, and the relative lack of research on sexual abuse of boys. Sexual victimization of boys by their mothers or other female relatives is especially rarely researched or reported. Sexual abuse of girls by their mothers, and other related and/or unrelated adult females is beginning to be researched and reported despite the highly taboo nature of female–female child sex abuse. In studies where students are asked about sex offenses, they report higher levels of female sex offenders than found in adult reports. This underreporting has been attributed to cultural denial of female-perpetrated child sex abuse, because "males have been socialized to believe they should be flattered or appreciative of sexual interest from a female." Journalist Cathy Young writes that under-reporting is contributed to by the difficulty of people, including jurors, in seeing a male as a "true victim".

Nineteen percent of the world's children live in India, which constitutes 42 percent of India's total population.

In 2007 the Ministry of Women and Child Development published the "Study on Child Abuse: India 2007." It sampled 12447 children, 2324 young adults and 2449 stakeholders across 13 states. It looked at different forms of child abuse: physical abuse, sexual abuse and emotional abuse and girl child neglect in five evidence groups, namely, children in a family environment, children in school, children at work, children on the street and children in institutions.

The study's main findings included: 53.22% of children reported having faced sexual abuse. Among them 52.94% were boys and 47.06% girls. Andhra Pradesh, Assam, Bihar and Delhi reported the highest percentage of sexual abuse among both boys and girls, as well as the highest incidence of sexual assaults. 21.90% of child respondents faced severe forms of sexual abuse, 5.69% had been sexually assaulted and 50.76% reported other forms of sexual abuse. Children on the street, at work and in institutional care reported the highest incidence of sexual assault. The study also reported that 50% of abusers are known to the child or are in a position of trust and responsibility and most children had not reported the matter to anyone. Despite years of lack of any specific child sexual abuse laws in India, which treated them separately from adults in case of sexual offense, the 'Protection of Children Against Sexual Offences Bill, 2011' was passed the Indian parliament on May 22, 2012.

International Law

Child sexual abuse is outlawed nearly everywhere in the world, generally with severe criminal penalties, including in some jurisdictions, life imprisonment or capital punishment. An adult's sexual intercourse with a child below the legal age of consent is defined as statutory rape, based on the principle that a child is not capable of consent and that any apparent consent by a child is not considered to be legal consent.

The United Nations Convention on the Rights of the Child (CRC) is an international treaty that legally obliges states to protect children's rights. Articles 34 and 35 of the CRC require states to protect children from all forms of sexual exploitation and sexual abuse. This includes outlawing the coercion of a child to perform sexual activity, the prostitution of children, and the exploitation of children in creating pornography. States are also required to prevent the abduction, sale, or trafficking of children. As of November 2008, 193 countries are bound by the CRC, including every member of the United Nations except the United States and Somalia.

Psychological/emotional abuse

Psychological abuse, also referred to as emotional abuse or mental abuse, is a form of abuse characterized by a person subjecting or exposing another to behavior that may result in psychological trauma, including anxiety, chronic depression, or post-traumatic stress disorder. Such abuse is often associated with situations of power imbalance, such as abusive relationships, bullying, child abuse and abuse in the workplace. There were "no consensus views about the definition of emotional abuse." As such, clinicians and researchers have offered sometimes divergent definitions of emotional abuse. However, the widely used Conflict Tactics Scale measures roughly twenty distinct acts of "psychological aggression" in three different categories:

- Verbal aggression (e.g., saying something that upsets or annoys someone else);
- Dominant behaviours (e.g., preventing someone to have contact with their family);
- Jealous behaviors (e.g., accusing a partner of maintaining other parallel relations).

The U.S. Department of Justice defines emotionally abusive traits as including causing fear by intimidation, threatening physical harm to self, partner, children, or partner's family or friends, destruction of pets and property, forcing isolation from family, friends, or school or work.

In 1996, Health Canada argued that emotional abuse is motivated by urges for "power and discontrol", and defines emotional abuse as including rejecting, degrading, terrorizing, isolating, corrupting/exploiting and "denying emotional responsiveness" as characteristic of emotional abuse.

Several studies have argued that, unlike physical and sexual maltreatment, an isolated incident does not constitute emotional abuse. Tomison and Tucci write, "emotional abuse is characterised by a climate or pattern of behaviour(s) occurring over time [...] Thus, 'sustained' and 'repetitive' are the crucial components of any definition of emotional abuse." Andrew Vachss, an author, attorney and former sex crimes investigator, defines emotional abuse as "the systematic diminishment of another. It may be intentional or subconscious (or both), but it is always a course of conduct, not a single event."

Subtler emotionally abusive tactics include insults, putdowns, arbitrary and unpredictable inconsistency, and gaslighting (the denial that previous abusive incidents occurred). Modern technology has led to new forms of abuse, by text messaging and online cyber-bullying.

Prevalence

Domestic abuse—defined as chronic mistreatment in marriage, families, dating and other intimate relationships —- can include emotionally abusive behavior. Psychological abuse does not always lead to physical abuse, but physical abuse in domestic relationships is nearly always preceded and accompanied by psychological abuse. Murphy and O'Leary report that psychological aggression by one partner is the most reliable predictor of the other partner's likelihood of first exhibiting physical aggression.

A 2005 study by Hamel reports that "men and women physically and emotionally abuse each other at equal rates". Basile found that psychological aggression was effectively bidirectional in cases where heterosexual and homosexual couples went to court for domestic disturbances. A 2007 study of Spanish college students (n = 1,886) aged 18–27 found that psychological aggression (as measured by the Conflict Tactics Scale) is so pervasive in dating relationships that it can be regarded as a normalized element of dating, and that women are substantially more likely to exhibit psychological aggression. Similar findings have been reported in other studies. Strauss et al. found that female intimate partners in heterosexual relationships were more likely than males to use psychological aggression, including threats to hit or throw an object. A study of young adults (N = 721) by Giordano et al. found that females in intimate heterosexual relationships were more likely than males to threaten to use a knife or gun against their partner.

Numerous studies done between the 1980 and 1994 report that lesbian relationships have higher overall rates of interpersonal aggression (including psychological aggression/emotional abuse) than heterosexual or gay male relationships. Furthermore, women who have been involved with both men and women reported higher rates of abuse from their female partners.

In 1996, the National Clearinghouse on Family Violence, for Health Canada, reported that 39% of married women or common-law wives suffered emotional abuse by husbands/partners; and a 1995 survey of women 15 and over (n = 1000) 36-43% reported emotional abuse during childhood or adolescence, and 39% experienced emotional abuse in marriage/dating; this report does not address boys or men suffering emotional abuse from families or intimate partners. A BBC radio documentary on domestic abuse, including emotional maltreatment, reports that 20% of men and 30% of women have been abused by a spouse or other intimate partner.

Straus and Field report that psychological aggression is a pervasive trait of American families: "verbal attacks on children, like physical attacks, are so prevalent as to be just about universal". A 2008 study by English, et al. found that fathers and mothers were equally likely to be verbally aggressive towards their children.

Rates of reported emotional abuse in the workplace vary, with studies showing 10% 24% and 36% of respondents indicating persistent and substantial emotional abuse from coworkers.

Keashly and Jagatic found that males and females commit "emotionally abusive behaviors" in the workplace at roughly similar rates. In a web-based survey, Namie found that women were more likely to engage in workplace bullying, such as name-calling, and that the average length of abuse was 16.5 months

Characteristics of Abusers

In their review of data from the Dunedin Multidisciplinary Health and Development Study (a longitudinal birth cohort study; n = 941) Moffitt et al. report that while men exhibit more aggression overall, gender is not a reliable predictor of interpersonal aggression, including psychological aggression. The study found that whether male or female, aggressive people share a cluster of traits, including high rates of suspicion and jealousy; sudden and drastic mood swings; poor self-control; and higher than average rates of approval of violence and aggression. Moffitt et al. also argue that antisocial men exhibit two distinct types of interpersonal aggression (one against strangers, the other against intimate female partners), while antisocial women are rarely aggressive against anyone other than intimate male partners.

Male and female perpetrators of emotional and physical abuse exhibit high rates of personality disorders. Rates of personality disorder in the general population are roughly 15%-20%, while roughly 80% of abusive men in court-ordered treatment programmes have personality disorders.

Abusers may aim to avoid household chores or exercise total control of family finances. Abusers can be very manipulative, often recruiting friends, law officers and court officials, even the victim's family to their side, while shifting blame to the victim.

Effects

English, et al. report that children whose families are characterized by interpersonal violence, including psychological aggression and verbal aggression, may exhibit a range of serious disorders, including chronic depression, anxiety, post-traumatic stress disorder, dissociation and anger. Additionally, English et al. report that the impact of emotional abuse "did not differ significantly" from that of physical abuse. Johnson et al. report that, in a survey of female patients (n = 825), 24% suffered emotional abuse, and this group experienced higher rates of gynecological problems. In their study of men emotionally abused by a wife/partner or parent (n = 116), Hines and Malley-Morrison report that victims exhibit high rates of post traumatic stress disorder, drug addiction and alcoholism.

Namie's study of workplace emotional abuse found that 31% of women and 21% of men who reported workplace emotional abuse exhibited three key symptoms of post-traumatic stress disorder (hypervigilance, intrusive imagery, and avoidance behaviors). A 1998 study of male college students (n = 70) by Simonelli & Ingram found that men who were emotionally abused by their female partners exhibited higher rates of chronic depression than the general population.

A study of college students (N = 80) by Goldsmith and Freyd report that many who have experienced emotional abuse do not characterize the mistreatment as abusive. Additionally, Goldsmith and Freyd show that these people also tend to exhibit higher than average rates of alexithymia (difficulty identifying and processing their own emotions).

Jacobson et al. found that women report markedly higher rates of fear during marital conflicts. However, a rejoinder argued that Jacobson's results were invalid due to men and women's drastically differing interpretations of questionnaires. Coker et al. found that the effects of mental abuse were similar whether the victim was male or female. Pimlott-Kubiak and Cortina found that severity and duration of abuse were the only accurate predictors of aftereffects of abuse; sex of perpetrator or victim were not reliable predictors.

Analysis of large survey (N = 25,876) by LaRoche found that women abused by men were slightly more likely to seek psychological help than were men abused by women (63% vs. 62%).

Popular and clinical perception

Several studies found double-standards in how people tend to view emotional abuse by men versus emotional abuse by women. Follingstad et al. found that, when rating hypothetical vignettes of psychological abuse in marriages, professional psychologists tend to rate male abuse of females as more serious than identical scenarios describing female abuse of males: "the stereotypical association between physical aggression and males appears to extend to an association of psychological abuse and males" Similarly, Sorenson and Taylor randomly surveyed a group of Los Angeles, California residents for their opinions of hypothetical vignettes of abuse in heterosexual relationships. Their study found that abuse committed by women, including emotional and psychological abuse such as controlling or humiliating behavior, was typically viewed as less serious or detrimental than identical abuse committed by men. Additionally, Sorenson and Taylor found that respondents had a broader range of opinions about female perpetrators, representing a lack of clearly defined mores when compared to responses about male perpetrators.

According to Walsh and Shluman, "The higher rates of female initiated aggression [including psychological aggression] may result, in part, from adolescents' attitudes about the unacceptability of male aggression and the relatively less negative attitudes toward female aggression".

Hamel's 2007 study found that "prevailing patriarchal conception of intimate partner violence" led to a systematic reluctance to study women who psychologically and physically abuse their male partners.

Dutton found that men who are emotionally or physically abused often encounter victim blaming that erroneously presumes the man either provoked or deserved the mistreatment of their female partners. Similarly, domestic violence victims will often blame their own behavior, rather than the violent actions of the abuser. Victims may try continually to alter their behavior and circumstances in order to please the abuser.

Simon argues that because aggression in abusive relationships can be carried out subtly and covertly through various manipulation and control tactics, victims often don't perceive the true nature of the relationship until conditions worsen considerably.

Cultural Causes

Some scholars argue that hundreds or thousands of years of male dominated societies have created negative attitudes towards women among many men, and that wife abuse stems from "normal psychological and behavioral patterns of most men... feminists seek to understand why men in general use physical force against their partners and what functions this serves for a society in a given historical context". Similarly, Dobash and Dobash claim that "Men who assault their wives are actually living up to cultural prescriptions that are cherished in Western society—aggressiveness, male dominance and female subordination—and they are using physical force as a means to enforce that dominance", while Walker claims that men exhibit a "socialized androcentric need for power".

While some women are aggressive and dominating to male partners the majority of abuse in heterosexual partnerships, at about 80% in the USA, is by men. Note that critics stress that this Department of Justice study examines crime figures, and does not specifically address domestic abuse figures. While the categories of crime and domestic abuse may cross-over, most instances of domestic abuse are not regarded as crimes or reported to police—critics thus argue that it's inaccurate to regard the DOJ study as a comprehensive statement on domestic abuse because compelling evidence shows that men and women tend to commit emotional and physical abuse in roughly equal rates. A 2002 study reports that ten percent of violence in the UK, overall, is by females against males. However, more recent data specifically regarding domestic abuse (including emotional abuse) report that 3 in 10 women, and 2 in 10 men, have experienced domestic abuse.

Some argue that fundamentalist views of religions, which have developed in male-dominated cultures, tend to reinforce emotional abuse, citing the Book of Genesis as an example of a text that has been used to justify men abusing women: "in sorrow thou shalt bring forth children: and thy desire shall be to thy husband, and he shall rule over thee". Critics also suggest that fundamentalist religious prohibitions against divorce make it more difficult for religious men or women to leave an abusive marriage: A 1985 survey of Protestant clergy in the United States by Jim M Alsdurf found that 21% of them agreed that "no amount of abuse would justify a woman's leaving her husband ever", and 26% agreed with the statement that "a wife should submit to her husband and trust that God would honour her action by either stopping the abuse or giving her the strength to endure it."

Many older and some not so old children's stories contain gender stereotyping, and music videos and computer games for children and teenagers have been criticised for continuing to portray men as aggressive and in control, while the females are there only for their sexual allure; women are portrayed as wanting to be chased and caught when they run away.

Critics argue that legal systems have in the past endorsed these traditions of male domination and it is only in recent years that abusers have begun to be punished for their behaviour. Some laws in past centuries have however specifically prohibited punitive wife-beating: "The Body of Liberties adopted in 1641 by the Massachusetts Bay colonists states, 'Every married woman shall be free from bodily correction or stripes by her husband, unless it be in his own defense from her assault.' In 1879, Harvard University law scholar wrote, "The cases in the American courts are uniform against the right of the husband to use any chastisement, moderate or otherwise, toward the wife, for any purpose."

While recognizing that feminist researchers have done valuable work and highlighted neglected topics critics suggest that the male cultural domination hypothesis for abuse is untenable as a generalized explanation for numerous reasons:

Many variables (racial, ethnic, cultural and subcultural, nationality, religion, family dynamics, mental illness, etc.) make it difficult or impossible to define male and female roles in any meaningful way that apply to the entire population.

Studies show that disagreements about power-sharing in relationships are more strongly associated with abuse than are imbalances of power.

Research has not discovered that male privilege is a necessary and sufficient sole cause of abuse of women. On the contrary, peer-reviewed studies have produced inconsistent results when directly examining patriarchal beliefs and wife abuse. Yllo and Straus argued that "low status" women in the United States suffered higher rates of spousal abuse; however, a rejoinder argued that Yllo and Straus's interpretive conclusions were "confusing and contradictory". Smith estimated that patriarchal beliefs were a causative factor for only 20% of wife abuse. Other studies failed to find a causal link between spouse abuse and traditionalist/conservative cultural beliefs. Campbell writes that "there is not a simple linear correlation between female status and rates of wife assault". Other studies had similar findings. Additionally, a study of Hispanic Americans revealed that traditionalist men exhibited lower rates of abuse towards women.

Studies show that treatment programs based on the patriarchal privilege model are flawed due to a weak connection between abusiveness and one's cultural or social attitudes.

Numerous empirical studies challenge the concept that male abuse or control of women is culturally sanctioned. Such studies show that abusive men are widely viewed as unsuitable partners for dating or marriage. A minority of abusive men qualify as pervasively misogynistic. The majority of men who commit spousal abuse agree that their behavior was inappropriate. A minority of men approve of spousal abuse under even limited circumstances. Furthermore, the majority of men are non-abusive towards girlfriends or wives for the duration of relationships, contrary to predictions that aggression or abuse towards women is an innate element of masculine culture.

Dutton argues that the numerous studies establishing that heterosexual and gay male relationships have lower rates of abuse than lesbian relationships, and the fact that women who've been involved with both men and women were more likely to have been abused by a woman "are difficult to explain in terms of male domination". Additionally, Dutton suggests that "patriarchy must interact with psychological variables in order to account for the great variation in power-violence data. It is suggested that some forms of psychopathology lead to some men adopting patriarchal ideology to justify and rationalize their own pathology".

Child Neglect

Child neglect is a form of child maltreatment. Child neglect can be defined as a deficit in meeting a child's basic needs. Furthermore, child neglect is the failure to provide basic physical health care, supervision, nutrition, emotional nurturing, education or safe housing. Society generally believes there are necessary behaviors a caregiver must provide a child in order for the child to develop (physically, socially, and emotionally). Child neglect depends on how a child and society perceives the parents' behavior; it is not how the parent believes they are behaving towards their child. Parental failure to provide when options are available is different from failure to provide when options are not available. Poverty is often an issue and leads parents to not being able to provide. The circumstances and intentionality must be examined before defining behavior as neglectful. Child neglect is the most frequent form of abuse of children,with children that are born to young mothers at a substantial risk for neglect. In 2008, the U.S. state and local child protective services received 3.3 million reports of children being abused or neglected. Seventy-one percent of the children were classified as victims of child neglect. Maltreated children/youth were about five times more likely to have a first emergency department presentation for suicide related behavior compared to their peers, in both boys and girls. Children/youth permanently removed from their parental home because of substantiated child maltreatment are at an increased risk of a first presentation to the emergency department for suicide related behavior.

Definition

Neglect is notoriously difficult to define as there are no clear, cross-cultural standards for desirable or minimally adequate child rearing practices. Research shows that neglect often co-exists with other forms of abuse and adversity. While neglect generally refers to the absence of parental care and the chronic failure to meet children's basic needs, defining those needs has not been straightforward. "Working Together" defines neglect as:

> ..the persistent failure to meet a child's basic physical and/or psychological needs, likely to result in the serious impairment of the child's health or development. Neglect may occur during pregnancy as a result of maternal substance abuse. Once a child is born, neglect may involve a parent or carer failing to provide adequate food, clothing and shelter (including exclusion from home or abandonment); protect a child from physical and emotional harm or danger; ensure adequate supervision (including the use of inadequate care-givers); or ensure access to appropriate medical care or treatment. It may also include neglect of, or unresponsiveness to, a child's basic emotional needs.

Child neglect (also called psychological abuse) is a form of child abuse that occurs when someone intentionally does not provide a child with food, water, shelter, clothing, medical care, or other necessities. Forms of child neglect include: Allowing the child to witness violence or severe abuse between parents or adult, ignoring, insulting, or threatening the child with violence, not providing the child with a safe environment and adult emotional support, and showing reckless disregard for the child's well-being.

Other definitions of child neglect are:

- "the failure of a person responsible for a child's care and upbringing to safeguard the child's emotional and physical health and general well-being"
- acts of commission, harm to a child may or may not be the intended consequence
- the persistent failure to meet a child's basic physical and/or psychological needs resulting in serious impairment of health and/or development.

Types

There are various types of child neglect.

- Physical neglect refers to the failure to provide a child with basic necessities of life such as food and clothing;
- Medical neglect is when caregivers do not meet children's basic health care needs;
- Emotional neglect is failing to provide emotional support such as emotional security and encouragement;
- Educational/ developmental neglect is the failure to provide a child with experiences for necessary growth and development, such as not sending a child to school or giving him or her an education.
- Depending on the laws and child protective policies in your area, leaving a young child unsupervised may be considered neglect, especially if doing so places the child in danger.

Causes

The causes of child neglect are complex and can be attributed to three different levels; an intrapersonal, an inter-personal/family and a social/ ecological level. Although the causes of neglect are varied, studies suggest that, amongst other things, parental mental health problems, substance use, domestic violence, unemployment, and poverty are factors which increase the likelihood of neglect. Children that result from unintended pregnancies are more likely to suffer from abuse and neglect, they are also more likely to live in poverty. Neglectful families often experience a variety or a combination of adverse factors.

Intra-personal

At the intra-personal level, the discussion around neglectful parent's characteristics often focuses on mothers, reflecting traditional notions of women as primary caregivers for children. "Neglectful attributes" have included an inability to plan, lack of confidence about the future, difficulty with managing money, emotional immaturity, lack of knowledge of children's needs, a large number of children, being a teenage mother, high levels of stress and poor socioeconomic circumstances. Mental health problems, particularly depression, have been linked with a parent's inability to meet a child's needs. Likewise, substance misuse is believed to play a crucial role in undermining a parent's ability to cope with parental responsibilities. While the literature largely focuses on mothers, the role of fathers in neglect as well as the impact of their absence remains largely unexplored. There is still little known about whether mothers and fathers neglect differently and how this affects children. Similarly, not much is known about whether girls and boys experience neglect differently. More research in this area and a gendered analysis of neglect would be useful.

Inter-personal/Family

At the inter-personal/family level, a significant number of neglectful families are headed by a lone mother or have a transient male. Unstable and abusive relationships have also been mentioned as increasing the risk of child neglect. The impact of living with domestic violence on children frequently includes either direct violence or forced witnessing of abuse, which is potentially very damaging to children. While the UK Department of Health connects children's exposure to domestic violence to parents' failure to protect them from emotional harm, the notion of "failure to protect" has been challenged as it focuses primarily on the responsibility of the abused parent, usually the mother, who is often herself at significant risk. A recent reform to the Domestic Violence, Crime and Victims Act has introduced a new offence of causing or allowing the death of a child or vulnerable adult, thus reinforcing the notion of "failure to protect". Research on domestic violence, however, has consistently shown that supporting the non-abusive parent is good child protection. There is some indication of the cyclical and inter-generational nature of neglect. A study on childhood abuse and later sensitivity to a child's emotions showed that mothers with a self-reported history of physical abuse had higher indications of insensitivity and lack of attunement to infants' emotional cues than mothers with no history of abuse. Although the literature suggests that neglectful parents may have been affected adversely by their own past experiences, more research is needed to explore the link between past experiences of maltreatment and neglectful parenting behaviours. Alcohol and drug abuse in care-givers are important risk-factors for recurrent child maltreatment after accounting for other known risk factors; the increased risk appears to be similar between alcohol and drug abuse.

Social/Ecological

At the social/ecological level, the association between poverty and neglect has frequently been made. The NSPCC maltreatment study supports the association between neglect and lower socio-economic class. US studies have shown that less affluent families are more likely to be found to maltreat their children, particularly in the form of neglect and physical abuse, than affluent families. Some argue that many forms of physical neglect, such as inadequate clothing, exposure to environmental hazards and poor hygiene may be directly attributed to poverty whereas others are more cautious in making a direct link. While poverty is believed to increase the likelihood of neglect, poverty does not predetermine neglect. Many low-income families are not neglectful but provide loving homes for their children. However, when poverty coexists with other forms of adversity, it can negatively impact parent's ability to cope with stressors and undermine their capacity to adequately respond to their child's needs. McSherry argues that the relationship between child neglect and poverty should be seen as circular and interdependent. Where care-giver alcohol abuse is identified, children are significantly more likely to experience multiple incidents of neglect compared with children where this is not identified, as were children where other family risk factors (including markers of socioeconomic disadvantage)are found.

Effects

Effects of child neglect can differ depending on the individual and how much treatment is provided, but generally speaking child neglect that occurs in the first two years of a child's life may be more of an important precursor of childhood aggression compared to later neglect, which may not have as strong a correlation. Children who suffer from neglect most often also have attachment difficulties, cognitive deficits, emotional/ behavioral problems, and physical consequences as a result of neglect. Early neglect has the potential to modify the body's stress response, specifically cortisol levels (stress hormones) which can cause abnormalities and alter the body's overall health. Research has shown that there is a relationship between neglect and disturbed patterns of infant-caretaker attachment. If parents lack sensitivity to their baby's needs, the baby will develop insecure-anxious attachment. The neglectful behavior the child experiences will contribute to their attachment difficulties and formation of relationships in the future, or lack thereof. In addition to biological and social effects, neglect affects intellectual ability and cognitive/academic deficits. Also, children who suffer from child neglect may also suffer from anxiety or impulse-control disorders. Another result of child neglect is what people call "failure to thrive". Infants who have deficits in growth and abnormal behaviors such as withdrawal, apathy and excessive sleep are failing to thrive, rather than developing to become "healthy" individuals.

A study by Robert Wilson, a professor at Rush University Medical Center in Chicago, and his colleagues, showed for the first time that children under the age of 18 when they were moderately neglected in some manner by their caregivers had a 3 times likely risk of stroke over those with moderately low levels, after controlling for some common risk factors (they interviewed 1,040 participants ages 55 or older; after 3 1/2 years, 257 of them died and 192 were autopsied, with 89 having stroke evidence upon autopsy and another 40 had a history of it). Neglect, bullying, and abuse have previously been linked to changes in the brain's grey matter and white matter and to accelerated aging.

Intervention Programs

Fortunately, there are early intervention programs and treatments for child neglect. In addition to individual, family, group counseling and social support services, behavioral skills training programs exist to eliminate problematic behavior and teach parents "appropriate" parenting behavior. Programs, such as Triple P (Parenting Program), a positive parenting program, works with parents whose children have discernible problems. It is a multilevel, parenting and family support strategy ("Triple P"). Neglectful families often experience multiple problems and deficits, lack of knowledge, skills and resources. If parents are educated on "proper" parenting and given the appropriate resources, it could help decrease the amount of child neglect cases. When deciding whether to leave a child home alone, you will want to consider your child's physical, mental, and emotional well-being, as well as laws and policies in your State regarding this issue.

Child Abuse Fatalities

A child abuse fatality occurs when a child's death is the result of abuse or neglect, or when abuse and/or neglect are contributing factors to a child's death. In the United States, 1,730 children died in 2008 due to factors related to abuse; this is a rate of 2 per 100,000 U.S. children. Family situations which place children at risk include moving, unemployment, having non-family members living in the household. A number of policies and programs have been put in place in the U.S. to try to better understand and to prevent child abuse fatalities, including: safe-haven laws, child fatality review teams, training for investigators, shaken baby syndrome prevention programs, and child abuse death laws which mandate harsher sentencing for taking the life of a child.

Effects of Child Abuse

There are strong associations between exposure to child abuse in all its forms and higher rates of many chronic conditions. The strongest evidence comes from the Adverse Childhood Experiences (ACE's) series of studies which show correlations between exposure to abuse or neglect and higher rates in adulthood of chronic conditions, high-risk health behaviors and shortened lifespan. A recent publication, Hidden Costs in Health Care: The Economic Impact of Violence and Abuse, makes the case that such exposure represents a serious and costly public-health issue that should be addressed by the healthcare system. Child abuse is a major life stressor that has consequences involving the mental health of an adult but, the majority of studies examining the negative consequences of abuse have been focused on adolescences and young adults. It has been identified that childhood sexual abuse is a risk factor for the development of substance-related problems during adolescence and adulthood. The early experiences of child abuse can trigger the development of an internalizing disorder, such as anxiety and depression. For example, adults with a history of some form of child abuse, whether sexual abuse, physical abuse, or neglect, have more chances of developing depression than an adult who has never been abused. Child abuse can also cause problems with the neurodevelopment of a child. Research shows that abused children often develop deficits with language, deregulation of mood, behaviour and also social/emotional disturbances. These risks are elevated when child abuse is combined with traumatic events and/or fetal alcohol exposure. A big concern with researchers is the degree to which maltreated children grow up to be maltreating adults or if they exhibit social signs of abuse or neglect. Studies show that 90 percent of maltreating adults were maltreated as children in their life. When children were 2 studies show that 16 percent of 267 high risk mothers mistreated thir own children, to different effects. The first two years of a child's life is when parents invest the least in their children. Almost 7 million American infants go to child care services, like day care, and a majority of that care is poor. Serious consequences occur when young children are maltreated, including developmental issues. 16 percent of those 267 high risk mothers mistreat their two year old children in different ways. 55 percent of the children experienced physical abuse, 55 percent experienced neglect, 43 percent experienced hostile and rejecting parenting, and 43 percent experienced unavailable parenting.

Psychological Effects

Children who have a history of neglect or physical abuse are at risk of developing psychiatric problems, or a disorganized attachment style. Disorganized attachment is associated with a number of developmental problems, including dissociative symptoms, as well as anxiety, depressive, and acting out symptoms. A study by Dante Cicchetti found that 80% of abused and maltreated infants exhibited symptoms of disorganized attachment. When some of these children become parents, especially if they suffer from posttraumatic stress disorder (PTSD), dissociative symptoms, and other sequelae of child abuse, they may encounter difficulty when faced with their infant and young children's needs and normative distress, which may in turn lead to adverse consequences for their child's social-emotional development. Despite these potential difficulties, psychosocial intervention can be effective, at least in some cases, in changing the ways maltreated parents think about their young children.

Victims of childhood abuse, it is claimed, also suffer from different types of physical health problems later in life. Some reportedly suffer from some type of chronic head, abdominal, pelvic, or muscular pain with no identifiable reason. Even though the majority of childhood abuse victims know or believe that their abuse is, or can be, the cause of different health problems in their adult life, for the great majority their abuse was not directly associated with those problems, indicating that sufferers were most likely diagnosed with other possible causes for their health problems, instead of their childhood abuse. One long-term study found that up to 80% of abused people had at least one psychiatric disorder at age 21, with problems including depression, anxiety, eating disorders, and suicide attempts. One Canadian hospital found that between 36% and 76% of women mental health outpatients had been abused, as had 58% of women and 23% of men schizophrenic inpatients.

The effects of child abuse vary, depending on the type of abuse. A 2006 study found that childhood emotional and sexual abuse were strongly related to adult depressive symptoms, while exposure to verbal abuse and witnessing of domestic violence had a moderately strong association, and physical abuse a moderate one. For depression, experiencing more than two kinds of abuse exerted synergetically stronger symptoms. Sexual abuse was particularly deleterious in its intrafamilial form, for symptoms of depression, anxiety, dissociation, and limbic irritability. Childhood verbal abuse had a stronger association with anger-hostility than any other type of abuse studied, and was second only to emotional abuse in its relationship with dissociative symptoms. More generally, in the case of 23 of the 27 illnesses listed in the questionnaire of a French INSEE survey, some statistically significant correlations were found between repeated illness and family traumas encountered by the child before the age of 18 years. According to Georges Menahem, the French sociologist who found out these correlations by studying health inequalities, these relationships show that inequalities in illness and suffering are not only social. Health inequality also has its origins in the family, where it is associated with the degrees of lasting affective problems (lack of affection, parental discord, the prolonged absence of a parent, or a serious illness affecting either the mother or father) that individuals report having experienced in childhood.

Physical Effects

Children who are physically abused are likely to receive bone fractures, particularly rib fractures, and may have a higher risk of developing cancer. Children who experience child abuse & neglect are 59% more likely to be arrested as juveniles, 28% more likely to be arrested as adults, and 30% more likely to commit violent crime.

The immediate physical effects of abuse or neglect can be relatively minor (bruises or cuts) or severe (broken bones, hemorrhage, or even death). In some cases the physical effects are temporary; however, the pain and suffering they cause a child should not be discounted. Meanwhile, the long-term impact of child abuse and neglect on physical health is just beginning to be explored. The long-term effects can be:

1. *Shaken baby syndrome.* Shaking a baby is a common form of child abuse that often results in permanent neurological damage (80% of cases) or death (30% of cases). Damage results from intracranial hypertension (increased pressure in the skull) after bleeding in the brain, damage to the spinal cord and neck, and rib or bone fractures.
2. *Impaired brain development.* Child abuse and neglect have been shown, in some cases, to cause important regions of the brain to fail to form

or grow properly, resulting in impaired development. These alterations in brain maturation have long-term consequences for cognitive, language, and academic abilities. NSCAW found more than three-quarters of foster children between 1 and 2 years of age to be at medium to high risk for problems with brain development, as opposed to less than half of children in a control sample.

3. *Poor physical health.* Several studies have shown a relationship between various forms of household dysfunction (including childhood abuse) and poor health. Adults who experienced abuse or neglect during childhood are more likely to suffer from physical ailments such as allergies, arthritis, asthma, bronchitis, high blood pressure, and ulcers.

On the other hand, there are some children who are raised in child abuse, but who manage to do unexpectedly well later in life regarding the preconditions. Such children have been termed dandelion children, as inspired from the way that dandelions seem to prosper irrespective of soil, sun, drought, or rain. Such children (or currently grown-ups) are of high interest in finding factors that mitigate the effects of child abuse.

Prevention

A support-group structure is needed to reinforce parenting skills and closely monitor the child's well-being. Visiting home nurse or social-worker visits are also required to observe and evaluate the progress of the child and his/her caretaking situation. The support-group structure and visiting home nurse or social-worker visits are not mutually exclusive. Many studies have demonstrated that the two measures must be coupled together for the best possible outcome. Children's school programs regarding "good touch...bad touch" can provide children with a forum in which to role-play and learn to avoid potentially harmful scenarios. Unintended conception increases the risk of subsequent child abuse, and large family size increases the risk of child neglect. Thus a comprehensive study for the National Academy of Sciences concluded that affordable contraceptive services should form the basis for child abuse prevention. "The starting point for effective child abuse programming is pregnancy planning," according to an analysis for US Surgeon General C. Everett Koop.

April has been designated Child Abuse Prevention Month in the United States since 1983. U.S. President Barack Obama continued that tradition by declaring April 2009 Child Abuse Prevention Month. One way the

Federal government of the United States provides funding for child-abuse prevention is through Community-Based Grants for the Prevention of Child Abuse and Neglect (CBCAP).

Resources for child-protection services are sometimes limited. According to Hosin (2007), "a considerable number of traumatized abused children do not gain access to protective child-protection strategies." Briere (1992) argues that only when "lower-level violence" of children ceases to be culturally tolerated will there be changes in the victimization and police protection of children.

Treatment to Victims of Child Abuse

A number of treatments are available to victims of child abuse. Trauma-focused cognitive behavioral therapy, first developed to treat sexually abused children, is now used for victims of any kind of trauma. It targets trauma-related symptoms in children including post-traumatic stress disorder (PTSD), clinical depression and anxiety. It also includes a component for non-offending parents. Several studies have found that sexually abused children undergoing TF-CBT improved more than children undergoing certain other therapies. Data on the effects of TF-CBT for children who experienced only non-sexual abuse was not available as of 2006. The purpose of dealing with the thoughts and feelings associated with the trauma is to deal with nightmares, flashbacks and other intrusive experiences that might be spontaneously brought on by any number of discriminative stimuli in the environment or in the individual's brain. This would aid the individual in becoming less fearful of specific stimuli that would arouse debilitating fear, anger, sadness or other negative emotion.In other words, the individual would have some control or mastery over those emotions.

Abuse-focused cognitive behavioral therapy was designed for children who have experienced physical abuse. It targets externalizing behaviors and strengthens prosocial behaviors. Offending parents are included in the treatment, to improve parenting skills/practices. It is supported by one randomized study.

Rational Cognitive Emotive Behavior Therapy consists of ten distinct but interdependent steps. These steps fall into one of three theoretical orientations (i.e., rational or solution focused, cognitive emotive, and behavioral) and are intended to provide abused children and their adoptive parents with positive behavior change, corrective interpersonal skills, and greater control over themselves and their relationships. They are: 1) determining and normalizing thinking and behaving, 2) evaluating language, 3) shifting attention away from problem talk 4) describing times when the attachment problem isn't happening, 5) focusing on how family members "successfully" solve problematic attachment behavior; 6) acknowledging "unpleasant emotions" (i.e., angry, sad, scared) underlying negative interactional patterns, 7) identifying antecedents (controlling conditions) and associated negative cognitive emotive connections in behavior (reciprocal role of thought and emotion in behavioral causation), 8) encouraging previously abused children to experience or "own" negative thoughts and associated aversive emotional feelings, 9) modeling and rewarding positive behavior change (with themselves and in relationships), and 10) encouraging and rewarding thinking and behaving differently. This type of therapy shifts victims thoughts away from the bad and changes their behavior.

Child-parent psychotherapy was designed to improve the child-parent relationship following the experience of domestic violence. It targets trauma-related symptoms in infants, toddlers, and preschoolers, including PTSD, aggression, defiance, and anxiety. It is supported by two studies of one sample.

Other forms of treatment include group therapy, play therapy, and art therapy. Each of these types of treatment can be used to better assist the client, depending on the form of abuse they have experienced. Play therapy and art therapy are ways to get children more comfortable with therapy by working on something that they enjoy (coloring, drawing, painting, etc.). The design of a child's artwork can be a symbolic representation of what they are feeling, relationships with friends or family, and more. Being able to discuss and analyze a child's artwork can allow a professional to get a better insight of the child.

Seeing a therapist is the first step on the process to recovery.Therapy is the art and science of helping children make sense of their feelings, thoughts, and behavior and learn how to control their behavior and improve interactions with others.The therapist has an important role in helping a child recover from the effects of abuse and neglect. The therapist serves a number of functions, including, helping the child address issues related to abuse and neglect, serving as a model for appropriate adult-child relationships, working to improve family relationships, and supporting positive and productive peer relationships and support systems. After a therapist has assessed a victim they can begin to plan the patients specific treatment that is best for them.

Ethical Concerns

One of the most challenging ethical dilemmas arising from child abuse relates to the parental rights of abusive parents or caretakers with regard to their children, particularly in medical settings. In the United States, the 2008 New Hampshire case of Andrew Bedner drew attention to this legal and moral conundrum. Bedner, accused of severely injuring his infant daughter, sued for the right to determine whether or not she remain on life support; keeping her alive, which would have prevented a murder charge, created a motive for Bedner to act that conflicted with the apparent interests of his child. Bioethicists Jacob M. Appel and Thaddeus Mason Pope recently argued, in separate articles, that such cases justify the replacement of the accused parent with an alternative decision-maker.

Child abuse also poses ethical concerns related to confidentiality, as victims may be physically or psychologically unable to report abuse to authorities. Accordingly, many jurisdictions and professional bodies have made exceptions to standard requirements for confidentiality and legal privileges in instances of child abuse. Medical professionals, including doctors, therapists, and other mental health workers typically owe a duty of confidentiality to their patients and clients, either by law and/or the standards of professional ethics, and cannot disclose personal information without the consent of the individual concerned. This duty conflicts with an ethical obligation to protect children from preventable harm. Accordingly, confidentiality is often waived when these professionals have a good faith suspicion that child abuse or neglect has occurred or is likely to occur and make a report to local child protection authorities. This exception allows professionals to breach confidentiality and make a report even when the child or his/her parent or guardian has specifically instructed to the contrary.

International Actions against Child Abuse

There are organizations at national, state, and county levels in the United States that provide community leadership in preventing child abuse and neglect. The National Alliance of Children's Trust Funds and Prevent Child Abuse America are two national organizations with member organizations at the state level.

Many investigations into child abuse are handled on the local level by Child Advocacy Centers. Started over 25 years ago at what is now known as the National Children's Advocacy Center in Huntsville, Alabama by District Attorney Robert "Bud" Cramer these multi-disciplinary teams have met to coordinate their efforts so that cases of child abuse can be investigated quickly and efficiently, ultimately reducing trauma to the child and garnering better convictions. These Child Advocacy Centers (known as CACs) have standards set by the National Children's Alliance.

Other organizations focus on specific prevention strategies. The National Center on Shaken Baby Syndrome focuses its efforts on the specific issue of preventing child abuse that is manifested as shaken baby syndrome. Mandated reporter training is a program used to prevent ongoing child abuse.

NICHD, also known as the National Institute of Child Health & Human Development is a broad organization, but helps victims of child abuse through one of its branches. Through the Child Development and Behavior (CDB) Branch, NICHD raises awareness efforts by supporting research projects to better understand the short- and long-term impacts of child abuse and neglect. They provide programs and observe National Child Abuse Prevention Month every April since 1984. The Children's Bureau leads activities for the Month, including the release of updated statistics about child abuse and neglect, candlelight vigils, and fundraisers to support prevention activities and treatment for victims. The Bureau also sponsors a "Blue Ribbon Campaign," in which people wear blue ribbons in memory of children who have died from abuse, or in honor of individuals and organizations that have taken important steps to prevent child abuse and neglect.

References

Crosson-Tower, C. (2008). *Understanding Child Abuse and Neglect.* Boston, MA: Pearson Education.

Finkelhor, D. (19 February 2008). *Childhood Victimization: Violence, Crime, and Abuse in the Lives of Young People.* Oxford University Press. p. 244.

Hoyano, L.; Keenan C. (2007). *Child Abuse: Law and Policy Across Boundaries.* Oxford University Press.

Korbin, Jill E. (1983). *Child abuse and neglect: cross-cultural perspectives.* Berkeley, CA: University of California Press.

Turton, Jackie (2008). *Child Abuse, Gender, and Society.* New York: Routledge. p. 161..

3

Child Marriage: A Violation of Child Rights

Child marriage and child betrothal customs occur in various times and places, whereby children are given in matrimony - before marriageable age as defined by the commentator and often before puberty. Today such customs are fairly widespread in parts of Africa, Asia, Oceania and South America: in former times it occurred also in Europe. It is frequently associated with arranged marriage. In some cases only one marriage-partner is a child, usually the female, due to importance placed upon female virginity, the perceived inability of women to work for money and to women's shorter reproductive life relative to men's. An increase in the advocacy of human rights, whether as women's rights or as children's rights, has caused traditions of child marriage to decrease in many areas. In 2011, The Elders formed Girls Not Brides, a global partnership of more than 190 non-governmental organisations committed to addressing child marriage.

Child marriages may depend upon socio-economic status. The aristocracy of some cultures, as in the European feudal era tended to use child marriage as a method to secure political ties. Families were able to cement political and/or financial ties by having their children marry. The betrothal is considered a binding contract upon the families and the children. The breaking of a betrothal can have serious consequences both for the families and for the betrothed individuals themselves.

Child marriage is a violation of human rights. In most cases young girls get married off to significantly older men when they are still children. Child marriages must be viewed within a context of force and coercion, involving pressure and emotional blackmail, and children that lack the choice or capacity to give their full consent. Child marriage must therefore always be considered forced marriage because valid consent is absent - and often considered unnecessary. Child marriage is common practice in Niger, Chad, Mali, Bangladesh, India, Guinea, Burkina Faso, Central African Republic, Mozambique, Nepal, Uganda and Cameroon, where over 50% of girls are married by the age of 18. More than 30% of girls are married by the age of 18 in another eighteen countries, mostly in Asia and Africa. Poverty, protection of girls, fear of loss of virginity before marriage and related family honour, and the provision of stability during unstable social periods are suggested as significant factors in determining a girl's risk of becoming married as a child. Statistics show that child marriage is most common among the poorest groups in society.

Child Marriage in European Judaism

In Jewish Ashkenazi communities in the Middle Ages, girls were married off very young. Despite the young threshold for marriage a large age gap between the spouses was opposed. Child marriage was possible in Judaism due to the very low marriageable age for females. A ketannah (literally meaning "little [one]") was any girl between the age of 3 years and that of 12 years plus one day; a ketannah was completely subject to her father's authority, and her father could arrange a marriage for her without her agreement. If the father was dead or missing, the brothers of the ketannah, collectively, had the right to arrange a marriage for her, as had her mother, although in these situations a ketannah would always have the right to annul her marriage even if it was the first. According to the Talmud a father is commanded not to marry his daughter to anyone until she grows up and says 'I want this one'. A marriage that takes place without the consent of the girl is not an effective legal marriage. If the marriage did end (due to divorce or the husband's death), any further marriages were optional; the ketannah had the right to annul them. The choice of a ketannah to annul a marriage, known in Hebrew as mi'un (literally meaning "refusal", "denial", "protest"), lead to a true annulment, not a divorce; a divorce document (get) was not necessary, and a ketannah who did this was not regarded by legal regulations as a divorcee, in relation to the marriage. Unlike divorce, mi'un was regarded with distaste by many rabbinic writers, even in the Talmud; in earlier classical Judaism, one major faction - the House of Shammai -

argued that such annulment rights only existed during the betrothal period (erusin) and not once the actual marriage (nissu'in) had begun.

Child Marriage in Africa

Despite many poor countries enacting marriageable age laws to limit marriage to a minimum age of 16 to 18, depending on jurisdiction, traditional marriages of girls of younger ages are widespread. Poverty, religion, tradition, and conflict make the rate of child marriage in Sub-Saharan Africa similar to that in South Asia.

In many tribal systems a man pays a bride price to the girl's family in order to marry her (comparable to the customs of dowry and dower.) In many parts of Africa, this payment, in cash, cattle, or other valuables, decreases as a girl gets older. Even before a girl reaches puberty, it is common for a married girl to leave her parents to be with her husband. Many marriages are related to poverty, with parents needing the bride price of a daughter to feed, clothe, educate, and house the rest of the family. Meanwhile, a male child in these countries is more likely to gain a full education, gain employment and pursue a working life, thus tending to marry later. In Mali, the female:male ratio of marriage before age 18 is 72:1; in Kenya, 21:1.

The various reports indicate that in many Sub-Saharan countries, there is a high incidence of marriage among girls younger than 15. Many governments have tended to overlook the particular problems resulting from child marriage, including obstetric fistulae, premature births, stillbirth, sexually transmitted diseases (including cervical cancer), and malaria.

In parts of Ethiopia and Nigeria numerous girls are married before the age of 15, some as young as the age of 7. In parts of Mali 39% of girls are married before the age of 15. In Niger and Chad, over 70% of girls are married before the age of 18.

In South Africa the law provides for respecting the marriage practices of traditional marriages, whereby a person might be married as young as 12 for females and 14 for males. Early marriage is cited as "a barrier to continuing education for girls (and boys)". This includes absuma (arranged marriages set up between cousins at birth), bride kidnapping and elopement decided on by the children.

Child Marriage in India

Child marriage is a common practice in many countries around the world, however it is especially prevalent in India, where more than one third of all child brides live. According to UNICEF, 47% of girls are married by 18 years of age, and 18% are married by 15 years of age. These marriages are often performed without the consent of the girls involved in the marriage. Indian law has made child marriage illegal, but it is still widely practiced across the nation. The highest rates are seen particularly in the rural states of Andhra Pradesh, Bihar, Madhya Pradesh, Rajasthan, and Uttar Pradesh. It affects both boys and girls, but statistics show that girls are far more likely to be forced into a child marriage than boys; however the percentage of girls forced into child marriage in India has declined in recent years. Many consider child marriage to be a human rights violation, resulting in death, health problems, poverty, violence, and lack of education.

Child marriage, also known as Bal Vivaha, is believed to have begun during the medieval ages of India. At this time, the political atmosphere was turbulent and ruled by Delhi Sultans in an absolute monarchy government. The sultans had an extreme commitment to their religion and forced many to convert, causing socio-cultural unrest, and Hindu women suffered the most. These days of the Delhi Sultans produced practices such as child marriage and lowered the status of women even further. They invented the ill omen of giving birth to a female baby and believed that young unmarried girls caused disaster. Child marriage became a widespread cultural practice with various reasons to justify it, and many marriages were performed while the girl was still an infant.

Indian feudalistic society became present, where characteristics such as honor, rivalry, and animosity were important qualities to possess, and because of this, families and kingdoms created strong military alliances to preserve or destroy power between them. To ensure the alliance was upheld by both sides, each family exchanged a young member of their household who was reared and educated at the other family's estate. The children were the assurance that the alliance between the families was honored, but in case it wasn't enough, the families made a marriage arrangement to deepen the alliance even further. They believed the marriage wouldn't work if they waited for the young children to grow up because they could possibly pick someone outside of the alliance. If they performed the marriage while the children were still young and susceptible to their parents' influence, the children would have no choice but to marry who their parents chose to strengthen the alliance.

The caste system is also believed to have contributed to the growth of child marriage. Castes, which are based on birth and heredity, do not allow two people to marry if they are from different castes. This system was threatened by young people's emotions and desires to marry outside their caste, so out of necessity, child marriage was created to ensure the caste system continued.

Parents of a child entering into a child marriage are often poor and use the marriage as a way to make her future better, especially in areas with little economic opportunities. During times of war, parents will often marry off their young child to protect her from the conflicts raging around her. Some families still use child marriage to build alliances, as they did during the medieval ages. Statistically, a girl in a child marriage has less of a chance to go to school, and parents think education will undermine her ability to be a traditional wife and mother. Virginity is an important part of Indian culture, and parents want to ensure their daughters do not have pre-marital sex, and child marriage is an easy way to fix this.

Child Marriage in Middle East

Roughly half of Yemeni girls are married before 18, some as young as eight. Yemeni law set the minimum age for marriage at 15 but tribal customs often flouted the law. In 1999 the minimum marriage age of fifteen for women was abolished; the onset of puberty, interpreted by conservatives to be at the age of nine, was set as a requirement for consummation of marriage. In practice "Yemeni law allows girls of any age to wed, but it forbids sex with them until the indefinite time they're 'suitable for sexual intercourse.'"

In April 2008 Nujood Ali, a 10-year-old girl, successfully obtained a divorce after being raped under these conditions. Her case prompted calls to raise the legal age for marriage to 18. Later in 2008, the Supreme Council for Motherhood and Childhood proposed to define the minimum age for marriage at 18 years. The law was passed in April 2009, with the age voted for as 17. But the law was dropped the following day following maneuvers by opposing parliamentarians. Negotiations to pass the legislation continue. Meanwhile, Yemenis inspired by Nujood's efforts continue to push for change, with Nujood involved in at least one rally. And one awareness campaign claims to have prevented some early marriages in the Yemeni governate of Amran.

The widespread prevalence of child marriage in the Kingdom of Saudi Arabia has been documented by human rights groups. Saudi clerics have justified the marriage of girls as young as 9, with sanction from the judiciary. There are laws defining the minimum age in Saudi Arabia as young as eight years.

Child Marriage in Oceania

In Indonesia the 1947 Law on Marriage stipulates that a woman must be at least 16 years old and a man must be at least 19 years old to marry. With the popular rise of social networking sites like Facebook underage marriage appears to be increasing in areas like Gunung Kidul, Yogyakarta. Couples have reported becoming acquainted through Facebook and continuing their relationships until girls became pregnant. Among the Atjeh of Sumatra girls formerly married before puberty. The husbands, though usually older, were still unfit for sexual union. Among the islanders of Fiji, also, marriage took place before puberty.

The Marquesas Islands have been noted for their sexual culture. Many sexual activities seen as taboo in western cultures are viewed appropriate by the native culture. One of these differences is that young children are introduced and educated to sex at a very young age. Contact with Western societies has changed many of these customs, so research into their pre-Western social history has to be done by reading antique writings. Children slept in the same room as their parents and were able to witness their parents while they had sex. Intercourse simulation became real penetration as soon as boys were physically able. Adults found simulation of sex by children to be funny. As children approached 11 attitudes shifted toward girls. When a child reaches adulthood, they are educated on sexual techniques by a much older adult.

Yuri Lisyansky in his memoirs reports that:

> "The next day, as soon as it was light, we were surrounded by a still greater multitude of these people. There were now a hundred females at least; and they practised all the arts of lewd expression and gesture, to gain admission on board. It was with difficulty I could get my crew to obey the orders I had given on this subject. Amongst these females were some not more than ten years of age. But youth, it seems, is here no test of innocence; these infants, as I may call them, rivalled their mothers in the wantonness of their motions and the arts of allurement. "

Adam Johann von Krusenstern in his book about the same expedition as Yuri's, reports that a father, brought a 10-12 year old girl on his ship, and she had sex with the crew. According to the book of Charles Pierre Claret de Fleurieu and Étienne Marchand, 8 year old girls had sex and other unnatural acts, in public.

Child Marriage in United States

Laws regarding child marriage vary in the different states of the United States. Generally, children 16 and over may marry with parental consent, with the age of 18 being the minimum in all but two states to marry without parental consent. Those under 16 generally require a court order in addition to parental consent.

Until 2008 the Fundamentalist Church of Jesus Christ of Latter Day Saints practiced child marriage through the concept of 'spiritual (religious only) marriages,' as soon as girls are ready to bear children, as part of its polygamy practice and laws have raised the age of legal marriage in response to criticism of the practice. In 2008 the Church changed its policy in the United States to no longer marry individuals younger than the local legal age. In 2007 church leader Warren Jeffs was convicted of being an accomplice to statutory rape of a minor due to arranging a marriage between a 14-year-old girl and a 19-year-old man. In March 2008 the state of Texas believed that children at the Yearning For Zion Ranch were being married to adults and were being abused. The state of Texas removed all 468 children from the ranch and placed them into temporary state custody. After the Austin's 3rd Court of Appeals and the Texas Supreme Court ruled that Texas acted improperly in removing them from the YFZ Ranch, the children were returned to their parents or relatives.

Consequences of Child Marriage

Young girls who get married will most likely be forced into having sexual intercourse with their, usually much older, husbands. This has severe negative health consequences as the girl is often not psychologically, physically and sexually mature. Child brides are likely to become pregnant at an early age and there is a strong correlation between the age of a mother and maternal mortality and morbidity. Girls aged l0-14 are five times more likely to die in pregnancy or childbirth than women aged 20-24 and girls aged 15-19 are twice as likely to die. The body of a young girl is not yet ready for pregnancy and childbirth, which leads to complications such as obstructed labour and obstetric fistula. Obstetric fistula can also be caused by the early sexual relations associated with child marriage, which take place sometimes even before menarche. Good prenatal care reduces the risk of childbirth complications, but in many instances, due to their limited autonomy or freedom of movement, young wives have no access to health services, which aggravates the risks of maternal complications and mortality for pregnant adolescents. Because young girls are not ready for the responsibilities and roles of being a wife, sexual partner and a mother, child marriage has a serious negative impact on their psychological well-being and personal development.

Early Maternal Deaths

Roza Olyai, an Indian gynecologist and the National Chairperson for the Adolescent Health Committee of the Federation of the Obstetric and Gynecological Societies of India said,

"Early marriage has many medical risks. The reproductive organs are not fully developed. The body is not ready. Teenage mothers, especially those below 18 years, risk hypertensive disorder, eclampsia, pre-eclampsia, and post-partum hemorrhage."

Girls who marry earlier in life are less likely to be informed about reproductive issues, and because of this, pregnancy-related deaths are known to be the leading cause of mortality among married girls between 15 and 19 years of age. These girls are twice more likely to die in childbirth than girls between 20 and 24 years of age. Girls younger than 15 years of age are 5 times more likely to die in childbirth.

HIV and AIDS

Girls entering into a child marriage are sometimes significantly younger than their husbands, who can be more sexually experienced. Marrying young and being sexually active can increase a girl's chance of becoming HIV-positive by more than 75%.

On top of pregnancy-related complications, young married girls are also at high risk of contracting HIV/AIDS. Girls are disproportionately affected by HIV/AIDS as compared to boys due to physical and social factors. Young married girls are even at higher risk because their older husbands may already be infected in previous sexual relationships. Furthermore, the age difference between the girl and the husband and her low economic status make it almost impossible for the girl to negotiate safe sex or demand fidelity.

Infant Health

Infants born to mothers under the age of 18 are 60% more likely to die in their first year than to mothers over the age of 19. If the children survive, they are more likely to suffer from low birth weight, malnutrition, and late physical and cognitive development.

Fertility Outcomes

A study conducted in India by the International Institute for Population Sciences and Macro International in 2005 and 2006 showed high fertility, low fertility control, and poor fertility outcomes data within child marriages. 90.8% of young married women reported no use of a contraceptive prior to having their first child. 23.9% reported having a child within the first year of marriage. 17.3% reported having three or more children over the course of the marriage. 23% reported a rapid repeat childbirth, and 15.2% reported an unwanted pregnancy. 15.3% reported a pregnancy termination (stillbirths, miscarriages or abortions). Fertility rates are higher in slums than in urban areas.

Lack of Education and Poverty

Marrying young is often associated with a lack of education and higher rates of poverty. Because of household responsibilities, pregnancy, and child rearing, young girls do not have access to schooling and income opportunities.

Violence

Young girls in a child marriage are more likely to experience domestic violence in their marriages as opposed to older women. A study conducted in India by the International Center for Research on Women showed that girls married before 18 years of age are twice as likely to be beaten, slapped, or threatened by their husbands and three times more likely to experience sexual violence. Young brides often show symptoms of sexual abuse and post-traumatic stress.

Human Rights Violation

Child marriage is a violation of human rights and is prohibited by a number of international conventions and other instruments. Nonetheless, it is estimated that in the next ten years more than 100 million girls are likely to be married before the age of 18

The Universal Declaration of Human Rights (1948) states that men and women of full age are entitled to equal rights as to marriage, during marriage and at its dissolution. Marriage shall be entered into only with the free and full consent of the intending parties.

The Convention on Consent to Marriage, Minimum Age for Marriage and Registration of Marriages (1964) says that no marriage shall be legally entered into without the full and free consent of both parties. States should specify a minimum age for marriage (not less than 15 years) and all marriages should be registered by the competent authority.

The Convention on the Elimination of All Forms of Discrimination of Women (1979) states that the betrothal and the marriage of a child shall have no legal effect, and all necessary action, including legislation, should be taken to specify a minimum age for marriage and to make the registration of marriages in an official registry compulsory. In their general recommendations of 1994, the Committee considers that the minimum age for marriage should be 18 years for both men and women.

The African Charter on the Rights and Welfare of the Child (1990) prohibits child marriage and the betrothal of girls and boys. Effective action, including legislation, should be taken to specify the minimum age of marriage to be 18 years.

Prevention Programs

Apni Beti, Apna Dhan (ABAD), which translates to "Our Daughter, Our Wealth," is one of India's first conditional cash transfer programs dedicated to delaying young marriages across the nation. In 1994, the Indian government implemented this program in the state of Haryana. On the birth of a mother's first, second, or third child, they are set to receive 500 rupees, or 11 USD, within the first 15 days to cover their post-delivery needs. Along with this, the government gives 2,500 rupees, or 55 USD, to invest in a long-term savings bond in the daughter's name, which can be later cashed for 25,000 rupees, or 550 USD, after her 18 birthday. She can only receive the money if she is not married. Anju Malhotra, an expert on child marriage and adolescent girls said of this program, "No other conditional cash transfer has this focus of delaying marriage... It's an incentive to encourage parents to value their daughters."

The International Center for Research on Women will evaluate Apni Beti, Apna Dhan over the course of the year 2012, when the program's initial participants turn 18, to see if the program, particularly the cash incentive, has motivated parents to delay their daughters' marriages. "We have evidence that conditional cash transfer programs are very effective in keeping girls in school and getting them immunized, but we don't yet have proof that this strategy works for preventing marriage," said Pranita Achyut, the program manager for Apni Beti, Apna Dhan. "If Haryana state's approach proves to be valuable, it could potentially be scaled up to make a significant difference in many more girls' lives – and not only in India."

References

D'Onofrio, Eve (2005), "Child Brides, Inegalitarianism, and the Fundamentalist Polygamous Family in the United States",*International Journal of Law, Policy and the Family* 19 (3): 373–394

Goswami, Ruchira, 2010, "Child Marriage in India: Mapping the Trajectory of Legal Reform" http://sanhati.com/excerpted/2207/

Nour, Nawal M. (2006), "Health Consequences of Child Marriage in Africa", *Emerging Infectious Diseases* 12(11): 1644–1649

Raj, Anita, Niranjan Saggurti, Donta Balaiah, Jay G. Silverman, 2010, "Prevalence of Child Marriage and its Impact on the Fertility and Fertility Control Behaviors of Young Women in India" http://www.ncbi.nlm.nih.gov/pmc/articles/PMC2759702/

UNICEF, "Early marriage: A childhood interrupted" http://www.unicef.org/india/child_protection_1536.htm

4

Trafficking of Children

Trafficking of children is a form of human trafficking and is defined as the "recruitment, transportation, transfer, harboring, and/or receipt" of a child for the purpose of exploitation. Though statistics regarding the magnitude of child trafficking are difficult to obtain, the International Labour Organization estimates that 1.2 million children are trafficked each year. The trafficking of children has been internationally recognized as a major human rights violation, one that exists in every region of the world. Yet, it is only within the past decade that the prevalence and ramifications of this practice have risen to international prominence, due to a dramatic increase in research and public action. A variety of potential solutions have accordingly been suggested and implemented, which can be categorized as four types of action: broad protection, prevention, law enforcement, and victim assistance. Major international documents regarding child trafficking include the 1989 U.N. Convention on the Rights of the Child, the 1999 I.L.O. Worst Forms of Child Labour Convention, and the 2000 U.N. Protocol to Prevent, Suppress and Punish Trafficking in Persons, especially Women and Children.

Defining Child Trafficking

The first major international legislation concerning child trafficking is part of the 2000 United Nations Palermo protocols, titled the Protocol to Prevent, Suppress and Punish Trafficking in Persons, especially Women and Children. Article 3(a) of this document defines child trafficking as the "recruitment, transportation, transfer, harboring and/or receipt" of a child for the purpose of exploitation. The definition for child trafficking given here applies only to cases of trafficking that are transnational and/or involve organized criminal groups; in spite of this, child trafficking is now typically recognized well outside of these parameters. The International Labour Organization expands upon this definition by asserting that movement and exploitation are key aspects of child trafficking. The definition of "child" used here is that listed in the 1989 U.N. Convention on the Rights of the Child which states, "a child means every human being below the age of 18 years, unless, under the law applicable to the child, majority is attained earlier." The distinction outlined in this definition is important, because some countries have chosen to set the "age of majority" lower than 18, thus influencing exactly what legally constitutes child trafficking.

Related Legal Instruments

Many international, regional, and national instruments have been implemented that relate to and affect the practice of child trafficking. These tools have been used to define what legally constitutes trafficking of children, such that appropriate legal action can be taken against those who engage in and promote this practice. These legal instruments are called by a variety of terms, including conventions, protocols, memorandums, joint actions, recommendations, and declarations. The most significant tools are listed below:

International Human Eights Instruments

These legal instruments were developed by the United Nations in an effort to outline the international human rights of human beings and, more specifically, children.

- U.N. Universal Declaration of Human Rights, 1948
- U.N. Convention on the Rights of the Child, 1989

Labour and Migration Treaties

The trafficking of children often involves both labour and migration. As such, these international frameworks clarify instances in which these practices are illegal.

- I.L.O. Minimum Age Convention, 1973

- I.L.O. Worst Forms of Child Labour Convention, 1999
- I.L.O. Worst Forms of Child Labour Recommendation No. 190, 1999
- I.L.O. Forced Labor Convention, 1930
- I.L.O. Migrant Workers Convention (Revised), 1949
- United Nations Convention on the Protection of the Rights of All Migrant Workers and Members of Their Families, 1990

Trafficking-specific Instruments

- Protocol to Prevent, Suppress and Punish Trafficking in Persons, especially Women and Children, 2000
- The Recommended Principles and Guidelines on Human Rights and Human Trafficking, 2002

Regional Instruments

A variety of regional instruments have also been developed to guide countries in decisions regarding child trafficking. Below are some of the major instruments, though many others exist:

- Council of Europe Convention on Action against Trafficking in Human Beings (Treaty series No. 197), 2005
- Communication to the European Parliament and the Council COM(2005) 514 Final
- Multilateral cooperation agreement to combat trafficking in persons, especially women and children, in West and Central Africa, 2006
- Mekong subregional cooperation agreement to fight human trafficking (COMMIT), 2004

National Law

National laws pertaining to child trafficking continue to develop worldwide, based on the international principles that have been established. Anti-trafficking legislation has been lauded as critical by the United Nations Global Initiative to Fight Human Trafficking, because it ensures that traffickers and trafficking victims are treated accordingly: for example, "if migration laws are used to pursue traffickers, it is often the case that the victims too are prosecuted as illegal migrants, whereas if there is a specific category of 'trafficker' and 'trafficked person,' then it is more likely that the victim will be treated as such." The existence of national laws regarding child trafficking also enables trafficking victims and/or their families to take appropriate civil action.

Types of Child Trafficking

Forced labour

Forced labour is a form of child trafficking. In fact, the end goal of child trafficking is often forced labour. Forced child labour refers specifically to children used for labour who are under the stipulated minimum age, usually 14 at the lowest. UNICEF estimates that, in 2011, 150 million children aged 5-14 in developing countries were involved in child labour. Within this number, the International Labour Organization reports that most child laborers - 60% - work in agriculture. However, the International Labour Organization also estimates that 115 million children are engaged in hazardous work, such as the sex or drug trade. Overall, child labor can take many forms, and includes domestic servitude, exploitation in agriculture, service, and manufacturing industries, sexual exploitation, use of children in the armed forces and drug trades, and child begging. In terms of global trends, the International Labour Organization estimates that in 2004-2008, there was a 3% reduction in the incidence of child labor; this stands in contrast to a previous I.L.O report which found that in 2000-2004, there was a 10% reduction in child labor. Thus, the International Labour Organization contends that, globally, child labour is slowly declining. Exempt from this statistic is sub-Saharan Africa, where the number of child laborers has remained relatively constant: 1 in 4 children aged 5-17 work in this region. Another major global trend concerns the number of child laborers in the 15-17 age group: in the past five years, a 20% increase in the number of these child laborers has been reported.

Sexual Exploitation

The Optional Protocol on the Sale of Children, Child Prostitution and Child Pornography is a protocol of the Convention on the Rights of the Child, formally adopted by the United Nations in 2000. Essentially, this protocol formally requires states to prohibit the sale of children, child prostitution, and child pornography. According to the International Labour Organization, sexual exploitation of children includes all of the following practices and activities:

- "The use of girls and boys in sexual activities remunerated in cash or in kind (commonly known as child prostitution) in the streets or indoors, in such places as brothels, discotheques, massage parlours, bars, hotels, restaurants, etc."
- "The trafficking of girls and boys and adolescents for the sex trade"
- "Child sex tourism"
- "The production, promotion and distribution of pornography involving children"
- "The use of children in sex shows (public or private)"

Though measuring the extent of this practice is difficult due to its criminal and covert nature, the International Labour Organization estimates that there are as many as 1.8 million children sexually trafficked worldwide, while UNICEF's 2006 State of the World's Children Report reports this number to be 2 million. The International Labor Organization has found that girls involved in other forms of child labour - such as domestic service or street vending - are at the highest risk of being pulled into commercial child sex trafficking. A variety of sources, including the I.L.O, and scholars Erin Kunze and D.M. Hughes, also contend that the increased use and availability of the Internet has served as a major resource for traffickers, ultimately increasing the incidence of child sex trafficking. In fact, in 2009, Illinois Sheriff Thomas J. Dart sued the owners of Craigslist, a popular online classifieds website, for its "allowance" and "facilitation" of prostitution, particularly in children. In response to public and legal pressure, Craigslist has since blocked all access to its "Adult Services" section.

Children in Armed Forces

The Optional Protocol on the Involvement of Children in Armed Conflict is a protocol of the Convention on the Rights of the Child, formally adopted by the United Nations in 2000. Essentially, the protocol states that while volunteers below the age of 18 can voluntarily join the armed forces, they cannot be conscripted. As the Protocol reads, "State parties shall take all feasible measures to ensure that member of their armed forces who have not attained the age of 18 years do not take a direct part in hostilities." Despite this, the International Labour Organization estimates that "tens of thousands" of girls and boys are currently forcibly enlisted in the armed forces in at least 17 countries around the world. Children conscripted into the armed forces can then be used in three distinct ways:

- Direct roles in hostilities (combat roles)
- Supporting roles (such as messengers or spies)
- For political advantage (such as for propaganda purposes)

Recent research conducted by the Coalition to Stop the Use of Child Soldiers has also noted that girl soldiers must be uniquely recognized, in that they are especially vulnerable to acts of sexual violence. The incidence of child soldiers has become especially relevant in popular culture following the Kony 2012 movement, which aims to arrest Joseph Kony, a Ugandan war criminal who is responsible for the trafficking of thousands of child soldiers and sex slaves.

Children in Drug Trades

Children are also used in drug trades in all regions of the world. Specifically, children are often trafficked into exploitation as either drug couriers or dealers, and then 'paid' in drugs, such that they become addicted and further entrapped. Due to the illicit nature of drug trafficking, children who are apprehended are often treated as criminals, when in reality they are often the ones in need of legal assistance. While comprehensive worldwide statistics regarding the prevalence of this practice are unknown, several useful regional studies have been conducted. For example, the I.L.O has recently investigated the use of Afghan children in the heroin trade and child involvement in the drug trades of Brazil. Scholar Luke Dowdney specifically studied children in the drug trade in Rio de Janeiro, Brazil; he found that children involved in the drug trades are at significantly higher risk of engaging in violence, particularly murder.

Child Begging

Forced child begging is a type of begging in which boys and girls under the age of eighteen are forced to beg through psychological and physical coercion. Begging is defined by the Buffalo Human Rights Law Review as "the activity of asking for money as charity on the street." There is evidence to suggest that forced begging is one industry that children are trafficked into, with a recent UNICEF study reporting that thirteen percent of trafficking victims in South Eastern Europe have been trafficked for the purpose of forced begging. The United Nations protocol affirms that "the recruitment, transportation, transfer, harboring or receipt of a child for the purpose of exploitation shall be considered 'trafficking in persons' even if this does not involve any of the means set forth in subparagraph (a) of this article." With this definition the transportation of a child to an urban center for the purposes of begging constitutes trafficking regardless of whether this process was enforced by a third party or family member. The severity of this form of trafficking is starting to gain global recognition, with the International Organization for Migration (IOM), the European Union, the International Labour Organization (ILO), and the United Nations, among others, beginning to emphasize its pertinence. The European Union's Brussels Declaration on Preventing and Combating Trafficking includes child begging as one form of trafficking, stating "trafficking in human beings is an abhorrent and worrying phenomenon involving coercive sexual exploitation, labor exploitation in conditions akin to slavery, exploitation in begging and juvenile delinquency as well as domestic servitude." This issue is especially difficult to regulate given that forced begging is often imposed by family members, with parental power leveraged over a child to ensure that begging is carried out.

By definition child begging occurs in persons younger than eighteen, though forced begging has been found by UNICEF to exist among children as young as the age of two. Incidences of this practice have been recorded by the World Bank in South and Central Asia, Europe, Latin America, the Caribbean, the Middle East, and West Africa.

Most research, such as studies done by UNICEF, suggests that boys are much more likely than girls to be trafficked for the purposes of begging; experts presume this is because there is a greater female presence in trafficking for the purposes of sexual exploitation. In Albania, where forced begging is a common practice, seventy percent of victims are male.

While concrete figures are difficult to determine, the International Labor Organization (ILO) recently reported that there are at least 600,000 children involved in forced begging. The problem may be much more extensive, however, with China's Ministry of Civil Affairs reporting that as many as 1.5 million children are forced into begging. Additionally, a recent study done in Senegal by Human Rights Watch projected that a minimum of 50,000 children within the country and neighboring nations have been trafficked for the purposes of begging. Begging is often the primary source of income for street children in a number of countries, with a current study conducted by UNICEF finding that 45.7% of children who work on the streets of Zimbabwe engaged in begging, though there is no way of knowing whether it was through forced means.

Gang networks involving forced begging have been found to occur in populations of 500 or greater.

Causes

Economic factors

Forced begging is a profitable practice in which exploiters are motivated by economic incentives. The business structures of major rings of children trafficked for the purpose of begging have been examined as comparable to a medium-size business enterprise. In the most severe cases networks of children forced to beg may generate $30-40,000 USD for the profiteer. Though family networks are not nearly as extensive, a study conducted in Albania showed that a family with multiple children begging can earn up to fifteen euros a day, an amount greater than the average national teacher salary. Anti-Slavery International asserts that because this income is relatively high many families believe it is the best option available given the lack of existing capabilities. Capability deprivation, meaning the routine absence of adequate resources that serve in facilitating opportunities, may account for cross-generational begging practices within families. UNICEF studies have found that begging is especially prevalent among families in which parents are incapacitated in some way, leading children to be the sole providers.

Political factors

According to the World Bank forced begging is most commonly found in the Middle East and countries of West Africa, where laws prohibiting begging are scarce and heavy regulation of trafficking absent. In Zimbabwe, where child begging is especially prominent, the United Nations has indicated many contradictions between the Labour Act of Zimbabwe and the United Nations Convention on the Rights of the Child. Many nations, such as Indonesia, have laws against begging on the books, but the repercussions for such entail temporary detainment and eventual release back onto the streets, which does little to combat the issue.

Cultural factors

There are several cultural factors that support begging. In Europe begging is found in a number of minority cultures, especially popular within Roma and nomadic communities. In Turkey familial networks of beggars have been documented across three generations, making it deeply ingrained within their survival schemas. It is important to note that while these may be culturally rooted practices, juvenile begging by way of familial pressure still falls under the realm of forced begging. The transport of children, even one's own, for the purposes of exploitation through begging is a form of trafficking outlined by the United Nations.

Religious factors

Some religious traditions teach achieving humility through begging; however, in Senegal the World Bank has found that this Islamic religious custom has been heavily exploited for the purposes of personal gain. This malpractice is conducted by numerous marabouts, Islamic religious teachers whose role is to provide boys between the ages of 7–17 with religious training. During this time it is common to teach these boys, known as talibes, humility through begging. In a number of Western African nations, however, concerns have been raised about the exploitative nature of this tradition. Cited incidences of abuse recorded by Human Rights Watch include talibes being forced to beg for upwards of ten hours a day, being beaten if they do not meet quotas set by marabouts, routinely denied adequate food and water, and required to sleep outdoors. It is highly debated by experts whether these young men ultimately receive the Quranic education they were initially promised. According to the United Nations definition even if there exists some religious justification for begging the additional abuses incurred fall under their condemned definition of trafficking, being that "once it is established that deception, coercion, force or other prohibited means were used, consent is irrelevant and cannot be used as a defense." Despite recent exposure surrounding the issue of forced begging instated by marabouts, families continue to send their children to these Quranic schools due to both a sense of religious obligation and a lack of alternative educational opportunities. Because these children are moving away from their homes and into urban centers where they are exploited by third parties this practice is purported by Human Rights Watch to be a human trafficking issue.

General abuses

UNICEF has found that children who are forced to beg by third parties are often removed from their families, surrender the majority of their income to their exploiter, endure unsafe work and living conditions, and are at times maimed to increase profits. The process of maiming, popularized by the film Slumdog Millionaire, is common given that according to the Buffalo Human Rights Law Review children with apparent special needs often make upwards of three times as much as other children who beg. In addition to inflictions such as blindness and loss of limbs, other physical abuses for the purposes of heightening profits include pouring chili pepper on a child's tongue to give the appearance of impeded speech, the use of opium to elicit cries, and administering forced injections of drugs that will increase a child's energy and alertness. Testimonies against trafficking ring gang leaders have discussed the detainment of individuals in small cells devoid of food, water, and light to make victims weak and feeble, and thus more likely to elicit donations.

The conditions in which begging takes place commonly expose children to further physical and verbal abuse, including sexual victimization and police brutality. Research completed by Human Rights Watch revealed that when begging hours are completed for the day children often do not have proper shelter, adequate food, or access to healthcare where they reside. Furthermore, many of the gangs which run networks of forced begging have heavy drug involvement, thus the children under their control are often turned into drug addicts in order for them to become further reliant on their exploiters.

Long-term implications

Studies have shown that children forced into begging primarily receive little to no education, with upwards of sixteen hours a day dedicated to time on the streets. With education being a leading method in escaping poverty child beggars have been shown to engage in a cyclical process of continuing this practice cross-generationally. Interviews conducted by UNICEF show that children who beg have little hope for the future and do not believe their circumstances will improve. Children who work on the streets typically have little or no knowledge of their rights, leaving them especially susceptible to exploitation both as juveniles and later as adults. Children who beg have also been found by UNICEF to have much higher instances of HIV-infection due to lack of awareness and supervision on the streets.

Solutions

A victim-centered human rights approach to combating trafficking has been internationally renowned as the best possible strategy when addressing this issue, with recourse focusing on punishing the exploiter and rehabilitating the child. Some countries who emphasize this method include the United States, with the U.S. Trafficking Victims Protection Act of 2000 affirming "victims of severe forms of trafficking should not be inappropriately incarcerated, fined, or otherwise penalized solely for unlawful acts committed as a direct result of being trafficked."

Other supported methods, such as those outlined by the Buffalo Human Rights Law Review, include relying on three Ps: protection, prosecution, and prevention. Protection starts with enforcing strict measures on the matters of both trafficking and begging. For many nations the first step is the criminalization of begging and trafficking. Prosecution should be instituted in the form of greater legal ramifications for traffickers, with punishment focused on the exploiter rather than the exploited. This becomes difficult with respect to victims of familial trafficking, considering this would require changes in care placement and strict monitoring of each displaced child's welfare. Many organizations affirm that prevention begins with discouraging donations and improving services so that children, and families as a whole, have greater capabilities. Though well intentioned, by giving child beggars money individuals only make this practice more profitable and soon these funds find their way into the hands of the child's abuser.

Government response

In Senegal, where the abuses against talibes are extensive, there have been several initiatives with the help of the World Bank to put an end this exploitation. First, there is intervention on a community level with education on the validity of some of these Quranic institutions provided to rural villages that typically send their children there. This is supplemented by improved regulation of schools within the nation to ensure that they remain places of education, followed by a greater enforcement of preexisting laws banning trafficking and exploitative begging. Finally, rehabilitation services have been provided with the help of CSOs to recovered children to provide them with the capabilities they have been denied.

In Zimbabwe policy has adapted to ensure the safety of all persons under the age of sixteen with the Children's Protection and Adoption Act, however, the government admits that a lack of resources and capital play a critical role in inadequate enforcement.

In Bangladesh, where there are an estimated 700,000 beggars, a law passed in 2009 banning the practice, though officials report some trouble with enforcement.

In China, the Ministry of Public Security has established a department that solely focuses on child trafficking. Recently the department has instituted a hotline where the public dials 110 to report suspected incidences of forced begging, which law enforcement officials are expected to investigate further. The police are trained to take the children into custody if a blood relationship with their guardian cannot be established, and educate parents on the illegality and dangers of begging if they are those responsible for the child's action. This policy instituted in April 2009 has since led to the recovery of 9,300 children.

NGO initiatives

Many NGOs have initiated movements focusing on informing the public on the dangers of donations. As recently reported by UNICEF "certain behaviors, such as giving money to child beggars can also indirectly motivate traffickers and controller to demand children." The Mirror Foundation's Stop Child Begging Project of Thailand is one such organization that emphasizes eliminating the demand. Their initiatives are focused on educating passersby on the forced begging of trafficked Cambodians within their country to decrease the likelihood of donations.

Other methods

In China, where the kidnapping and forced begging of children has been routinely documented, a multi-media movement has begun. Here, blogs are utilized to publicize over 3,000 photos of children whose families believe have been abducted for the purpose of begging, with hundreds of thousands of followers who remain on the look out for these children in major urban centers. This campaign has enabled at least six children to be recovered and reunited with their families.

In instances where begging is religiously sanctioned it has been suggested by USAid that religious leaders should outwardly condemn this practice. For talibes religious leaders have been asked to take a stance against begging using passages sited in the Quran, such as "Except paradise, you should not beg anything for the sake of Allah" (8:23), which would help strip the practice of its religious foundation.

Mechanisms of Child Trafficking

In general, child trafficking takes place in three stages: recruitment, movement, and exploitation. Recruitment occurs when a child is approached by a recruiter, or in some cases, directly approaches a recruiter themselves. Recruitment is initiated in many different ways: adolescents may be under pressure to contribute to their families, children may be kidnapped or abducted into trafficking, or families may be trafficked together. Then, movement will occur - locally, regionally, and/or internationally - through a variety of transportation types, including by car, train, boat, or foot. Ultimately, the final goal of child trafficking is exploitation, whereby traffickers use the services of children to garner illegal profit. Exploitation can take place in a variety of forms, including forced labor, sexual exploitation, and child begging, among other practices.

Supply and Demand Framework

Child trafficking is often conceptualized using the economic model of supply and demand. Specifically, those who are trafficked constitute the "supply," while the traffickers, and all those who profit from the exploitation, provide the "demand." Two types of demand are defined: consumer demand and derived demand. Consumer demand is generated by people who actively or passively buy the products or services of trafficked labor. An example of this would be a tourist purchasing a t-shirt that has been made by a trafficked child. Derived demand, on the other hand, is generated by people who directly profit from the practice of trafficking, such as pimps or corrupt factory owners. Scholar Kevin Bales has extensively studied the application of this economic framework to instances of human trafficking; he contends that it is central to an accurate understanding of how trafficking is initiated and sustained. Bales, along with scholars Elizabeth M. Wheaton, Edward J. Schauer, and Thomas V. Galli, have asserted that national governments should more actively implement policies that reduce both types of demand, thus working towards the elimination of trafficking.

Social Mechanisms

Various international organizations, including the International Labor Organization and the United Nations Global Initiative to Fight Human Trafficking have linked child trafficking to poverty: Living in poverty has been found to increase children's vulnerability to trafficking. However, poverty is only one of many social "risk factors" that can lead to trafficking. As UNICEF and the World Bank note, "Often children experience several risk factors at the same time, and one of them may act as a trigger that sets the trafficking event in motion. This is sometimes called 'poverty plus,' a situation in which poverty does not by itself lead to a person being trafficked, but where a 'plus' factor such as illness combines with poverty to increase vulnerability." UNICEF, UN.GIFT and several scholars, including Una Murray and Mike Dottridge, also contend that an accurate understanding of child trafficking must incorporate an analysis of gender inequality. Specifically, in many countries, girls are at a higher risk of being trafficked, particularly into sexual exploitation. In addition, these international agencies and scholars contend that giving women and men an equal voice in anti-trafficking policy is critical to reducing the incidence of child trafficking.

Prevalence of Child Trafficking

It is difficult to obtain reliable estimates concerning the number of children trafficked each year, primarily due to the covert and criminal nature of this practice. It often takes years to gather and compile estimates regarding child trafficking and, as a result, data can seem both inadequate and outdated. This process of gathering data is only complicated by the fact that very few countries publish national estimates of child trafficking. As a result, the available statistics are widely thought to underestimate the actual scope of the problem.

Trafficking of children has been documented in every region of the world. The most reliable figure regarding the prevalence of this practice is provided by the International Labour Organization, which estimates that 1.2 million children are trafficked each year; this estimate includes cross-border and internal trafficking.

Regionally, the International Labour Organization has provided the following estimates for trafficking of children by region per year:

- Asia/Pacific: 250,000 children
- Latin America & the Caribbean: 550,000 children
- Africa: 200,000 children
- Transition economies: 200,000 children
- Developed/industrialized economies: n/a

As the numbers above indicate, child trafficking occurs the most frequently in Latin America and the Caribbean. Child trafficking is also the most prevalent in developing countries, though it does occur in developed and industrialized economies as well. Notably, the United States Department of State publishes an annual "Trafficking in Persons" report which provides ample data regarding the prevalence of human and child trafficking in the majority of countries.

According to anthropologist Samuel Pyeatt Menefee, in the late 17th and 18th centuries, in Britain, parents in poverty "sold their children (actually, their children's services, but to all intents and purposes their persons as well)". Sale motivations were more economic than for wife sales and prices, drawing from limited data, "appear to have been fairly high." Many of the boys sold were climbing boys for chimney sweeps until they were no longer small enough. Prostitution was another reason for selling a child, usually a girl. One sale was of a niece; another was the sale by a man of the daughter of a woman domestic partner who also ran his business. Some children were stolen and then sold. Purchasing was apparently also done through "baby-farming operations."

Impacts

Children and Families

According to UN.GIFT, child trafficking has the most significant impact on trafficked children and their families. First, trafficking can result in the death or permanent injury of the trafficked child. This can stem from a dangerous "movement" stage of trafficking or from specific aspects of the "exploitation" stage, such as hazardous working conditions. Moreover, trafficked children are often denied access to healthcare, effectively increasing their chances of serious injury and death. Trafficked children are also often subject to domestic violence; they may be beaten or starved in order to ensure obedience. In addition, these children frequently encounter substance abuse; they may be given drugs as "payment" or to ensure that they become addicted and thus dependent on their trafficker(s). As opposed to many other forms of crime, the trauma experienced by children who are trafficked is often prolonged and repeated, leading to severe psychological impacts. UN.GIFT reports that trafficked children often suffer from depression, anxiety, and post-traumatic stress disorder, among other conditions.

Effects on families are also severe. Some families believe that sending or allowing their children to relocate in order to find work will bring in additional income, while in reality many families will never see their trafficked children again. In addition, UN.GIFT has found that certain forms of trafficking, particularly sexual exploitation in girls, bring "shame" to families. Thus, in certain cases, children who are able to escape trafficking may return to their families only to find that they are rejected and ostracized.

Communities

Child trafficking has also been shown to have a major effect on communities. If multiple children in a community are trafficked, it can result in the entire community being corrupted, and thus devastated, by trafficking. Social development efforts are hindered, as trafficked children's educations are cut short. As a result of this lack of education, children who escape trafficking may be less able to secure employment later in life. In addition, trafficked girls face special obstacles, in that their prospects for marriage might be diminished if the community becomes aware that they have been trafficked, particularly into sexual exploitation.

Nations

On a national level, economic development is severely hindered by the lack of education of trafficked children; this results in a major loss of potentially productive future workers. Children who are able to successfully return to their families often pose a significant financial burden, due to their lack of education, and the illnesses and injuries they may have incurred during trafficking work. There are major costs associated with the rehabilitation of these trafficked children, so that they are able to successfully participate in their communities. Furthermore, the persistence of child trafficking indicates the presence of sustained criminal activity and criminal networks, which, in most cases, are also associated with drugs and violence. As a result, UN.GIFT has cited child trafficking as a significant indicator of national and global security threats.

Proposed Solutions

Solutions to child trafficking, or "anti-trafficking actions", can be roughly classified into four categories:

- *Broad protection*: "To prevent children and former victims from being (re)trafficked"

- *Prevention*: "Of the crime of child trafficking and the exploitation that is its end result"
- *Law enforcement*: "In particular within a labour context and relating to labour laws and regulations"
- *Victim assistance*: "Covering the kinds of responses necessary to help trafficked children and to reduce their vulnerability to being re-trafficked"

Broad protection actions are geared towards children who could potentially be trafficked, and include raising awareness about child trafficking, particularly in vulnerable communities. This type of outreach also includes policies geared towards improving the economic statuses of vulnerable families, so that reasonable alternatives are available to them, other than sending their children to work. Examples of this include increasing employment opportunities for adults and conditional cash transfer programs. Another major broad protection program that has been readily endorsed by UN.GIFT, the I.L.O, and UNICEF involves facilitating gender equality, specifically by enhancing both boys' and girls' access to affordable, quality education.

Preventative actions are more focused on addressing the actual practice of child trafficking, specifically by implementing legal frameworks that are aimed to both deter and prosecute traffickers. This involves the adoption and implementation of the International Labour Organization's international labour standards, as well as the development of safe and legal migration practices.

Law enforcement refers to the actual prosecution of traffickers; UNICEF maintains that successful prosecution of child traffickers is the surest way to send a message that child trafficking will not be tolerated. Traffickers can be "caught" at any one of the three steps of trafficking: recruitment, movement, and/or exploitation; anti-trafficking laws as well as child labour laws must then be appropriately enforced. The development of grassroots "surveillance" systems has also been suggested by UNICEF which would enable communities to immediately report signs of child trafficking to legal authorities.

Victim assistance begins first with victim identification; child trafficking laws must specifically and appropriately define what constitutes a "trafficking victim." Legal processes must then be in place for removing children from trafficking situations, and returning them either to their families or other appropriate settings. Victims should also be provided with individualized and supportive physical and psychological rehabilitation. Finally, steps should be taken to avoid "double victimization" - in other words, to ensure that formerly trafficked children are treated as victims, and not as criminals. An example of "double victimization" would be a child who was illegally trafficked into sexual exploitation in the United States, and then, once free from trafficking, is prosecuted for being an illegal migrant.

References

Bales, Kevin (1999). *Disposable People: New Slavery in the Global Economy*. Berkeley, CA: University of California Press

Cherneva, Iveta. "Human Trafficking For Begging." Buffalo Human Rights Law Review 17 (2011): 25. LexisNexis Academic: Law Reviews.

I.L.O.. *Commercial Sexual Exploitation of Children and Adolescents: The I.L.O.'s Response*. Retrieved March 12, 2012.

United Nations (2000). *U.N. Protocol to Prevent, Suppress and Punish Trafficking in Persons, especially Women and Children*. Retrieved February 9, 2012.

Wheaton, Elizabeth M.; Edward J. Schauer, Thomas V. Galli (2010). "Economics of Human Trafficking". *International Migration* 48 (4). Retrieved April 12, 2012.

5

Child Abduction and International Family Law

Child abduction or Child theft is the unauthorized removal of a minor (a child under the age of legal adulthood) from the custody of the child's natural parents or legally appointed guardians. The term child abduction confounds two legal and social categories which differ by their perpetrating contexts: abduction by members of the child's family or abduction by strangers.

1. *Parental Child Abduction*: A family relative's (usually parent's) unauthorized custody of a child without parental agreement and contrary to family law ruling, which largely removes the child from care, access and contact of the other parent and family side. Occurring around parental separation or divorce, such parental or familial child abduction may include parental alienation, a form of child abuse seeking to disconnect a child from targeted parent and denigrated side of family.
2. Abduction or kidnapping by strangers (from outside the family, natural or legal guardians) who steal a child for criminal purposes which may include:
   - extortion, to elicit a ransom from the guardians for the child's return
   - illegal adoption, a stranger steals a child with the intent to rear the child as their own or to sell to a prospective adoptive parent
   - human trafficking, a stranger steals a child with the intent to exploit the child themselves or by trade in a list of possible abuses

including slavery, forced labor, sexual abuse, or even illegal organ trading

- murder

Abductions by Strangers

The stereotypical version of child abduction by a stranger is the classic form of "kidnapping," exemplified by the Lindbergh kidnapping, in which the child is detained, transported some distance, held for ransom or with intent to keep the child permanently. These instances are, however, rare.

The earliest nationally publicised kidnapping of a child by a stranger for the purpose of extracting a ransom payment from the parents was the Pool case of 1819, which took place in Baltimore, Maryland. Margaret Pool, 20-months-old, was kidnapped on May 20 by Nancy Gamble (19-years-old) and secreted with the assistance of Marie Thomas. On May 22, the parents, James and Mary Pool, placed an ad in the Baltimore Patriot newspaper offering a $20 reward for Mary's return. When the child was recovered on May 23—through the efforts of members of the community who conducted a search—it was revealed that the child had been badly whipped by Gamble and bore bloody wounds. Both Gamble and Thomas were tried for the crime of kidnapping and found guilty. The motive for the crime was demonstrated to be financial. She had kidnapped the child with the intention of waiting for a reward to be offered, then would return the child and collect the money. This is a technique favored by many ransom child kidnappers before the use of written ransom demands became the favored method.. Nancy Gamble's crime and subsequent trial were reported in detail in Baltimore Patriot. The June 26 article, as well as others on the case that had appeared in the Patriot, were reprinted in newspapers in other states including: Connecticut, Maryland, Massachusetts, New Hampshire, New Jersey, New York, Pennsylvania, Vermont, Virginia and Washington D.C.

There are reports that abduction of children to be used or sold as slaves is common in parts of Africa.

The Lord's Resistance Army, a rebel paramilitary group operating mainly in northern Uganda, is notorious for its abductions of children for use as child soldiers or sex slaves. According to the Sudan Tribune, as of 2005, more than 30,000 children have been kidnapped by the LRA and their leader, Joseph Kony.

A very small number of abductions result in most cases from women who kidnap babies (or other young children) to bring up as their own. These women are often unable to have children of their own, or have miscarried, and seek to satisfy their unmet psychological need by abducting a child rather than by adopting. The crime is often premeditated, with the woman often simulating pregnancy to reduce suspicion when a baby suddenly appears in the household.

Historically, a few states have accepted child abduction as a form of punishment for political opponents or for profit. A notable case is Francoist Spain, during which an estimated 300,000 children were abducted from their parents.

Some other abductions have been to make children available by child-selling for adoption by other people, often unwittingly on the part of the new parents.

Parental Child Abduction

By far the most common kind of child abduction is parental child abduction (200,000 in 2010 alone) and often occurs when the parents separate or begin divorce proceedings. A parent may remove or retain the child from the other seeking to gain an advantage in expected or pending child-custody proceedings or because that parent fears losing the child in those expected or pending child-custody proceedings; a parent may refuse to return a child at the end of an access visit or may flee with the child to prevent an access visit or fear of domestic violence and abuse.

Parental child abductions may be within the same city, within the state region or within the same country, or may be international. Studies performed for the U.S. Department of Justice's Office of Juvenile Justice and Delinquency Prevention reported that in 1999, 53% percent of family abducted children were gone less than one week, and 21% were gone one month or more.

International Child Abduction

The term international child abduction is generally synonymous with international parental kidnapping, child snatching, and child stealing. However, the more precise legal usage of international child abduction originates in private international law and refers to the illegal removal of children from their home by an acquaintance or family member to a foreign country. In this context, "illegal" is normally taken to mean "in breach of custodial rights" and "home" is defined as the child's habitual residence. As implied by the "breach of custodial rights," the phenomenon of international child abduction generally involves an illegal removal that creates a jurisdictional conflict of laws whereby multiple authorities and jurisdictions could conceivably arrive at seemingly reasonable and conflicting custodial decisions with geographically limited application. Such a result often strongly affects a child's access and connection to half their family and may causes the loss of their former language, culture, name and nationality, it violates numerous children's rights, and can cause severe psychological and emotional trauma to the child and family left behind.

There is a common misconception that because the abductor in these cases is usually not a stranger the children are not in danger. The harmful consequences for children and families have been shown in several studies and child abduction has been characterized as a form of parental alienation and child abuse. Adding international dimensions to the detrimental effects of child abduction significantly increases the detrimental effects on children and families. The modern day ease of international travel and corollary increase in international marriages is leading to a rapid rise in the number of international child abductions.

What is today called "parental kidnapping," "international child abduction,", "parental child abduction" and "parental child trafficking" has existed as long as different legal jurisdictions and international borders have — though often under different names. None of these names achieved the modern day broad acceptance of terms like international child abduction. Lacking a common set of terminology or specifically designed laws to address the, at the time, poorly defined problem, researchers on the history of cross-border child abduction must search for terms like "custodial interference," "contempt of child custody orders," "legal kidnapping" or, in cases where children were viewed more as property than as individual subjects of rights, name variations on theft, child-maintenance debt and smuggling, among others.

Lawmakers struggled to typify and discuss international child abduction and discussions at the Hague Conference on Private International Law noted that, what some were referring to with variations on "legal kidnapping," was an oxymoron since that which is legal cannot be kidnapping and that which is kidnapping cannot be legal. The response to these concerns was the coining of the term "international child abduction." The terms first prominent use was in the title of the 1980 Hague Convention on the Civil Aspects of International Child Abduction. The term is not, however, used anywhere in the actual text of the convention itself in preference of the more technical terms "wrongful removal" or "wrongful retention" which were better suited for describing the mechanics of the Convention's system. The use of the term is now widespread in international law.

Impact on Society, Families and Children

As the result of the harmful effects on children, parental kidnapping has been characterized as a form of child abuse and an extreme form of parental alienation. Abducted children suffer emotionally and sometimes physically at the hands of their abducting parents. Many are told the other parent is dead or has abandoned them. Uprooted from their entire life, home, family and friends, abducted children are often even given new names by their abductors and instructed to hide their real names or where they used to live. Generally the abductor avoids mentioning the victim parent and waits for time to erase difficult questions, such as "When can we see mom/dad again?". These children become hostages. It is beyond their comprehension that a parent who truly cares and loves them cannot discover their whereabouts. Childhood cannot be recaptured. Abductions rob a child of their sense of history, intimacy, values and morals, self-awareness, opportunity of knowing one's beginnings and the love and contact of extended family—a loss virtually no child possesses the ability to protect themselves against.

Huntington lists some of the deleterious effects of abduction on child victims:

1. Depression;
2. Loss of community;
3. Loss of stability, security, and trust;
4. Excessive fearfulness, even of ordinary occurrences;
5. Loneliness;
6. Anger;
7. Helplessness;
8. Disruption in identity formation; and
9. Fear of abandonment.

Many of these effects can be subsumed by the problems relevant to reactive attachment disorder, stress, fear of abandonment, learned helplessness, and guilt.

The extended support systems of abducting and victim parents can also become part of the dispute. Believing primarily one side of the abduction story, family, friends, and professionals in each parents individual country may lose their objectivity. As a result, protective concerns expressed by the abandoned parent may be viewed as undue criticism, interference, and histrionics preventing the victim parent from effectively relieving the trauma imposed on their innocent child by the abduction.

Mediation in Child Abduction Cases

Mediation is a process during which abductors and the left behind family, assisted by mediator(s), attempt to resolve conflicts independent of the judicial system. Mediators create a constructive atmosphere for discussions and ensure fair dealings between parents. The mediators do not make decisions; instead, they confine themselves to assisting the parties in working out for themselves a fair and sensible solution to their problems. More specifically, the mediation can address not only the child's primary residence, but also the child's contact with both parents, visitation arrangements, agreements concerning the child's maintenance, schooling, further education, bi-cultural and bi-lingual upbringing, necessary arrangements for financial support etc.

Mediation can be helpful in international child abduction cases. In the context of mediation families can deal with the question of return and also find solutions to other issues relating to their children.

Legal Justifications for Abduction

International law has generally recognized that there may be extenuating circumstances where a child abduction may have been necessary or justifiable due to extenuating circumstances. The 1902 Convention on the Guardianship of minors limited such considerations to strictly emergency situations. Starting with the 1924 Declaration on the Rights of the Child and the 1959 United Nations Declaration on the Rights of the Child there was a growing recognition at the international level of the shift in nation's domestic laws away from parental authority and towards an emphasis on protecting the child, even from their own parents. This foreshadowed the

1989 UN Convention on the Rights of the Child and led to the establishment of exceptional circumstances in Article 13 of the Hague Abduction Convention where the removal of children would not be considered child abduction and allow the child to remain in their new country.

The principal purpose of the Abduction Convention is to cause the prompt return of a child to his or her "habitual residence." In certain exceptional cases under Article 13b, the court's mandatory return obligation is changed to a discretionary obligation, specifically, "the judicial or administrative authority of the requested State is not bound to order the return of the child if the person, institution or other body which opposes its return establishes that there is a grave risk that his or her return would expose the child to physical or psychological harm or otherwise place the child in an intolerable situation." It is important to note that the duty to return a child is not abrogated by a finding under Art. 13(b) but merely changes from mandatory to discretionary. Since the general intent of the Convention is to cause the return of a child to his or her "habitual residence," unless there are some powerful and compelling reasons otherwise the court is normally and routinely expected to exercise its discretion and return the child to his or her "habitual residence".

In the primary source of interpretation for the Convention, the Explanatory Report, Professor E. Perez-Vera noted the following:

> "it would seem necessary to underline the fact that the three types of exception to the rule concerning the return of the child must be applied only so far as they go and no further. This implies above all that they are to be interpreted in a restrictive fashion if the Convention is not to become a dead letter. In fact, the Convention as a whole rests upon the unanimous rejection of this phenomenon of illegal child removals and upon the conviction that the best way to combat them at an international level is to refuse to grant them legal recognition. The practical application of this principle requires that the signatory States be convinced that they belong, despite their differences, to the same legal community within which the authorities of each State acknowledge that the authorities of one of them - those of the child's habitual residence - are in principle best placed to decide upon questions of custody and access. As a result, a systematic invocation of the said exceptions, substituting the forum chosen by the abductor for that of the child's residence, would lead to the collapse of the whole structure of the Convention by depriving it of the spirit of mutual confidence which is its inspiration."

In spite of the spirit and intent of the Convention as conveyed by the Convention itself and further reinforced by the Perez-Vera report, Article 13b is frequently used by abductors as a vehicle to litigate the child's best interests or custody. Although Article 13(b) inquiries are not intended to deal with issues or factual questions appropriate for custody proceedings, many countries use article 13b to request psychological profiles, detailed evaluations of parental fitness, evidence concerning lifestyle and the nature and quality of relationships. These misinterpretations of the Abduction Convention's exceptions have rendered the Convention largely ineffective in accomplishing its objectives. The best interests of a child, which is explicitly never mentioned in the Convention, is an essentially subjective standard that judges often use to facilitate foreign nations' manipulation of the treaty and create a pretext for discretionary decisions. This discretion often takes the form of gender, cultural and national biases. The result is substantive non-compliance with the Abduction Convention.

Domestic Violence

At the time the Hague Abduction Convention was drafted domestic violence was never explicitly considered as an affirmative defense for child abduction. This deficiency has been attributed to the drafters of the Convention not foreseeing that the child's primary caretaker would abduct the child to escape the domestic violence of a non-custodial parent. Part of this lack of foresight is caused by the fact that, at the time of the Conventions drafting, joint custody laws were rare. One parent was usually both the custodial parent and primary caretaker while the other, non-custodial parent, had rights of access. The move towards joint custody laws conferred both the parent who acted as the primary caretaker and their ex-partner with custodial rights and, by extension, a right to request the return of children wrongfully removed from their place of habitual residence. In addition to not accounting for a shift in child custody law towards shared parenting and joint custody, the framers of the Convention also did little to account for the motivation for abducting a child, generally assuming that all abductions were harmful to children when, in fact, the child's primary caretaker may be acting altruistically by fleeing with a child to protect themselves from a dangerous domestic situation.

Internationalization of Family Law

In all family law disputes a determination must be made as to which legal systems and laws should be applied to the dispute. This question becomes orders of magnitude more complicated when aspects, or parties, of the case occur in, or hail from, multiple legal jurisdictions.

Today's international family law norms were heavily influenced by the concepts of domicile and nationality. In Europe these ideas were refined during the nineteenth century by Italian politician, Pasquale Mancini, who believed matters of personal status were to be governed by the nationality of the person. During the same period in the US and Latin America the prevailing principle was that jurisdiction over personal matters was determined by domicile which, in the Americas, was acquired immediately upon moving to a foreign jurisdiction even if neither citizenship nor nationality were acquired.

Starting in the late eighteenth century until the early 1920s a number of efforts were made to develop a series of international treaties governing international conflicts of law in Europe. Treaties that favored nationality as the determining jurisdictional factor either never got of the ground, were not widely signed or had substantial practical problems with countries renouncing them after signing. At the same time the inter-American system in Latin America produced the Bustamante Code of 1928 and the Montevideo Conventions of 1939 and 1940. Of particular note in these later Conventions was the introduction of a definition of "domicile" that started with a reference to the "habitual residence" for civil status. Lessons learned in prior efforts to create successful multilateral treaties culminated in a number of successful treaties in the mid-1900s, such as the 1961 Convention on the Protection of Minors, the New York Convention of 1956 on the Recovery Abroad of Maintenance drafted under the auspices of the United Nations, and the Hague Convention of 1961 concerning the powers of authorities and the law applicable in respect of the protection of minors ("1961 Convention.")

The 1961 Convention brought an innovation in terminology by creating a compromise between advocates of "nationality" as the determining factor for jurisdiction and advocates for the modern fact-centric model of "habitual residence." It also included expanded language to encompass both judicial and administrative authorities in response to the Boll case, in which Sweden claimed its public administrative law was exempt from the 1902 Convention on the Guardianship of minors because it only governed domestic private judicial law and not public administrative law. The 1961 Convention also emphasized the concept of the "interests of the child" as a basis for authorities of the child's nationality to overrule the authorities of the child's habitual residence. Of particularly special note, the drafters of the 1961 Convention expressly considered a provision addressing the removal of a child from their habitual residence with an intent to evade rightful jurisdiction—primarily for child custody reasons. This first attempt to codify international child abduction failed due to an inability to agree on a definition or manner of describing the phenomenon, with a number of countries that adhered to the principle of nationality regulating personal child and family law unable to classify their nationals removing children from foreign countries to their home state as fraudulent evasion.

In actual cases of international child abduction, this lack of a specific provision on child abduction in the 1961 treaty resulted in countries regularly interpreting the "habitual residence" concept of the Convention in a manner that allowed parents to take children to a foreign country and immediately acquire "habitual residence." This allowed judicial forum shopping and created perverse incentives for removing children from their homes to foreign jurisdictions in order to game the family law system and obtain a more favorable custodial outcome than could be gained in the jurisdiction of the child's home.

In the 1970s, dissatisfaction with these results led to efforts to create conventions on the foreign recognition and enforcement of judgments to make it harder for courts to favor a parent solely because that parent is a national suing in his or her home state. Canada also proposed that the Hague Conference work on a Convention to address what it termed "legal kidnapping." The Hague received Canada's request enthusiastically and, inspired by a Swiss proposal originally submitted at the Council of Europe in 1976 coined a new term in international family law — "international child abduction."

In 1980 the Hague Conference drafted a convention to address the problem of international child abduction: the Hague Convention on the Civil Aspects of International Child Abduction - commonly referred to as the Abduction Convention. The Swiss idea of restoring the status quo ante after a "wrongful removal" or "wrongful retention" became a mainstay of the Abduction Convention. Under the convention, an application could be made for the return of a child who had been wrongfully removed or retained so long as the applicant possessed rights of custody, and provided that those rights were being "actually exercised" at the time of the abduction. The concept of "actually exercised" in reference to custodial rights itself was an innovation in terminology. Having met these requirements a child was to be returned "forthwith" except in exceptional circumstances.

Inspired by the Hague Evidence Convention and the Hague Service Convention's of 1965 and 1970, the Abduction Convention required the establishment of a single Central Authority in each country that would handle two-way communications with domestic courts, administrative agencies and foreign Central Authorities. Furthermore, each Central Authority was required to take "any and all actions" to secure the goals of the treaty and cooperate with other Central Authority's to do the same. All of these new obligations emphasized the need for international cooperation amongst state parties in achieving the objectives of the Convention.

Established in 1989 the Convention on the Rights of the Child reflected the growing international consensus that children be viewed as a subject of rights and not merely as an object of rights or of protective action. The UNCRC roused an unprecedented response with 187 countries ratifying it within seven years forming an essential backdrop in international children's law. Article 11 of the Convention explicitly requires State Parties to combat the illicit transfer and retention of children and promote the conclusion of bilateral or multilateral agreements or accession to existing agreements that do so, Article 35 stipulates that "States Parties shall take all appropriate national, bilateral and multilateral measures to prevent the abduction, sale or traffic of children for any purpose or in any form."

The 1996 Convention on Jurisdiction, Applicable Law, Recognition, Enforcement and Co-operation in respect of Parental Responsibility and Measures is the third of the modern Hague Conventions on international family law, following in the footsteps of the Abduction Convention and the Adoption Convention. It is much broader in scope than the first two conventions and covers a wide range of civil measures related to the protection of children including: orders concerning parental responsibility and contact, public measures of protection or care, matters of legal representation and the protection of children's property.

The Convention has uniform rules determining which country's authorities are competent to take the necessary measures of protection. The Convention also determines which country's laws are to be applied and provides for the recognition and enforcement of measures taken in one

Contracting State in all the other Contracting States. The co-operation provisions of the Convention provide the basic framework for the exchange of information and the necessary degree of collaboration between administrative authorities in the Contracting States. Reflecting an ever increasing emphasis on the need for international cooperation as an essential element in the success of these measures the Convention has a full chapter on cooperation consisting of eleven articles.

Convention on the Civil Aspects of International Child Abduction

(Concluded 25 October 1980)

The States signatory to the present Convention,

Firmly convinced that the interests of children are of paramount importance in matters relating to their custody,

Desiring to protect children internationally from the harmful effects of their wrongful removal or retention and to establish procedures to ensure their prompt return to the State of their habitual residence, as well as to secure protection for rights of access,

Have resolved to conclude a Convention to this effect, and have agreed upon the following provisions -

Chapter I - Scope of the Convention

Article 1

The objects of the present Convention are -

a) to secure the prompt return of children wrongfully removed to or retained in any Contracting State; and

b) to ensure that rights of custody and of access under the law of one Contracting State are effectively respected in the other Contracting States.

Article 2

Contracting States shall take all appropriate measures to secure within their territories the implementation of the objects of the Convention. For this purpose they shall use the most expeditious procedures available.

Article 3

The removal or the retention of a child is to be considered wrongful where:

a) it is in breach of rights of custody attributed to a person, an institution or any other body, either jointly or alone, under the law of the State in which the child was habitually resident immediately before the removal or retention; and

b) at the time of removal or retention those rights were actually exercised, either jointly or alone, or would have been so exercised but for the removal or retention.

The rights of custody mentioned in sub-paragraph *a)* above, may arise in particular by operation of law or by reason of a judicial or administrative decision, or by reason of an agreement having legal effect under the law of that State.

Article 4

The Convention shall apply to any child who was habitually resident in a Contracting State immediately before any breach of custody or access rights. The Convention shall cease to apply when the child attains the age of 16 years.

Article 5

For the purposes of this Convention -

a) "rights of custody" shall include rights relating to the care of the person of the child and, in particular, the right to determine the child's place of residence;

b) "rights of access" shall include the right to take a child for a limited period of time to a place other than the child's habitual residence.

Chapter II - Central Authorities

Article 6

A Contracting State shall designate a Central Authority to discharge the duties which are imposed by the Convention upon such authorities.

Federal States, States with more than one system of law or States having autonomous territorial organisations shall be free to appoint more than one Central Authority and to specify the territorial extent of their powers. Where a State has appointed more than one Central Authority, it shall designate the Central Authority to which applications may be addressed for transmission to the appropriate Central Authority within that State.

Article 7

Central Authorities shall co-operate with each other and promote co-operation amongst the competent authorities in their respective States to secure the prompt return of children and to achieve the other objects of this Convention.

In particular, either directly or through any intermediary, they shall take all appropriate measures -

a) to discover the whereabouts of a child who has been wrongfully removed or retained;

b) to prevent further harm to the child or prejudice to interested parties by taking or causing to be taken provisional measures;

c) to secure the voluntary return of the child or to bring about an amicable resolution of the issues;

d) to exchange, where desirable, information relating to the social background of the child;

e) to provide information of a general character as to the law of their State in connection with the application of the Convention;

f) to initiate or facilitate the institution of judicial or administrative proceedings with a view to obtaining the return of the child and, in a proper case, to make arrangements for organising or securing the effective exercise of rights of access;

g) where the circumstances so require, to provide or facilitate the provision of legal aid and advice, including the participation of legal counsel and advisers;

h) to provide such administrative arrangements as may be necessary and appropriate to secure the safe return of the child;

i) to keep each other informed with respect to the operation of this Convention and, as far as possible, to eliminate any obstacles to its application.

Chapter III - Return of Children

Article 8

Any person, institution or other body claiming that a child has been removed or retained in breach of custody rights may apply either to the Central

Authority of the child's habitual residence or to the Central Authority of any other Contracting State for assistance in securing the return of the child.

The application shall contain -

a) information concerning the identity of the applicant, of the child and of the person alleged to have removed or retained the child;

b) where available, the date of birth of the child;

c) the grounds on which the applicant's claim for return of the child is based;

d) all available information relating to the whereabouts of the child and the identity of the person with whom the child is presumed to be.

The application may be accompanied or supplemented by -

e) an authenticated copy of any relevant decision or agreement;

f) a certificate or an affidavit emanating from a Central Authority, or other competent authority of the State of the child's habitual residence, or from a qualified person, concerning the relevant law of that State;

g) any other relevant document.

Article 9

If the Central Authority which receives an application referred to in Article 8 has reason to believe that the child is in another Contracting State, it shall directly and without delay transmit the application to the Central Authority of that Contracting State and inform the requesting Central Authority, or the applicant, as the case may be.

Article 10

The Central Authority of the State where the child is shall take or cause to be taken all appropriate measures in order to obtain the voluntary return of the child.

Article 11

The judicial or administrative authorities of Contracting States shall act expeditiously in proceedings for the return of children.

If the judicial or administrative authority concerned has not reached a decision within six weeks from the date of commencement of the proceedings, the applicant or the Central Authority of the requested State, on its own initiative or if asked by the Central Authority of the requesting

State, shall have the right to request a statement of the reasons for the delay. If a reply is received by the Central Authority of the requested State, that Authority shall transmit the reply to the Central Authority of the requesting State, or to the applicant, as the case may be.

Article 12

Where a child has been wrongfully removed or retained in terms of Article 3 and, at the date of the commencement of the proceedings before the judicial or administrative authority of the Contracting State where the child is, a period of less than one year has elapsed from the date of the wrongful removal or retention, the authority concerned shall order the return of the child forthwith.

The judicial or administrative authority, even where the proceedings have been commenced after the expiration of the period of one year referred to in the preceding paragraph, shall also order the return of the child, unless it is demonstrated that the child is now settled in its new environment.

Where the judicial or administrative authority in the requested State has reason to believe that the child has been taken to another State, it may stay the proceedings or dismiss the application for the return of the child.

Article 13

Notwithstanding the provisions of the preceding Article, the judicial or administrative authority of the requested State is not bound to order the return of the child if the person, institution or other body which opposes its return establishes that -

a) the person, institution or other body having the care of the person of the child was not actually exercising the custody rights at the time of removal or retention, or had consented to or subsequently acquiesced in the removal or retention; or

b) there is a grave risk that his or her return would expose the child to physical or psychological harm or otherwise place the child in an intolerable situation.

The judicial or administrative authority may also refuse to order the return of the child if it finds that the child objects to being returned and has attained an age and degree of maturity at which it is appropriate to take account of its views.In considering the circumstances referred to in this Article, the judicial and administrative authorities shall take into account the information relating to the social background of the child provided by the Central Authority or other competent authority of the child's habitual residence.

Article 14

In ascertaining whether there has been a wrongful removal or retention within the meaning of Article 3, the judicial or administrative authorities of the requested State may take notice directly of the law of, and of judicial or administrative decisions, formally recognised or not in the State of the habitual residence of the child, without recourse to the specific procedures for the proof of that law or for the recognition of foreign decisions which would otherwise be applicable.

Article 15

The judicial or administrative authorities of a Contracting State may, prior to the making of an order for the return of the child, request that the applicant obtain from the authorities of the State of the habitual residence of the child a decision or other determination that the removal or retention was wrongful within the meaning of Article 3 of the Convention, where such a decision or determination may be obtained in that State. The Central Authorities of the Contracting States shall so far as practicable assist applicants to obtain such a decision or determination.

Article 16

After receiving notice of a wrongful removal or retention of a child in the sense of Article 3, the judicial or administrative authorities of the Contracting State to which the child has been removed or in which it has been retained shall not decide on the merits of rights of custody until it has been determined that the child is not to be returned under this Convention or unless an application under this Convention is not lodged within a reasonable time following receipt of the notice.

Article 17

The sole fact that a decision relating to custody has been given in or is entitled to recognition in the requested State shall not be a ground for refusing to return a child under this Convention, but the judicial or administrative authorities of the requested State may take account of the reasons for that decision in applying this Convention.

Article 18

The provisions of this Chapter do not limit the power of a judicial or administrative authority to order the return of the child at any time.

Article 19

A decision under this Convention concerning the return of the child shall not be taken to be a determination on the merits of any custody issue.

Article 20

The return of the child under the provisions of Article 12 may be refused if this would not be permitted by the fundamental principles of the requested State relating to the protection of human rights and fundamental freedoms.

Chapter IV - Rights of Access

Article 21

An application to make arrangements for organising or securing the effective exercise of rights of access may be presented to the Central Authorities of the Contracting States in the same way as an application for the return of a child.

The Central Authorities are bound by the obligations of co-operation which are set forth in Article 7 to promote the peaceful enjoyment of access rights and the fulfilment of any conditions to which the exercise of those rights may be subject. The Central Authorities shall take steps to remove, as far as possible, all obstacles to the exercise of such rights.

The Central Authorities, either directly or through intermediaries, may initiate or assist in the institution of proceedings with a view to organising or protecting these rights and securing respect for the conditions to which the exercise of these rights may be subject.

Chapter V - General Provisions

Article 22

No security, bond or deposit, however described, shall be required to guarantee the payment of costs and expenses in the judicial or administrative proceedings falling within the scope of this Convention.

Article 23

No legalisation or similar formality may be required in the context of this Convention.

Article 24

Any application, communication or other document sent to the Central Authority of the requested State shall be in the original language, and shall be accompanied by a translation into the official language or one of the official languages of the requested State or, where that is not feasible, a translation into French or English.

However, a Contracting State may, by making a reservation in accordance with Article 42, object to the use of either French or English, but not both, in any application, communication or other document sent to its Central Authority.

Article 25

Nationals of the Contracting States and persons who are habitually resident within those States shall be entitled in matters concerned with the application of this Convention to legal aid and advice in any other Contracting State on the same conditions as if they themselves were nationals of and habitually resident in that State.

Article 26

Each Central Authority shall bear its own costs in applying this Convention.

Central Authorities and other public services of Contracting States shall not impose any charges in relation to applications submitted under this Convention. In particular, they may not require any payment from the applicant towards the costs and expenses of the proceedings or, where applicable, those arising from the participation of legal counsel or advisers. However, they may require the payment of the expenses incurred or to be incurred in implementing the return of the child.

However, a Contracting State may, by making a reservation in accordance with Article 42, declare that it shall not be bound to assume any costs referred to in the preceding paragraph resulting from the participation of legal counsel or advisers or from court proceedings, except insofar as those costs may be covered by its system of legal aid and advice.

Upon ordering the return of a child or issuing an order concerning rights of access under this Convention, the judicial or administrative authorities may, where appropriate, direct the person who removed or retained the child, or who prevented the exercise of rights of access, to pay necessary expenses incurred by or on behalf of the applicant, including travel expenses, any costs incurred or payments made for locating the child, the costs of legal representation of the applicant, and those of returning the child.

Article 27

When it is manifest that the requirements of this Convention are not fulfilled or that the application is otherwise not well founded, a Central Authority is not bound to accept the application. In that case, the Central Authority shall forthwith inform the applicant or the Central Authority through which the application was submitted, as the case may be, of its reasons.

Article 28

A Central Authority may require that the application be accompanied by a written authorisation empowering it to act on behalf of the applicant, or to designate a representative so to act.

Article 29

This Convention shall not preclude any person, institution or body who claims that there has been a breach of custody or access rights within the meaning of Article 3 or 21 from applying directly to the judicial or administrative authorities of a Contracting State, whether or not under the provisions of this Convention.

Article 30

Any application submitted to the Central Authorities or directly to the judicial or administrative authorities of a Contracting State in accordance with the terms of this Convention, together with documents and any other information appended thereto or provided by a Central Authority, shall be admissible in the courts or administrative authorities of the Contracting States.

Article 31

In relation to a State which in matters of custody of children has two or more systems of law applicable in different territorial units -

a) any reference to habitual residence in that State shall be construed as referring to habitual residence in a territorial unit of that State;

b) any reference to the law of the State of habitual residence shall be construed as referring to the law of the territorial unit in that State where the child habitually resides.

Article 32

In relation to a State which in matters of custody of children has two or more systems of law applicable to different categories of persons, any reference to the law of that State shall be construed as referring to the legal system specified by the law of that State.

Article 33

A State within which different territorial units have their own rules of law in respect of custody of children shall not be bound to apply this Convention where a State with a unified system of law would not be bound to do so.

Article 34

This Convention shall take priority in matters within its scope over the *Convention of 5 October 1961 concerning the powers of authorities and the law applicable in respect of the protection of minors*, as between Parties to both Conventions. Otherwise the present Convention shall not restrict the application of an international instrument in force between the State of origin and the State addressed or other law of the State addressed for the purposes of obtaining the return of a child who has been wrongfully removed or retained or of organising access rights.

Article 35

This Convention shall apply as between Contracting States only to wrongful removals or retentions occurring after its entry into force in those States.

Where a declaration has been made under Article 39 or 40, the reference in the preceding paragraph to a Contracting State shall be taken to refer to the territorial unit or units in relation to which this Convention applies.

Article 36

Nothing in this Convention shall prevent two or more Contracting States, in order to limit the restrictions to which the return of the child may be subject, from agreeing among themselves to derogate from any provisions of this Convention which may imply such a restriction.

Chapter VI - Final Clauses

Article 37

The Convention shall be open for signature by the States which were

Members of the Hague Conference on Private International Law at the time of its Fourteenth Session.

It shall be ratified, accepted or approved and the instruments of ratification, acceptance or approval shall be deposited with the Ministry of Foreign Affairs of the Kingdom of the Netherlands.

Article 38

Any other State may accede to the Convention.

The instrument of accession shall be deposited with the Ministry of Foreign Affairs of the Kingdom of the Netherlands.

The Convention shall enter into force for a State acceding to it on the first day of the third calendar month after the deposit of its instrument of accession.

The accession will have effect only as regards the relations between the acceding State and such Contracting States as will have declared their acceptance of the accession. Such a declaration will also have to be made by any Member State ratifying, accepting or approving the Convention after an accession. Such declaration shall be deposited at the Ministry of Foreign Affairs of the Kingdom of the Netherlands; this Ministry shall forward, through diplomatic channels, a certified copy to each of the Contracting States.

The Convention will enter into force as between the acceding State and the State that has declared its acceptance of the accession on the first day of the third calendar month after the deposit of the declaration of acceptance.

Article 39

Any State may, at the time of signature, ratification, acceptance, approval or accession, declare that the Convention shall extend to all the territories for the international relations of which it is responsible, or to one or more of them. Such a declaration shall take effect at the time the Convention enters into force for that State.

Such declaration, as well as any subsequent extension, shall be notified to the Ministry of Foreign Affairs of the Kingdom of the Netherlands.

Article 40

If a Contracting State has two or more territorial units in which different systems of law are applicable in relation to matters dealt with in this Convention, it may at the time of signature, ratification, acceptance, approval or accession declare that this Convention shall extend to all its territorial units or only to one or more of them and may modify this declaration by submitting another declaration at any time.

Any such declaration shall be notified to the Ministry of Foreign Affairs of the Kingdom of the Netherlands and shall state expressly the territorial units to which the Convention applies.

Article 41

Where a Contracting State has a system of government under which executive, judicial and legislative powers are distributed between central and other authorities within that State, its signature or ratification, acceptance or approval of, or accession to this Convention, or its making of any declaration in terms of Article 40 shall carry no implication as to the internal distribution of powers within that State.

Article 42

Any State may, not later than the time of ratification, acceptance, approval or accession, or at the time of making a declaration in terms of Article 39 or 40, make one or both of the reservations provided for in Article 24 and Article 26, third paragraph. No other reservation shall be permitted.

Any State may at any time withdraw a reservation it has made. The withdrawal shall be notified to the Ministry of Foreign Affairs of the Kingdom of the Netherlands.

The reservation shall cease to have effect on the first day of the third calendar month after the notification referred to in the preceding paragraph.

Article 43

The Convention shall enter into force on the first day of the third calendar month after the deposit of the third instrument of ratification, acceptance, approval or accession referred to in Articles 37 and 38.

Thereafter the Convention shall enter into force -

(1) for each State ratifying, accepting, approving or acceding to it subsequently, on the first day of the third calendar month after the deposit of its instrument of ratification, acceptance, approval or accession;

(2) for any territory or territorial unit to which the Convention has been extended in conformity with Article 39 or 40, on the first day of the third calendar month after the notification referred to in that Article.

Article 44

The Convention shall remain in force for five years from the date of its entry into force in accordance with the first paragraph of Article 43 even for States which subsequently have ratified, accepted, approved it or acceded to it.

If there has been no denunciation, it shall be renewed tacitly every five years.

Any denunciation shall be notified to the Ministry of Foreign Affairs of the Kingdom of the Netherlands at least six months before the expiry of the five year period. It may be limited to certain of the territories or territorial units to which the Convention applies.

The denunciation shall have effect only as regards the State which has notified it. The Convention shall remain in force for the other Contracting States.

Article 45

The Ministry of Foreign Affairs of the Kingdom of the Netherlands shall notify the States Members of the Conference, and the States which have acceded in accordance with Article 38, of the following -

(1) the signatures and ratifications, acceptances and approvals referred to in Article 37;

(2) the accessions referred to in Article 38;

(3) the date on which the Convention enters into force in accordance with Article 43;

(4) the extensions referred to in Article 39;

(5) the declarations referred to in Articles 38 and 40;

(6) the reservations referred to in Article 24 and Article 26, third paragraph, and the withdrawals referred to in Article 42;

(7) the denunciations referred to in Article 44.

In witness whereof the undersigned, being duly authorised thereto, have signed this Convention.

Done at The Hague, on the 25th day of October, 1980, in the English and French languages, both texts being equally authentic, in a single copy which shall be deposited in the archives of the Government of the Kingdom of the Netherlands, and of which a certified copy shall be sent, through diplomatic channels, to each of the States Members of the Hague Conference on Private International Law at the date of its Fourteenth Session.

Convention on Jurisdiction, Applicable Law, Recognition, Enforcement And Co-Operation in Respect of Parental Responsibility and Measures for the Protection of Children

(Concluded 19 October 1996)

The States signatory to the present Convention,

Considering the need to improve the protection of children in international situations,

Wishing to avoid conflicts between their legal systems in respect of jurisdiction, applicable law, recognition and enforcement of measures for the protection of children,

Recalling the importance of international co-operation for the protection of children,

Confirming that the best interests of the child are to be a primary consideration,

Noting that the *Convention of 5 October 1961 concerning the powers of authorities and the law applicable in respect of the protection of minors* is in need of revision,

Desiring to establish common provisions to this effect, taking into account the *United Nations Convention on the Rights of the Child* of 20 November 1989,

Have agreed on the following provisions -

Chapter I - Scope of the Convention

Article 1

(1) The objects of the present Convention are -

- *a)* to determine the State whose authorities have jurisdiction to take measures directed to the protection of the person or property of the child;
- *b)* to determine which law is to be applied by such authorities in exercising their jurisdiction;

c) to determine the law applicable to parental responsibility;

d) to provide for the recognition and enforcement of such measures of protection in all Contracting States;

e) to establish such co-operation between the authorities of the Contracting States as may be necessary in order to achieve the purposes of this Convention.

(2) For the purposes of this Convention, the term 'parental responsibility' includes parental authority, or any analogous relationship of authority determining the rights, powers and responsibilities of parents, guardians or other legal representatives in relation to the person or the property of the child.

Article 2

The Convention applies to children from the moment of their birth until they reach the age of 18 years.

Article 3

The measures referred to in Article 1 may deal in particular with -

a) the attribution, exercise, termination or restriction of parental responsibility, as well as its delegation;

b) rights of custody, including rights relating to the care of the person of the child and, in particular, the right to determine the child's place of residence, as well as rights of access including the right to take a child for a limited period of time to a place other than the child's habitual residence;

c) guardianship, curatorship and analogous institutions;

d) the designation and functions of any person or body having charge of the child's person or property, representing or assisting the child;

e) the placement of the child in a foster family or in institutional care, or the provision of care by *kafala* or an analogous institution;

f) the supervision by a public authority of the care of a child by any person having charge of the child;

g) the administration, conservation or disposal of the child's property.

Article 4

The Convention does not apply to -

a) the establishment or contesting of a parent-child relationship;

b) decisions on adoption, measures preparatory to adoption, or the annulment or revocation of adoption;

c) the name and forenames of the child;

d) emancipation;

e) maintenance obligations;

f) trusts or succession;

g) social security;

h) public measures of a general nature in matters of education or health;

i) measures taken as a result of penal offences committed by children;

j) decisions on the right of asylum and on immigration.

Chapter II - Jurisdiction

Article 5

(1) The judicial or administrative authorities of the Contracting State of the habitual residence of the child have jurisdiction to take measures directed to the protection of the child's person or property.

(2) Subject to Article 7, in case of a change of the child's habitual residence to another Contracting State, the authorities of the State of the new habitual residence have jurisdiction.

Article 6

(1) For refugee children and children who, due to disturbances occurring in their country, are internationally displaced, the authorities of the Contracting State on the territory of which these children are present as a result of their displacement have the jurisdiction provided for in paragraph 1 of Article 5.

(2) The provisions of the preceding paragraph also apply to children whose habitual residence cannot be established.

Article 7

(1) In case of wrongful removal or retention of the child, the authorities of the Contracting State in which the child was habitually resident

immediately before the removal or retention keep their jurisdiction until the child has acquired a habitual residence in another State, and

a) each person, institution or other body having rights of custody has acquiesced in the removal or retention; or

b) the child has resided in that other State for a period of at least one year after the person, institution or other body having rights of custody has or should have had knowledge of the whereabouts of the child, no request for return lodged within that period is still pending, and the child is settled in his or her new environment.

(2) The removal or the retention of a child is to be considered wrongful where -

a) it is in breach of rights of custody attributed to a person, an institution or any other body, either jointly or alone, under the law of the State in which the child was habitually resident immediately before the removal or retention; and

b) at the time of removal or retention those rights were actually exercised, either jointly or alone, or would have been so exercised but for the removal or retention.

The rights of custody mentioned in sub-paragraph *a* above, may arise in particular by operation of law or by reason of a judicial or administrative decision, or by reason of an agreement having legal effect under the law of that State.

(3) So long as the authorities first mentioned in paragraph 1 keep their jurisdiction, the authorities of the Contracting State to which the child has been removed or in which he or she has been retained can take only such urgent measures under Article 11 as are necessary for the protection of the person or property of the child.

Article 8

(1) By way of exception, the authority of a Contracting State having jurisdiction under Article 5 or 6, if it considers that the authority of another Contracting State would be better placed in the particular case to assess the best interests of the child, may either

- request that other authority, directly or with the assistance of the Central Authority of its State, to assume jurisdiction to take such measures of protection as it considers to be necessary, or

- suspend consideration of the case and invite the parties to introduce such a request before the authority of that other State.

(2) The Contracting States whose authorities may be addressed as provided in the preceding paragraph are

a) a State of which the child is a national,

b) a State in which property of the child is located,

c) a State whose authorities are seised of an application for divorce or legal separation of the child's parents, or for annulment of their marriage,

d) a State with which the child has a substantial connection.

(3) The authorities concerned may proceed to an exchange of views.

(4) The authority addressed as provided in paragraph 1 may assume jurisdiction, in place of the authority having jurisdiction under Article 5 or 6, if it considers that this is in the child's best interests.

Article 9

(1) If the authorities of a Contracting State referred to in Article 8, paragraph 2, consider that they are better placed in the particular case to assess the child's best interests, they may either

- request the competent authority of the Contracting State of the habitual residence of the child, directly or with the assistance of the Central Authority of that State, that they be authorised to exercise jurisdiction to take the measures of protection which they consider to be necessary, or

- invite the parties to introduce such a request before the authority of the Contracting State of the habitual residence of the child.

(2) The authorities concerned may proceed to an exchange of views.

(3) The authority initiating the request may exercise jurisdiction in place of the authority of the Contracting State of the habitual residence of the child only if the latter authority has accepted the request.

Article 10

(1) Without prejudice to Articles 5 to 9, the authorities of a Contracting State exercising jurisdiction to decide upon an application for divorce or legal separation of the parents of a child habitually resident in another Contracting State, or for annulment of their marriage, may, if

the law of their State so provides, take measures directed to the protection of the person or property of such child if

a) at the time of commencement of the proceedings, one of his or her parents habitually resides in that State and one of them has parental responsibility in relation to the child, and

b) the jurisdiction of these authorities to take such measures has been accepted by the parents, as well as by any other person who has parental responsibility in relation to the child, and is in the best interests of the child.

(2) The jurisdiction provided for by paragraph 1 to take measures for the protection of the child ceases as soon as the decision allowing or refusing the application for divorce, legal separation or annulment of the marriage has become final, or the proceedings have come to an end for another reason.

Article 11

(1) In all cases of urgency, the authorities of any Contracting State in whose territory the child or property belonging to the child is present have jurisdiction to take any necessary measures of protection.

(2) The measures taken under the preceding paragraph with regard to a child habitually resident in a Contracting State shall lapse as soon as the authorities which have jurisdiction under Articles 5 to 10 have taken the measures required by the situation.

(3) The measures taken under paragraph 1 with regard to a child who is habitually resident in a non-Contracting State shall lapse in each Contracting State as soon as measures required by the situation and taken by the authorities of another State are recognised in the Contracting State in question.

Article 12

(1) Subject to Article 7, the authorities of a Contracting State in whose territory the child or property belonging to the child is present have jurisdiction to take measures of a provisional character for the protection of the person or property of the child which have a territorial effect limited to the State in question, in so far as such measures are not incompatible with measures already taken by authorities which have jurisdiction under Articles 5 to 10.

(2) The measures taken under the preceding paragraph with regard to a child habitually resident in a Contracting State shall lapse as soon as the authorities which have jurisdiction under Articles 5 to 10 have taken a decision in respect of the measures of protection which may be required by the situation.

(3) The measures taken under paragraph 1 with regard to a child who is habitually resident in a non-Contracting State shall lapse in the Contracting State where the measures were taken as soon as measures required by the situation and taken by the authorities of another State are recognised in the Contracting State in question.

Article 13

(1) The authorities of a Contracting State which have jurisdiction under Articles 5 to 10 to take measures for the protection of the person or property of the child must abstain from exercising this jurisdiction if, at the time of the commencement of the proceedings, corresponding measures have been requested from the authorities of another Contracting State having jurisdiction under Articles 5 to 10 at the time of the request and are still under consideration.

(2) The provisions of the preceding paragraph shall not apply if the authorities before whom the request for measures was initially introduced have declined jurisdiction.

Article 14

The measures taken in application of Articles 5 to 10 remain in force according to their terms, even if a change of circumstances has eliminated the basis upon which jurisdiction was founded, so long as the authorities which have jurisdiction under the Convention have not modified, replaced or terminated such measures.

Chapter III - Applicable Law

Article 15

(1) In exercising their jurisdiction under the provisions of Chapter II, the authorities of the Contracting States shall apply their own law.

(2) However, in so far as the protection of the person or the property of the child requires, they may exceptionally apply or take into

consideration the law of another State with which the situation has a substantial connection.

(3) If the child's habitual residence changes to another Contracting State, the law of that other State governs, from the time of the change, the conditions of application of the measures taken in the State of the former habitual residence.

Article 16

(1) The attribution or extinction of parental responsibility by operation of law, without the intervention of a judicial or administrative authority, is governed by the law of the State of the habitual residence of the child.

(2) The attribution or extinction of parental responsibility by an agreement or a unilateral act, without intervention of a judicial or administrative authority, is governed by the law of the State of the child's habitual residence at the time when the agreement or unilateral act takes effect.

(3) Parental responsibility which exists under the law of the State of the child's habitual residence subsists after a change of that habitual residence to another State.

(4) If the child's habitual residence changes, the attribution of parental responsibility by operation of law to a person who does not already have such responsibility is governed by the law of the State of the new habitual residence.

Article 17

The exercise of parental responsibility is governed by the law of the State of the child's habitual residence. If the child's habitual residence changes, it is governed by the law of the State of the new habitual residence.

Article 18

The parental responsibility referred to in Article 16 may be terminated, or the conditions of its exercise modified, by measures taken under this Convention.

Article 19

(1) The validity of a transaction entered into between a third party and another person who would be entitled to act as the child's legal representative under the law of the State where the transaction was concluded cannot be contested, and the third party cannot be held liable,

on the sole ground that the other person was not entitled to act as the child's legal representative under the law designated by the provisions of this Chapter, unless the third party knew or should have known that the parental responsibility was governed by the latter law.

(2) The preceding paragraph applies only if the transaction was entered into between persons present on the territory of the same State.

Article 20

The provisions of this Chapter apply even if the law designated by them is the law of a non-Contracting State.

Article 21

(1) In this Chapter the term "law" means the law in force in a State other than its choice of law rules.

(2) However, if the law applicable according to Article 16 is that of a non-Contracting State and if the choice of law rules of that State designate the law of another non-Contracting State which would apply its own law, the law of the latter State applies. If that other non-Contracting State would not apply its own law, the applicable law is that designated by Article 16.

Article 22

The application of the law designated by the provisions of this Chapter can be refused only if this application would be manifestly contrary to public policy, taking into account the best interests of the child.

Chapter IV - Recognition and Rnforcement

Article 23

(1) The measures taken by the authorities of a Contracting State shall be recognised by operation of law in all other Contracting States.

(2) Recognition may however be refused -

   a) if the measure was taken by an authority whose jurisdiction was not based on one of the grounds provided for in Chapter II;

   b) if the measure was taken, except in a case of urgency, in the context of a judicial or administrative proceeding, without the child having been provided the opportunity to be heard, in violation of fundamental principles of procedure of the requested State;

c) on the request of any person claiming that the measure infringes his or her parental responsibility, if such measure was taken, except in a case of urgency, without such person having been given an opportunity to be heard;

d) if such recognition is manifestly contrary to public policy of the requested State, taking into account the best interests of the child;

e) if the measure is incompatible with a later measure taken in the non-Contracting State of the habitual residence of the child, where this later measure fulfils the requirements for recognition in the requested State;

f) if the procedure provided in Article 33 has not been complied with.

Article 24

Without prejudice to Article 23, paragraph 1, any interested person may request from the competent authorities of a Contracting State that they decide on the recognition or non-recognition of a measure taken in another Contracting State. The procedure is governed by the law of the requested State.

Article 25

The authority of the requested State is bound by the findings of fact on which the authority of the State where the measure was taken based its jurisdiction.

Article 26

(1) If measures taken in one Contracting State and enforceable there require enforcement in another Contracting State, they shall, upon request by an interested party, be declared enforceable or registered for the purpose of enforcement in that other State according to the procedure provided in the law of the latter State.

(2) Each Contracting State shall apply to the declaration of enforceability or registration a simple and rapid procedure.

(3) The declaration of enforceability or registration may be refused only for one of the reasons set out in Article 23, paragraph 2.

Article 27

Without prejudice to such review as is necessary in the application of the preceding Articles, there shall be no review of the merits of the measure taken.

Article 28

Measures taken in one Contracting State and declared enforceable, or registered for the purpose of enforcement, in another Contracting State shall be enforced in the latter State as if they had been taken by the authorities of that State. Enforcement takes place in accordance with the law of the requested State to the extent provided by such law, taking into consideration the best interests of the child.

Chapter V -Co-operation

Article 29

(1) A Contracting State shall designate a Central Authority to discharge the duties which are imposed by the Convention on such authorities.

(2) Federal States, States with more than one system of law or States having autonomous territorial units shall be free to appoint more than one Central Authority and to specify the territorial or personal extent of their functions. Where a State has appointed more than one Central Authority, it shall designate the Central Authority to which any communication may be addressed for transmission to the appropriate Central Authority within that State.

Article 30

(1) Central Authorities shall co-operate with each other and promote co-operation amongst the competent authorities in their States to achieve the purposes of the Convention.

(2) They shall, in connection with the application of the Convention, take appropriate steps to provide information as to the laws of, and services available in, their States relating to the protection of children.

Article 31

The Central Authority of a Contracting State, either directly or through public authorities or other bodies, shall take all appropriate steps to -

a) facilitate the communications and offer the assistance provided for in Articles 8 and 9 and in this Chapter;

b) facilitate, by mediation, conciliation or similar means, agreed solutions for the protection of the person or property of the child in situations to which the Convention applies;

c) provide, on the request of a competent authority of another Contracting State, assistance in discovering the whereabouts of a child where it appears that the child may be present and in need of protection within the territory of the requested State.

Article 32

On a request made with supporting reasons by the Central Authority or other competent authority of any Contracting State with which the child has a substantial connection, the Central Authority of the Contracting State in which the child is habitually resident and present may, directly or through public authorities or other bodies,

a) provide a report on the situation of the child;

b) request the competent authority of its State to consider the need to take measures for the protection of the person or property of the child.

Article 33

(1) If an authority having jurisdiction under Articles 5 to 10 contemplates the placement of the child in a foster family or institutional care, or the provision of care by *kafala* or an analogous institution, and if such placement or such provision of care is to take place in another Contracting State, it shall first consult with the Central Authority or other competent authority of the latter State. To that effect it shall transmit a report on the child together with the reasons for the proposed placement or provision of care.

(2) The decision on the placement or provision of care may be made in the requesting State only if the Central Authority or other competent authority of the requested State has consented to the placement or provision of care, taking into account the child's best interests.

Article 34

(1) Where a measure of protection is contemplated, the competent authorities under the Convention, if the situation of the child so requires, may request any authority of another Contracting State which has information relevant to the protection of the child to communicate such information.

(2) A Contracting State may declare that requests under paragraph 1 shall be communicated to its authorities only through its Central Authority.

Article 35

(1) The competent authorities of a Contracting State may request the authorities of another Contracting State to assist in the implementation of measures of protection taken under this Convention, especially in securing the effective exercise of rights of access as well as of the right to maintain direct contacts on a regular basis.

(2) The authorities of a Contracting State in which the child does not habitually reside may, on the request of a parent residing in that State who is seeking to obtain or to maintain access to the child, gather information or evidence and may make a finding on the suitability of that parent to exercise access and on the conditions under which access is to be exercised. An authority exercising jurisdiction under Articles 5 to 10 to determine an application concerning access to the child, shall admit and consider such information, evidence and finding before reaching its decision.

(3) An authority having jurisdiction under Articles 5 to 10 to decide on access may adjourn a proceeding pending the outcome of a request made under paragraph 2, in particular, when it is considering an application to restrict or terminate access rights granted in the State of the child's former habitual residence.

(4) Nothing in this Article shall prevent an authority having jurisdiction under Articles 5 to 10 from taking provisional measures pending the outcome of the request made under paragraph 2.

Article 36

In any case where the child is exposed to a serious danger, the competent authorities of the Contracting State where measures for the protection of the child have been taken or are under consideration, if they are informed that the child's residence has changed to, or that the child is present in another State, shall inform the authorities of that other State about the danger involved and the measures taken or under consideration.

Article 37

An authority shall not request or transmit any information under this Chapter if to do so would, in its opinion, be likely to place the child's person or property in danger, or constitute a serious threat to the liberty or life of a member of the child's family.

Article 38

(1) Without prejudice to the possibility of imposing reasonable charges for the provision of services, Central Authorities and other public authorities of Contracting States shall bear their own costs in applying the provisions of this Chapter.

(2) Any Contracting State may enter into agreements with one or more other Contracting States concerning the allocation of charges.

Article 39

Any Contracting State may enter into agreements with one or more other Contracting States with a view to improving the application of this Chapter in their mutual relations. The States which have concluded such an agreement shall transmit a copy to the depositary of the Convention.

Chapter VI - General Provisions

Article 40

(1) The authorities of the Contracting State of the child's habitual residence, or of the Contracting State where a measure of protection has been taken, may deliver to the person having parental responsibility or to the person entrusted with protection of the child's person or property, at his or her request, a certificate indicating the capacity in which that person is entitled to act and the powers conferred upon him or her.

(2) The capacity and powers indicated in the certificate are presumed to be vested in that person, in the absence of proof to the contrary.

(3) Each Contracting State shall designate the authorities competent to draw up the certificate.

Article 41

Personal data gathered or transmitted under the Convention shall be used only for the purposes for which they were gathered or transmitted.

Article 42

The authorities to whom information is transmitted shall ensure its confidentiality, in accordance with the law of their State.

Article 43

All documents forwarded or delivered under this Convention shall be exempt from legalisation or any analogous formality.

Article 44

Each Contracting State may designate the authorities to which requests under Articles 8, 9 and 33 are to be addressed.

Article 45

(1) The designations referred to in Articles 29 and 44 shall be communicated to the Permanent Bureau of the Hague Conference on Private International Law.

(2) The declaration referred to in Article 34, paragraph 2, shall be made to the depositary of the Convention.

Article 46

A Contracting State in which different systems of law or sets of rules of law apply to the protection of the child and his or her property shall not be bound to apply the rules of the Convention to conflicts solely between such different systems or sets of rules of law.

Article 47

In relation to a State in which two or more systems of law or sets of rules of law with regard to any matter dealt with in this Convention apply in different territorial units -

(1) any reference to habitual residence in that State shall be construed as referring to habitual residence in a territorial unit;

(2) any reference to the presence of the child in that State shall be construed as referring to presence in a territorial unit;

(3) any reference to the location of property of the child in that State shall be construed as referring to location of property of the child in a territorial unit;

(4) any reference to the State of which the child is a national shall be construed as referring to the territorial unit designated by the law of that State or, in the absence of relevant rules, to the territorial unit with which the child has the closest connection;

(5) any reference to the State whose authorities are seised of an application for divorce or legal separation of the child's parents, or for annulment of their marriage, shall be construed as referring to the territorial unit whose authorities are seised of such application;

(6) any reference to the State with which the child has a substantial connection shall be construed as referring to the territorial unit with which the child has such connection;

(7) any reference to the State to which the child has been removed or in which he or she has been retained shall be construed as referring to the relevant territorial unit to which the child has been removed or in which he or she has been retained;

(8) any reference to bodies or authorities of that State, other than Central Authorities, shall be construed as referring to those authorised to act in the relevant territorial unit;

(9) any reference to the law or procedure or authority of the State in which a measure has been taken shall be construed as referring to the law or procedure or authority of the territorial unit in which such measure was taken;

(10) any reference to the law or procedure or authority of the requested State shall be construed as referring to the law or procedure or authority of the territorial unit in which recognition or enforcement is sought.

Article 48

For the purpose of identifying the applicable law under Chapter III, in relation to a State which comprises two or more territorial units each of which has its own system of law or set of rules of law in respect of matters covered by this Convention, the following rules apply -

a) if there are rules in force in such a State identifying which territorial unit's law is applicable, the law of that unit applies;

b) in the absence of such rules, the law of the relevant territorial unit as defined in Article 47 applies.

Article 49

For the purpose of identifying the applicable law under Chapter III, in relation to a State which has two or more systems of law or sets of rules of law applicable to different categories of persons in respect of matters covered by this Convention, the following rules apply -

a) if there are rules in force in such a State identifying which among such laws applies, that law applies;

b) in the absence of such rules, the law of the system or the set of rules of law with which the child has the closest connection applies.

Article 50

This Convention shall not affect the application of the *Convention of 25 October 1980 on the Civil Aspects of International Child Abduction*, as between Parties to both Conventions. Nothing, however, precludes provisions of this Convention from being invoked for the purposes of obtaining the return of a child who has been wrongfully removed or retained or of organising access rights.

Article 51

In relations between the Contracting States this Convention replaces the *Convention of 5 October 1961 concerning the powers of authorities and the law applicable in respect of the protection of minors*, and the*Convention governing the guardianship of minors*, signed at The Hague 12 June 1902, without prejudice to the recognition of measures taken under the Convention of 5 October 1961 mentioned above.

Article 52

(1) This Convention does not affect any international instrument to which Contracting States are Parties and which contains provisions on matters governed by the Convention, unless a contrary declaration is made by the States Parties to such instrument.

(2) This Convention does not affect the possibility for one or more Contracting States to conclude agreements which contain, in respect of children habitually resident in any of the States Parties to such agreements, provisions on matters governed by this Convention.

(3) Agreements to be concluded by one or more Contracting States on matters within the scope of this Convention do not affect, in the relationship of such States with other Contracting States, the application of the provisions of this Convention.

(4) The preceding paragraphs also apply to uniform laws based on special ties of a regional or other nature between the States concerned.

Article 53

(1) The Convention shall apply to measures only if they are taken in a State after the Convention has entered into force for that State.

(2) The Convention shall apply to the recognition and enforcement of measures taken after its entry into force as between the State where the measures have been taken and the requested State.

Article 54

(1) Any communication sent to the Central Authority or to another authority of a Contracting State shall be in the original language, and shall be accompanied by a translation into the official language or one of the official languages of the other State or, where that is not feasible, a translation into French or English.

(2) However, a Contracting State may, by making a reservation in accordance with Article 60, object to the use of either French or English, but not both.

Article 55

(1) A Contracting State may, in accordance with Article 60,

a) reserve the jurisdiction of its authorities to take measures directed to the protection of property of a child situated on its territory;

b) reserve the right not to recognise any parental responsibility or measure in so far as it is incompatible with any measure taken by its authorities in relation to that property.

(2) The reservation may be restricted to certain categories of property.

Article 56

The Secretary General of the Hague Conference on Private International Law shall at regular intervals convoke a Special Commission in order to review the practical operation of the Convention.

Chapter VII - Final Clauses

Article 57

(1) The Convention shall be open for signature by the States which were Members of the Hague Conference on Private International Law at the time of its Eighteenth Session.

(2) It shall be ratified, accepted or approved and the instruments of ratification, acceptance or approval shall be deposited with the Ministry of Foreign Affairs of the Kingdom of the Netherlands, depositary of the Convention.

Article 58

(1) Any other State may accede to the Convention after it has entered into force in accordance with Article 61, paragraph 1.

(2) The instrument of accession shall be deposited with the depositary.

(3) Such accession shall have effect only as regards the relations between the acceding State and those Contracting States which have not raised an objection to its accession in the six months after the receipt of the notification referred to in sub-paragraph *b* of Article 63. Such an objection may also be raised by States at the time when they ratify, accept or approve the Convention after an accession. Any such objection shall be notified to the depositary.

Article 59

(1) If a State has two or more territorial units in which different systems of law are applicable in relation to matters dealt with in this Convention, it may at the time of signature, ratification, acceptance, approval or accession declare that the Convention shall extend to all its territorial units or only to one or more of them and may modify this declaration by submitting another declaration at any time.

(2) Any such declaration shall be notified to the depositary and shall state expressly the territorial units to which the Convention applies.

(3) If a State makes no declaration under this Article, the Convention is to extend to all territorial units of that State.

Article 60

(1) Any State may, not later than the time of ratification, acceptance, approval or accession, or at the time of making a declaration in terms of Article 59, make one or both of the reservations provided for in Articles 54, paragraph 2, and 55. No other reservation shall be permitted.

(2) Any State may at any time withdraw a reservation it has made. The withdrawal shall be notified to the depositary.

(3) The reservation shall cease to have effect on the first day of the third calendar month after the notification referred to in the preceding paragraph.

Article 61

(1) The Convention shall enter into force on the first day of the month following the expiration of three months after the deposit of the third instrument of ratification, acceptance or approval referred to in Article 57.

(2) Thereafter the Convention shall enter into force -

a) for each State ratifying, accepting or approving it subsequently, on the first day of the month following the expiration of three months after the deposit of its instrument of ratification, acceptance, approval or accession;

b) for each State acceding, on the first day of the month following the expiration of three months after the expiration of the period of six months provided in Article 58, paragraph 3;

c) for a territorial unit to which the Convention has been extended in conformity with Article 59, on the first day of the month following the expiration of three months after the notification referred to in that Article.

Article 62

(1) A State Party to the Convention may denounce it by a notification in writing addressed to the depositary. The denunciation may be limited to certain territorial units to which the Convention applies.

(2) The denunciation takes effect on the first day of the month following the expiration of twelve months after the notification is received by the depositary. Where a longer period for the denunciation to take effect is specified in the notification, the denunciation takes effect upon the expiration of such longer period.

Article 63

The depositary shall notify the States Members of the Hague Conference on Private International Law and the States which have acceded in accordance with Article 58 of the following -

a) the signatures, ratifications, acceptances and approvals referred to in Article 57;

b) the accessions and objections raised to accessions referred to in Article 58;

c) the date on which the Convention enters into force in accordance with Article 61;

d) the declarations referred to in Articles 34, paragraph 2, and 59;

e) the agreements referred to in Article 39;

f) the reservations referred to in Articles 54, paragraph 2, and 55 and the withdrawals referred to in Article 60, paragraph 2;

g) the denunciations referred to in Article 62.

In witness whereof the undersigned, being duly authorised thereto, have signed this Convention.

Done at The Hague, on the 19th day of October 1996, in the English and French languages, both texts being equally authentic, in a single copy which shall be deposited in the archives of the Government of the Kingdom of the Netherlands, and of which a certified copy shall be sent, through diplomatic channels, to each of the States Members of the Hague Conference on Private International Law at the date of its Eighteenth Session.

References

Adair Dyer. "The Internationalization of Family Law". US Davis Law Review. Retrieved 2010-08-08.

Ernie Allen. "The kid is with a parent, how bad can it be?" The Crisis of Family Abductions. National Center for Missing and Exploited Children. Retrieved 2012-05-11.

"Hague Abduction Convention text". Hcch.net. Retrieved 2010-04-20.

Leto, Marisa (2000-04-01). "Whose best interest? International child abduction under the Hague Convention". Chicago Journal of International Law. Retrieved 2010-09-24.

Merle H. Weiner (2000). "International Child Abduction and the Escape from Domestic Violence". Fordham Law Review. Retrieved 2010-08-21.

Parental Child Abduction is Child Abuse. Nancy Faulkner, Ph.D. Presented to the United Nations Convention on Child Rights in Special Session, June 9, 1999

William M. Hilton (1997). "The Limitations on Art. 13(b) of The Convention on the Civil Aspects of International Child Abduction done at the Hague on 25 Oct 1980". Retrieved 2009-06-12.

6

Child Labour and Violation of Human Rights

Child labour can be defined as the employment of children under the age of 18 years, it is considered by many people as the exploitation of children, and it is also considered to violate universal schooling and children rights. Children perform duties in factories, agriculture, domestic work, tourist guides, businesses and restaurants as waiters, extreme forms of child labour include child soldiers, trafficking and child prostitution. There however exist other forms of constructive forms of child labour is evident where we have children who are actors or singers.In developing countries children work in order to earn money to support their families, however in developed countries children work in order to be financially independent from their parents, in developing countries the major push factor to child labour is poverty, this may occur where adults who are parents and labourers do not earn enough to support their families and as a result they end up sending their children to work other than go to school.

Theories of Normative Ethics

Normative ethics concentrates on classifying whether actions are wrong or right, the normative theories tends to observe the norms of actions to determine whether these actions are morally right or morally wrong, there are a number of normative theories, and they include consequential theory, deontology theory or duty theory and virtue ethic theories.

Consequential Theories

The consequential theories states that an action is morally right if the actions themselves have an outcome that is beneficial, there are three consequential theories and they include the utilitarian theory, Altruism theory and the egoism theory. The utilitarian theory states that an action is right if the outcome of the action is beneficial to everyone, the egoism theory states that morally right actions are those whose outcome maximises benefits to the person performing them. And finally the Altruism theory states that an action is considered morally right if the outcome of the action is favourable to every person except the person performing the action.

According to utilitarian theory child labour is morally wrong in that it does not beneficial to everyone, the children suffer and in some cases they are not paid, further these children should be attending school or performing school related duties other than working, there is a need to educate and train these children in order to prepare them for the job market and employing them before they complete their education will mean that this is violating their rights.

An example is the India gap kid clothing company where according to the UK reporters there was beating of children in the industry and further children were not paid for their work, child labour, the employers take advantage that children punishment is allowed in many countries and because children are not aware of their rights they are forced to undertake hard work.

Employers prefer to employ children because they provide cheap labour and also they are easy to control, children are also seen to be more obedient than adults, they therefore employ the children for the purpose of cutting down costs and also because the children are easy to control than the adults because adults are related with initiatives which include protests and formation of trade union. The employers benefit in this case and this is in line with the Altruism theory states that an action is considered morally right if the outcome of the action is favourable to every person except the person performing the action.

The egoism theory which states that morally right actions are those whose outcome maximises benefits to the person performing them supports child labour in developing countries, this is because the children achieve financial dependence from their parents and also have a chance to earn money to achieve what they like than bother their children, the egoistic theory therefore supports child labour in developed countries where the child benefits and also the parents whose financial burden is reduced, in developed countries where children work to support their family it is morally right to engage children in such employment opportunities but it must be noted that child labour should not violate their rights to education and also overworking them.

In a case where a rubber plantation in Liberia where the firestone company was said to be the owner of the rubber plantation, Child labour was evident where the company set a high quota that its workers had to achieve in order to get paid, for this reason therefore the workers working in the plantation brought in their family including their children in order to meet the quota set, a critical view of this situation in accordance with the Consequential theories it is clear that the labourers followed the rules set by the company and their only option to meet these set rules was to bring in their children, therefore child labour here is justified by this theory where parents feared loosing their job and the action to involve children would benefit the family and the company at the same time.

Deontological Theories

The second branch of theory is the deontological theories which is also referred to as the duty theory, they state that when making decisions about actions one has to consider the duties and the rights of the others, these theories include the Contractarianism theory, natural rights theory and the categorical imperative theory. The natural right theory states that human beings have natural rights that should be followed when undertaking actions and The Contractarianism theory states that morally right actions are those that we would accept if we were unbiased.

According to this theory the involvement of children at work is wrong, one because it endangers the children both physically and mentally, in a case where children are trafficked and used as prostitutes and as soldiers this violates the laws of nature, children are supposed to go to school and receive necessary training in order to prepare them to become employees, in contrast child labour has turned the children into sexual harassment where they are turned into prostitutes violating natural laws.

Child labour according to the Deontological theories violates the natural laws of nature, this is because children are yet to be adults where the children are young and do not know their rights, involving them at work places will result into the violation of their rights because most employers tend to exploit them by forcing them to undertake hard work and even not pay them, they further know that children are easy to control than adults and that children will obey, the adult workers know their rights and will not be exploited and they will organise demonstration and even form trade unions that fight for their rights.

Virtue Ethic Theory

The virtue ethic theory states that morally right actions are those that follow the defined rules and laws of action, according to this theory it is evident that child labour is wrong, this is because in most countries laws have been set that children should not work and therefore anyone employing or letting their children work is violating these laws

Developing countries have lagged behind in the campaign towards reducing child labour, which is the reason why they have a high numbers of children working. for this reason therefore the developed countries have adopted ways in which they can discourage this, for example in 1990 there was a mass boycott of oranges from brazil by developed countries, the reason was that orange producing firms used children labour in the production process, also in 2000 there was boycott of cocoa produced in ivory coast by developed countries, these countries noted that children in cocoa plantations employed children in the cultivation of coca and that children were held as captives to work in these farms, for this reason therefore the developed countries banned the importation of coca from ivory coast but later the ban was removed after the country agreed to stop child labour

The theories of normative ethics do not support child labour, for this reason therefore there should be an increased effort to ban child labour in the whole world because it is not morally right, in most cases children are not paid for their work and are disciplined for not working hard, the employers know that they can pay less for employing children and also that children are obedient than adults and for this reason they will employ children, the employers therefore avoid trade unions and protests from workers in case they exploit their workers, for this reason therefore no child should be allowed to work and this will stop exploitation of children worldwide.

In developing countries where children work to support their families the government should come up with policy measures to improve employment and standards of living, this will result into a reduction of child labour in most countries and a healthy working labour force will be evident in future.

Status of Child Labour

Child labour refers to the employment of children at regular and sustained labour. This practice is considered exploitative by many international organizations and is illegal in many countries. Child labour was utilized to varying extents through most of history, but entered public dispute with the advent of universal schooling, with changes in working conditions during the industrial revolution, and with the emergence of the concepts of workers' and children's rights.

In many developed countries, it is considered inappropriate or exploitative if a child below a certain age works (excluding household chores or school-related work). An employer is usually not permitted to hire a child below a certain minimum age. This minimum age depends on the country and the type of work involved. States ratifying the Minimum Age Convention adopted by the International Labour Organization in 1973, have adopted minimum ages varying from 14 to 16. Child labor laws in the United States set the minimum age to work in an establishment without restrictions and without parents' consent at age 16.

Agile boys were employed by the chimney sweeps; small children were employed to scramble under machinery to retrieve cotton bobbins; and children were also employed to work in coal mines to crawl through tunnels too narrow and low for adults. Children also worked as errand boys, crossing sweepers, shoe blacks, or selling matches, flowers and other cheap goods. Some children undertook work as apprentices to respectable trades, such as building or as domestic servants (there were over 120,000 domestic servants in London in the mid 18th Century). Working hours were long: builders worked 64 hours a week in summer and 52 in winter, while domestic servants worked 80 hour weeks.

A high number of children works as prostitutes. Children as young as three were put to work. In coal mines children began work at the age of five and generally died before the age of 25. Many children (and adults) worked 16 hour days. As early as 1802 and 1819 Factory Acts were passed to regulate the working hours of workhouse children in factories and cotton mills to 12 hours per day. These acts were largely ineffective and after radical agitation, by for example the "Short Time Committees" in 1831, a Royal Commission recommended in 1833 that children aged 11–18 should work a maximum of 12 hours per day, children aged 9–11 a maximum of eight hours, and children under the age of nine were no longer permitted to work. This act however only applied to the textile industry, and further agitation led to another act in 1847 limiting both adults and children to 10 hour working days. By 1900, there were 1.7 million child labourers reported in American industry under the age of fifteen. The number of children under the age of 15 who worked in industrial jobs for wages climbed to 2 million in 1910.

Child labour is still common in some parts of the world, it can be factory work, mining, prostitution, quarrying, agriculture, helping in the parents' business, having one's own small business (for example selling food), or doing odd jobs. Some children work as guides for tourists, sometimes combined with bringing in business for shops and restaurants (where they may also work as waiters). Other children are forced to do tedious and repetitive jobs such as: assembling boxes, polishing shoes, stocking a store's products, or cleaning. However, rather than in factories and sweatshops, most child labour occurs in the informal sector, "selling many things on the streets, at work in agriculture or hidden away in houses—far from the reach of official labour inspectors and from media scrutiny." And all the work that they did was done in all types of weather; and was also done for minimal pay. As long as there is family poverty there will be child labour.

According to UNICEF, there are an estimated 158 million children aged 5 to 14 in child labour worldwide, excluding child domestic labour. The United Nations and the International Labour Organization consider child labour exploitative, with the UN stipulating, in article 32 of the Convention on the Rights of the Child that:

> ...States Parties recognize the right of the child to be protected from economic exploitation and from performing any work that is likely to be hazardous or to interfere with the child's education, or to be harmful to the child's health or physical, mental, spiritual, moral or social development. Although globally there is an estimated 250 milllion children working.

In the 1990s every country in the world except for Somalia and the United States became a signatory to the Convention on the Rights of the Child, or CRC. However according to the United Nations Foundation Somalia signed the convention in 2002, the delay of the signing was believed to been due to Somalia not having a government to sign the convention. The CRC provides the strongest, most consistent international legal language prohibiting illegal child labour; however it does not make child labour illegal.

Poor families often rely on the labours of their children in order to survive. Sometimes it is their only income.

In a recent paper, Basu and Van (1998) argue that the primary cause of child labour is parental poverty. That being so, they caution against the use of a legislative ban against child labour, and argue that should be used only when there is reason to believe that a ban on child labour will cause adult wages to rise and so compensate adequately the households of the poor children. Child labour is still widely used today in many countries, including India and Bangladesh. CACL estimated that there are between 70 and 80 million child labourers in India.

Child labour accounts for 22% of the workforce in Asia, 32% in Africa, 17% in Latin America, 1% in US, Canada, Europe and other wealthy nations. The proportion of child labourers varies a lot among countries and even regions inside those countries.

BBC recently reported on Primark using child labour in the manufacture of clothing. In particular a £4.00 hand embroidered shirt was the starting point of a documentary produced by BBC's Panorama (TV series) programme. The programme asks consumers to ask themselves, "Why am I only paying £4 for a hand embroidered top? This item looks handmade. Who made it for such little cost?", in addition to exposing the violent side of the child labour industry in countries where child exploitation is prevalent. As a result of the programme, Primark took action and sacked the relevant companies, and reviewed their supplier procedures.

The Firestone Tire and Rubber Company operate a metal plantation in Liberia which is the focus of a global campaign called Stop Firestone. Workers on the plantation are expected to fulfil a high production quota or their wages will be halved, so many workers brought children to work. The International Labor Rights Fund filed a lawsuit against Firestone (The International Labor Fund vs. The Firestone Tire and Rubber Company) in November 2005 on behalf of current child labourers and their parents who had also been child labourers on the plantation. On June 26, 2007, the judge in this lawsuit in Indianapolis, Indiana denied Firestone's motion to dismiss the case and allowed the lawsuit to proceed on child labour claims.

On November 21, 2005, an Indian NGO activist Junned Khan, with the help of the Labour Department and NGO Pratham mounted the country's biggest ever raid for child labour rescue in the Eastern part of New Delhi, the capital of India. The process resulted in rescue of 480 children from over 100 illegal embroidery factories operating in the crowded slum area of Seelampur. For next few weeks, government, media and NGOs were in a frenzy over the exuberant numbers of young boys, as young as 5-6 year olds, released from bondage. This rescue operation opened the eyes of the world to the menace of child labour operating right under the nose of the largest democracy in the whole world.

After the news of child labourers working in embroidery industry was uncovered in the Sunday Observer on 28 October 2007, BBA activists swung into action. The GAP Inc. in a statement accepted that the child labourers were working in production of GAP Kids blouses and has already made a statement to pull the products from the shelf. In spite of the documentation of the child labourers working in the high-street fashion and admission by all concerned parties, only the SDM could not recognise these children as working under conditions of slavery and bondage.

Distraught and desperate that these collusions by the custodians of justice, founder of BBA Kailash Satyarthi, Chairperson of Global March Against Child Labour appealed to the Honourable Chief Justice of Delhi High Court through a letter at 11.00 pm. This order by the Honourable Chief Justice comes when the government is taking an extremely retrogressive stance on the issue of child labour in sweatshops in India and threatening 'retaliatory measures' against child rights organisations.

In a parallel development, Global March Against Child Labour and BBA are in dialogue with the GAP Inc. and other stakeholders to work out a positive strategy to prevent the entry of child labour in to sweatshops and device a mechanism of monitoring and remedial action. GAP Inc. Senior Vice President, Dan Henkle in a statement said: "We have been making steady progress, and the children are now under the care of the local government. As our policy requires, the vendor with which our order was originally placed will be required to provide the children with access to schooling and job training, pay them an ongoing wage and guarantee them jobs as soon as they reach the legal working age. We will now work with the local government and with Global March to ensure that our vendor fulfils these obligations."

On October 28, Joe Eastman, president of Gap North America, responded, “We strictly prohibit the use of child labor. This is non-negotiable for us—and we are deeply concerned and upset by this allegation. As we’ve demonstrated in the past, Gap has a history of addressing challenges like this head-on, and our approach to this situation will be no exception. In 2006, Gap Inc. ceased business with 23 factories due to code violations. We have 90 people located around the world whose job is to ensure compliance with our Code of Vendor Conduct. As soon as we were alerted to this situation, we stopped the work order and prevented the product from being sold in stores. While violations of our strict prohibition on child labor in factories that produce product for the company are extremely rare, we have called an urgent meeting with our suppliers in the region to reinforce our policies.”

In early August 2008, Iowa Labor Commissioner David Neil announced that his department had found that Agriprocessors, a kosher meatpacking company in Postville which had recently been raided by Immigration and Customs Enforcement, had employed 57 minors, some as young as 14, in violation of state law prohibiting anyone under 18 from working in a meatpacking plant. Neil announced that he was turning the case over to the state Attorney General for prosecution, claiming that his department’s inquiry had discovered “egregious violations of virtually every aspect of Iowa’s child labor laws.” Agriprocessors claimed that it was at a loss to understand the allegations.

In 1997, research indicated that the number of child labourers in the silk-weaving industry in the district of Kanchipuram in India exceeded 40,000. This included children who were bonded labourers to loom owners. Rural Institute for Development Education undertook many activities to improve the situation of child labourers. Working collaboratively, RIDE brought down the number of child labourers to less than 4,000 by 2007

In December 2009, campaigners in the UK called on two leading high street retailers to stop selling clothes made with cotton which may have been picked by children. Anti-Slavery International and the Environmental Justice Foundation (EJF) accused H&M and Zara of using cotton suppliers in Bangladesh. It is also suspected that many of their raw materials originates from Uzbekistan, where children aged 10 are forced to work in the fields. The activists were calling to ban the use of Uzbek cotton and implement a “track and trace” systems to guarantee an ethical responsible source of the material.

H&M said it "does not accept" child labour and "seeks to avoid" using Uzbek cotton, but admitted it did "not have any reliable methods" to ensure Uzbek cotton did not end up in any of its products. Inditex, the owner of Zara, said its code of conduct banned child labour.

Causes of Child Labour

Primary Causes

International Labour Organisation (ILO) suggests poverty is the greatest single cause behind child labour. For impoverished households, income from a child's work is usually crucial for his or her own survival or for that of the household. Income from working children, even if small, may be between 25 to 40% of these household income. Other scholars such as Harsch on African child labour, and Edmonds and Pavcnik on global child labour have reached the same conclusion.

Lack of meaningful alternatives, such as affordable schools and quality education, according to ILO, is another major factor driving children to harmful labour. Children work because they have nothing better to do. Many communities, particularly rural areas where between 60-70% of child labour is prevalent, do not possess adequate school facilities. Even when schools are sometimes available, they are too far away, difficult to reach, unaffordable or the quality of education is so poor that parents wonder if going to school is really worth it.

Cultural Causes

In European history when child labour was common, as well as in contemporary child labour of modern world, certain cultural beliefs have rationalised child labour and thereby encouraged it. Some view that work is good for the character-building and skill development of children. In many cultures, particular where informal economy and small household businesses thrive, the cultural tradition is that children follow in their parents' footsteps; child labour then is a means to learn and practice that trade from a very early age. Similarly, in many cultures the education of girls is less valued or girls are simply not expected to need formal schooling, and these girls pushed into child labour such as providing domestic services.

Macroeconomic Causes

Biggeri and Mehrotra have studied the macroeconomic factors that encourage child labour. They focus their study on five Asian nations including India, Pakistan, Indonesia, Thailand and Philippines. They suggest that child labour is a serious problem in all five, but it is not a new problem. Macroeconomic causes encouraged widespread child labour across the world, over most of human history. They suggest that the causes for child labour include both the demand and the supply side. While poverty and unavailability of good schools explain the child labour supply side, they suggest that the growth of low paying informal economy rather than higher paying formal economy is amongst the causes of the demand side. Other scholars too suggest that inflexible labour market, sise of informal economy, inability of industries to scale up and lack of modern manufacturing technologies are major macroeconomic factors affecting demand and acceptability of child labour.

Child Labour Incidents

Cocoa Production

In 1998, UNICEF reported that Ivory Coast farmers used enslaved children – many from surrounding countries. In late 2000 a BBC documentary reported the use of enslaved children in the production of cocoa—the main ingredient in chocolate— in West Africa. Other media followed by reporting widespread child slavery and child trafficking in the production of cocoa. In 2001, the US State Department estimated there were 15,000 child slaves cocoa, cotton and coffee farms in the Ivory Coast, and the Chocolate Manufacturers Association acknowledged that child slavery is used in the cocoa harvest.

Malian migrants have long worked on cocoa farms in the Ivory Coast, but in 2000 cocoa prices had dropped to a 10-year low and some farmers stopped paying their employees. The Malian counsel had to rescue some boys who had not been paid for five years and who were beaten if they tried to run away. Malian officials believed that 15,000 children, some as young as 11 years old, were working in the Ivory Coast in 2001. These children were often from poor families or the slums and were sold to work in other countries. Parents were told the children would find work and send money home, but once the children left home, they often worked in conditions resembling slavery. In other cases, children begging for food were lured from bus stations and sold as slaves. In 2002, the Ivory Coast had 12,000 children with no relatives nearby, which suggested they were trafficked, likely from neighboring Mali, Burkina Faso and Togo.

The cocoa industry was accused of profiting from child slavery and trafficking. The European Cocoa Association dismissed these accusations as "false and excessive" and the industry said the reports were not representative of all areas. Later the industry acknowledged the working conditions for children were unsatisfactory and children's rights were sometimes violated and acknowledged the claims could not be ignored. In a BBC interview, the ambassador for Ivory Coast to the United Kingdom called these reports of widespread use of slave child labour by 700,000 cocoa farmers as absurd and inaccurate.

In 2001, a voluntary agreement called the Harkin-Engel Protocol, was accepted by the international cocoa and chocolate industry to eliminate the worst forms of child labour, as defined by ILO's Convention 182, in West Africa. This agreement created a foundation named International Cocoa Initiative in 2002. The foundation claims it has, as of 2011, active programs in 290 cocoa growing communities in Côte d'Ivoire and Ghana, reaching a total population of 689,000 people to help eliminate the worst forms of child labour in cocoa industry. Other organisations claim progress has been made, but the protocol's 2005 deadlines have not yet been met.

Mining in Africa

In 2008, Bloomberg claimed child labour in copper and cobalt mines that supplied Chinese companies in Congo. The children are creuseurs, that is they dig the ore by hand, carry sacks of ores on their backs, and these are then purchased by these companies. Over 60 of Katanga's 75 processing plants are owned by Chinese companies and 90 percent of the region's minerals go to China. An African NGO report claimed 80,000 child labourers under the age of 15, or about 40% of all miners, were supplying ore to Chinese companies in this African region.

BBC, in 2012, accused Glencore of using child labour in its mining and smelting operations of Africa. Glencore denied it used child labour, and said it has strict policy of not using child labour. The company claimed it has a strict policy whereby all copper was mined correctly, placed in bags with numbered seals and then sent to the smelter. Glencore mentioned being aware of child miners who were part of a group of artisanal miners who had without authorisation raided the concession awarded to the company since 2010; Glencore has been pleading with the government to remove the artisanal miners from the concession.

Small-scale artisanal mining of gold is another source of dangerous child labour in poor rural areas in certain parts of the world. This form of mining uses labour-intensive and low-tech methods. It is informal sector of the economy. Human Rights Watch group estimates that about 12 percent of global gold production comes from artisanal mines. In west Africa, in countries such as Mali - the third largest exporter of gold in Africa - between 20,000 and 40,000 children work in artisanal mining. Locally known as orpaillage, children as young as 6 years old work with their families. These children and families suffer chronic exposure to toxic chemicals including mercury, and do hazardous work such as digging shafts and working underground, pulling up, carrying and crushing the ore. The poor work practices harm the long term health of children, as well as release hundreds of tons of mercury every year into local rivers, ground water and lakes. Gold is important to the economy of Mali and Ghana. For Mali, it is the second largest earner of its export revenue. For many poor families with children, it is the primary and sometimes the only source of income.

Meatpacking

In early August 2008, Iowa Labour Commissioner David Neil announced that his department had found that Agriprocessors, a kosher meatpacking company in Postville which had recently been raided by Immigration and Customs Enforcement, had employed 57 minors, some as young as 14, in violation of state law prohibiting anyone under 18 from working in a meatpacking plant. Neil announced that he was turning the case over to the state Attorney General for prosecution, claiming that his department's inquiry had discovered "egregious violations of virtually every aspect of Iowa's child labour laws." Agriprocessors claimed that it was at a loss to understand the allegations. Agriprocessors' CEO went to trial on these charges in state court on 4 May 2010. After a five-week trial he was found not guilty of all 57 charges of child labour violations by the Black Hawk County District Court jury in Waterloo, Iowa, on 7 June 2010.

GAP

A 2007 report claimed some GAP products had been produced by child labourers. GAP acknowledged the problem and announced it is pulling the products from its shelf. The report found Gap had rigorous social audit systems since 2004 to eliminate child labour in its supply chain. However, the report concluded that the system was being abused by unscrupulous subcontractors.

GAP's policy, the report claimed, is that if it discovers child labour was used by its supplier in its branded clothes, the contractor must remove the child from the workplace, provide it with access to schooling and a wage, and guarantee the opportunity of work on reaching a legal working age.

In 2007, The New York Times reported that GAP, after the child labour discovery, created a $200,000 grant to improve working conditions in the supplier community.

H&M

In December 2009, campaigners in the UK called on two leading high street retailers to stop selling clothes made with cotton which may have been picked by children. Anti-Slavery International and the Environmental Justice Foundation (EJF) accused H&M and Zara of using cotton suppliers in Bangladesh. It is also suspected that many of their raw materials originates from Uzbekistan, where children aged 10 are forced to work in the fields. The activists were calling to ban the use of Uzbek cotton and implement a "track and trace" systems to guarantee an ethical responsible source of the material.

H&M said it "does not accept" child labour and "seeks to avoid" using Uzbek cotton, but admitted it did "not have any reliable methods" to ensure Uzbek cotton did not end up in any of its products. Inditex, the owner of Zara, said its code of conduct banned child labour.

Silk Weaving

A 2003 Human Rights Watch report claimed children as young as five years old were employed and worked for up to 12 hours a day and six to seven days a week in silk industry. These children, claimed HRW, were bonded child labour in India, easy to find in Karnataka, Uttar Pradesh and Tamil Nadu.

In 2010, a German news investigative report claimed that in silk weaving industry, non-governmental organisations (NGOs) had found up to 10,000 children working in the 1,000 silk factories in 1998. In other places, thousands of bonded child labour were present in 1994. After UNICEF and NGOs got involved, after 2005, child labour figure is drastically lower, with the total estimated to be fewer than a thousand child labourers. The released children were back in school, claims the report.

Primark

In 2008, the BBC reported on Primark using child labour in the manufacture of clothing. In particular, a £4 hand-embroidered shirt was the starting point of a documentary produced by BBC's Panorama programme. The programme asks consumers to ask themselves, "Why am I only paying £4 for a hand embroidered top? This item looks handmade. Who made it for such little cost?", in addition to exposing the violent side of the child labour industry in countries where child exploitation is prevalent.

As a result of the BBC report, Royal Television Society awarded it a prise, and Primark took immediate action and fired three Indian suppliers in 2008.

Primark continued to investigate the allegations for three years, concluding that BBC report was a fake. In 2011, following an investigation by the BBC Trust's Editorial Standards Committee, the BBC announced, "Having carefully scrutinised all of the relevant evidence, the committee concluded that, on the balance of probabilities, it was more likely than not that the Bangalore footage was not authentic." BBC subsequently apologised for faking footage, and returned the television award for investigative reporting.

Eliminating Child Labour

Concerns have often been raised over the buying public's moral complicity in purchasing products assembled or otherwise manufactured in developing countries with child labour. However, others have raised concerns that boycotting products manufactured through child labour may force these children to turn to more dangerous or strenuous professions, such as prostitution or agriculture. For example, a UNICEF study found that after the Child Labour Deterrence Act was introduced in the US, an estimated 50,000 children were dismissed from their garment industry jobs in Bangladesh, leaving many to resort to jobs such as "stone-crushing, street hustling, and prostitution", jobs that are "more hazardous and exploitative than garment production". The study suggests that boycotts are "blunt instruments with long-term consequences, that can actually harm rather than help the children involved."

According to Milton Friedman, before the Industrial Revolution virtually all children worked in agriculture. During the Industrial Revolution many of these children moved from farm work to factory work. Over time, as real wages rose, parents became able to afford to send their children to school instead of work and as a result child labour declined, both before and after legislation. Austrian school economist Murray Rothbard said that British and American children of the pre- and post-Industrial Revolution lived and suffered in infinitely worse conditions where jobs were not available for them and went "voluntarily and gladly" to work in factories.

British historian and socialist E. P. Thompson in The Making of the English Working Class draws a qualitative distinction between child domestic work and participation in the wider (waged) labour market. Further, the usefulness of the experience of the industrial revolution in making predictions about current trends has been disputed. Social historian Hugh Cunningham, author of Children and Childhood in Western Society Since 1500, notes that:

"Fifty years ago it might have been assumed that, just as child labour had declined in the developed world in the late nineteenth and early twentieth centuries, so it would also, in a trickle-down fashion, in the rest of the world. Its failure to do that, and its re-emergence in the developed world, raise questions about its role in any economy, whether national or global."

According to Thomas DeGregori, an economics professor at the University of Houston, in an article published by the Cato Institute, a libertarian think-tank operating in Washington D.C., "it is clear that technological and economic change are vital ingredients in getting children out of the workplace and into schools. Then they can grow to become productive adults and live longer, healthier lives. However, in poor countries like Bangladesh, working children are essential for survival in many families, as they were in our own heritage until the late 19th century. So, while the struggle to end child labour is necessary, getting there often requires taking different routes—and, sadly, there are many political obstacles.

The International Labour Organisation's International Programme on the Elimination of Child Labour (IPEC), founded in 1992, aims to eliminate child labour. It operates in 88 countries and is the largest program of its kind in the world. IPEC works with international and government agencies, NGOs, the media, and children and their families to end child labour and provide children with education and assistance.

Concerns have often been raised over the buying public's moral complicity in purchasing products assembled or otherwise manufactured in developing countries with child labour. However, others have raised concerns that boycotting products manufactured through child labour may force these children to turn to more dangerous or strenuous professions, such as prostitution or agriculture. For example, a UNICEF study found that after the Child Labor Deterrence Act was introduced in the US, an estimated 50,000 children were dismissed from their garment industry jobs in Bangladesh, leaving many to resort to jobs such as "stone-crushing, street hustling, and prostitution", jobs that are "more hazardous and exploitative than garment production". The study suggests that boycotts are "blunt instruments with long-term consequences, that can actually harm rather than help the children involved."

According to Milton Friedman, before the Industrial Revolution virtually all children worked in agriculture. During the Industrial Revolution many of these children moved from farm work to factory work. Over time, as real wages rose, parents became able to afford to send their children to school instead of work and as a result child labour declined, both before and after legislation.

Austrian school economist Murray Rothbard also defended child labour, stating that British and American children of the pre- and post-Industrial Revolution lived and suffered in infinitely worse conditions where jobs were not available for them and went "voluntarily and gladly" to work in factories.

However, the British historian and socialist E. P. Thompson in The Making of the English Working Class draws a qualitative distinction between child domestic work and participation in the wider (waged) labour market. Further, the usefulness of the experience of the industrial revolution in making predictions about current trends has been disputed. Economic historian Hugh Cunningham, author of *Children and Childhood in Western Society Since 1500*, notes that:

> "Fifty years ago it might have been assumed that, just as child labour had declined in the developed world in the late nineteenth and early twentieth centuries, so it would also, in a trickle-down fashion, in the rest of the world. Its failure to do that, and its re-emergence in the developed world, raise questions about its role in any economy, whether national or global."

According to Thomas DeGregori, an economics professor at the University of Houston, in an article published by the Cato Institute, a libertarian think-tank operating in Washington D.C., "it is clear that technological and economic change are vital ingredients in getting children out of the workplace and into schools. Then they can grow to become productive adults and live longer, healthier lives. However, in poor countries like Bangladesh, working children are essential for survival in many families, as they were in our own heritage until the late 19th century. So, while the struggle to end child labour is necessary, getting there often requires taking different routes—and, sadly, there are many political obstacles.

Lawrence Reed, president of the Foundation for Economic Education contends that the infamously brutal child labour conditions during the early industrial revolution were those of "apprentice children" (who were forced to work, even actually sold as slaves, by government-owned Workhouses) and not those of "free-work children" (those who worked voluntarily). So, the government and State-managed institutions, and not Laissez-faire capitalism, is to blame. He further contends that, although work conditions of free-work children were far from ideal, those have been wildly exaggerated in such "authoritative" sources as the Sadler report, a fact that even the anti-capitalist Friedrich Engels acknowledged.

The International Labour Organization's International Programme on the Elimination of Child Labour (IPEC) was created in 1992 with the overall goal of the progressive elimination of child labour, which was to be achieved through strengthening the capacity of countries to deal with the problem and promoting a worldwide movement to combat child labour. IPEC currently has operations in 88 countries, with an annual expenditure on technical cooperation projects that reached over US$61 million in 2008. It is the largest programme of its kind globally and the biggest single operational programme of the ILO.

The number and range of IPEC's partners have expanded over the years and now include employers' and workers' organizations, other international and government agencies, private businesses, community-based organizations, NGOs, the media, parliamentarians, the judiciary, universities, religious groups and, of course, children and their families.

IPEC's work to eliminate child labour is an important facet of the ILO's Decent Work Agenda. Child labour not only prevents children from acquiring the skills and education they need for a better future, it also perpetuates poverty and affects national economies through losses in competitiveness, productivity and potential income. Withdrawing children from child labour, providing them with education and assisting their families with training and employment opportunities contribute directly to creating decent work for adults.

Child Labour Laws and Initiatives

Almost every country in the world has laws relating to and aimed at preventing child labour. International Labour Organisation has helped set international law, which most countries have signed on and ratified.

According to ILO minimum age convention (C138) of 1973, child labour refers to any work performed by children under the age of 12, non-light work done by children aged 12–14, and hazardous work done by children aged 15–17. Light work was defined, under this Convention, as any work that does not harm a child's health and development, and that does not interfere with his or her attendance at school. This convention has been ratified by 135 countries.

The United Nations adopted the Convention on the Rights of the Child in 1990, which was subsequently ratified by 193 countries. Article 32 of the convention addressed child labour, as follows:

> ...Parties recognise the right of the child to be protected from economic exploitation and from performing any work that is likely to be hazardous or to interfere with the child's education, or to be harmful to the child's health or physical, mental, spiritual, moral or social development.

Under Article 1 of the 1990 Convention, a child is defined as "... every human being below the age of eighteen years unless, under the law applicable to the child, majority is attained earlier." Article 28 of this Convention requires States to, "make primary education compulsory and available free to all."

Three countries yet to domestically ratify the 1990 Convention include Somalia, South Sudan and the United States.

In 1999, ILO helped lead the Worst Forms Convention 182 (C182), which has so far been signed upon and domestically ratified by 151 countries including the United States. This international law prohibits worst forms of child labour, defined as all forms of slavery and slavery-like practices, such as child trafficking, debt bondage, and forced labour, including forced recruitment of children into armed conflict. The law also prohibits use of a child for prostitution or the production of pornography, child labour in illicit activities such as drug production and trafficking; and in hazardous work.

In addition to setting the international law, the United Nations initiated International Program on the Elimination of Child Labour (IPEC) in 1992. This initiative aims to progressively eliminate child labour through strengthening national capacities to address some of the causes of child labour. Amongst the key initiative is the so-called time bounded program countries, where child labour is most prevalent and schooling opportunities lacking. The initiative seeks to achieve amongst other things, universal primary school availability. The IPEC has expanded to at least the following target countries: Bangladesh, Brazil, China, Egypt, India, Indonesia, Mexico, Nigeria, Pakistan, Democratic Republic of Congo, El Salvador, Nepal, Tanzania, Dominican Republic, Costa Rica, Philippines, Senegal, South Africa and Turkey.

Exceptions Granted

In 2004, the United States passed an amendment to the Fair Labour Standards Act of 1938. The amendment allows certain children aged 14–18 to work in or outside a business where machinery is used to process wood. The law aims to respect the religious and cultural needs of the Amish community of the United States. The Amish believe that one effective way to educate children is on the job. The new law allows Amish children the ability to work with their families, once they are past eighth grade in school.

Similarly, in 1996, member countries of the European Union, per Directive 94/33/EC, agreed to a number of exceptions for young people in its child labour laws. Under these rules, children of various ages may work in cultural, artistic, sporting or advertising activities if authorised by competent authority. Children above the age of 13 may perform light work for a limited number of hours per week in other economic activities as defined at the discretion of each country. Additionally, the European law exception allows children aged 14 years or over to work as part of a work/ training scheme. The EU Directive clarified that these exceptions do not allow child labour where the children may experience harmful exposure to dangerous substances.

Scholars disagree on the best legal course forward to address child labour. Some suggest the need for laws that place a blanket ban on any work by children less than 18 years old. Others suggest the current international laws are enough, and the need for more engaging approach to achieve the ultimate goals.

Some scholars suggest any labour by children aged 18 year or less is wrong since this encourages illiteracy, inhumane work and lower investment in human capital. Child labour, claim these activists, also leads to poor labour standards for adults, depresses the wages of adults in developing countries as well as the developed countries, and dooms the third world economies to low-skill jobs only capable of producing poor quality cheap exports. More children that work in poor countries, the fewer and worse-paid are the jobs for adults in these countries. In other words, there are moral and economic reasons that justify a blanket ban on labour from children aged 18 years or less, everywhere in the world.

Other scholars suggest that these arguments are flawed, ignores history and more laws will do more harm than good. According to them, child labour is merely the symptom of a greater disease named poverty. If laws ban all lawful work that enables the poor to survive, informal economy, illicit operations and underground businesses will thrive. These will increase abuse of the children. In poor countries with very high incidence rates of child labour - such as Ethiopia, Chad, Niger and Nepal - schools are not available, and the few schools that exist offer poor quality education or are unaffordable. The alternatives for children who currently work, claim these studies, are worse: grinding subsistence farming, militia or prostitution. Child labour is not a choice, it is a necessity, the only option for survival. It is currently the least undesirable of a set of very bad choices.

These scholars suggest, from their studies of economic and social data, that early 20th century child labour in Europe and the United States ended in large part as a result of economic development of formal regulated economy, technology development and general prosperity. Child labour laws and ILO conventions came later. Edmonds suggests, even in contemporary times, incidence of child labour in Vietnam has rapidly reduced following economic reforms and GDP growth. These scholars suggest economic engagement, emphasis on opening quality schools rather than more laws, and expanding economically relevant skill development opportunities in the third world. International legal actions, such as trade sanctions increase child labour. "The Incredible Bread Machine" a book published by "World Research, Inc." in 1974:

> "Child labor was a particular target of early reformers. William Cooke Tatlor wrote at the time about these reformers who, witnissing children ar work in the factories, thought to themselves: 'How much more delightful would have

been the gambol of the free limbs on the hillside; the sight of the green mead with its spangles of buttercups and daisies; the song of the bird and the humming bee...' But for many of these children the factory system meant quite literally the only chance for survival. Today we overlook the fact that death from starvation and exposure was a common fate before the Industrial Revolution, for the pre capitalist economy was barely able to support the population. Yes, children were working. Formerly they would have starved. It was only as goods were produced in greater abundance at lower cost that men could support their families without sending their children to work. It was not the reformer or the politician that ended the grim necessity for child labor; it was capitalism."

Worst Forms of Child Labor Convention, 1999

The Convention concerning the Prohibition and Immediate Action for the Elimination of the Worst Forms of Child Labour, known in short as the Worst Forms of Child Labour Convention, was adopted by the International Labour Organization (ILO) in 1999 as ILO Convention No 182. It is one of 8 ILO fundamental conventions.

By ratifying this Convention No. 182, a country commits itself to taking immediate action to prohibit and eliminate the worst forms of child labour. The Convention is enjoying the fastest pace of ratifications in the ILO's history since 1919.

The ILO's International Programme on the Elimination of Child Labour (IPEC) is responsible for assisting countries in this regard as well as monitoring compliance. One of the methods used by IPEC to assist countries in this regard are Time-bound Programmes.

The ILO also adopted the Worst Forms of Child Labour Recommendation No 190 in 1999. This recommendation contains, among others, recommendations on the types of hazards that should be considered for inclusion within a country-based definition of Worst Form Hazards faced by Children at Work.

The full-text of the convention is given below.

The General Conference of the International Labor Organisation,

Having been convened at Geneva by the Governing Body of the International Labor Office, and having met in its 87th Session on 1 June 1999, and

Considering the need to adopt new instruments for the prohibition and elimination of the worst forms of child labor, as the main priority for national and international action, including international cooperation and assistance, to complement the Convention and the Recommendation concerning Minimum Age for Admission to Employment, 1973, which remain fundamental instruments on child labor, and

Considering that the effective elimination of the worst forms of child labor requires immediate and comprehensive action, taking into account the importance of free basic education and the need to remove the children concerned from all such work and to provide for their rehabilitation and social integration while addressing the needs of their families, and

Recalling the resolution concerning the elimination of child labor adopted by the International Labor Conference at its 83rd Session in 1996, and

Recognising that child labor is to a great extent caused by poverty and that the long-term solution lies in sustained economic growth leading to social progress, in particular poverty alleviation and universal education, and

Recalling the Convention on the Rights of the Child adopted by the United Nations General Assembly on 20 November 1989, and

Recalling the ILO Declaration on Fundamental Principles and Rights at Work and its Follow-up, adopted by the International Labor Conference at its 86th Session in 1998, and

Recalling that some of the worst forms of child labor are covered by other international instruments, in particular the Forced Labor Convention, 1930, and the United Nations Supplementary Convention on the Abolition of Slavery, the Slave Trade, and Institutions and Practices Similar to Slavery, 1956, and

Having decided upon the adoption of certain proposals with regard to child labor, which is the fourth item on the agenda of the session, and

Having determined that these proposals shall take the form of an international Convention,

Adopts this seventeenth day of June of the year one thousand nine hundred and ninety-nine the following Convention, which may be cited as the Worst Forms of Child Labor Convention, 1999.

Article 1

Each Member which ratifies this Convention shall take immediate and effective measures to secure the prohibition and elimination of the worst forms of child labor as a matter of urgency.

Article 2

For the purposes of this Convention, the term "child" shall apply to all persons under the age of 18.

Article 3

For the purposes of this Convention, the term "*the worst forms of child labor*" comprises:

(a) All forms of slavery or practices similar to slavery, such as the sale and trafficking of children, debt bondage and serfdom and forced or compulsory labor, including forced or compulsory recruitment of children for use in armed conflict;

(b) The use, procuring or offering of a child for prostitution, for the production of pornography or for pornographic performances;

(c) The use, procuring or offering of a child for illicit activities, in particular for the production and trafficking of drugs as defined in the relevant international treaties;

(d) Work which, by its nature or the circumstances in which it is carried out, is likely to harm the health, safety or morals of children.

Article 4

1. The types of work referred to under Article 3(d) shall be determined by national laws or regulations or by the competent authority, after consultation with the organisations of employers and workers concerned, taking into consideration relevant international standards, in particular Paragraphs 3 and 4 of the Worst Forms of Child Labor Recommendation, 1999.
2. The competent authority, after consultation with the organisations of employers and workers concerned, shall identify where the types of work so determined exist.
3. The list of the types of work determined under paragraph 1 of this Article shall be periodically examined and revised as necessary, in consultation with the organisations of employers and workers concerned.

Article 5

Each Member shall, after consultation with employers' and workers' organisations, establish or designate appropriate mechanisms to monitor the implementation of the provisions giving effect to this Convention.

Article 6

1. Each Member shall design and implement programes of action to eliminate as a priority the worst forms of child labor.
2. Such programes of action shall be designed and implemented in consultation with relevant government institutions and employers' and workers' organisations, taking into consideration the views of other concerned groups as appropriate.

Article 7

1. Each Member shall take all necessary measures to ensure the effective implementation and enforcement of the provisions giving effect to this Convention including the provision and application of penal sanctions or, as appropriate, other sanctions.
2. Each Member shall, taking into account the importance of education in eliminating child labor, take effective and time-bound measures to:
   (a) Prevent the engagement of children in the worst forms of child labor;
   (b) Provide the necessary and appropriate direct assistance for the removal of children from the worst forms of child labor and for their rehabilitation and social integration;
   (c) Ensure access to free basic education, and, wherever possible and appropriate, vocational training, for all children removed from the worst forms of child labor;
   (d) Identify and reach out to children at special risk; and
   (e) Take account of the special situation of girls.
3. Each Member shall designate the competent authority responsible for the implementation of the provisions giving effect to this Convention.

Article 8

Members shall take appropriate steps to assist one another in giving effect to the provisions of this Convention through enhanced international cooperation and/or assistance including support for social and economic development, poverty eradication programes and universal education.

Article 9

The formal ratifications of this Convention shall be communicated to the Director-General of the International Labor Office for registration.

Article 10

1. This Convention shall be binding only upon those Members of the International Labor Organisation whose ratifications have been registered with the Director-General of the International Labor Office.
2. It shall come into force 12 months after the date on which the ratifications of two Members have been registered with the Director-General.
3. Thereafter, this Convention shall come into force for any Member 12 months after the date on which its ratification has been registered.

Article 11

1. A Member which has ratified this Convention may denounce it after the expiration of ten years from the date on which the Convention first comes into force, by an act communicated to the Director-General of the International Labor Office for registration. Such denunciation shall not take effect until one year after the date on which it is registered.
2. Each Member which has ratified this Convention and which does not, within the year following the expiration of the period of ten years mentioned in the preceding paragraph, exercise the right of denunciation provided for in this Article, will be bound for another period of ten years and, thereafter, may denounce this Convention at the expiration of each period of ten years under the terms provided for in this Article.

Article 12

1. The Director-General of the International Labor Office shall notify all Members of the International Labor Organisation of the registration of all ratifications and acts of denunciation communicated by the Members of the Organisation.

2. When notifying the Members of the Organisation of the registration of the second ratification, the Director-General shall draw the attention of the Members of the Organisation to the date upon which the Convention shall come into force.

Article 13

The Director-General of the International Labor Office shall communicate to the Secretary-General of the United Nations, for registration in accordance with article 102 of the Charter of the United Nations, full particulars of all ratifications and acts of denunciation registered by the Director-General in accordance with the provisions of the preceding Articles.

Article 14

At such times as it may consider necessary, the Governing Body of the International Labor Office shall present to the General Conference a report on the working of this Convention and shall examine the desirability of placing on the agenda of the Conference the question of its revision in whole or in part.

Article 15

1. Should the Conference adopt a new Convention revising this Convention in whole or in part, then, unless the new Convention otherwise provides:
   (a) The ratification by a Member of the new revising Convenmtion shall ipso jure involve the immediate denunciation of this Convention, notwithstanding the provisions of Article 11 above, if and when the new revising Convention shall have come into force;
   (b) As from the date when the new revising Convention comes into force, this Convention shall cease to be open to ratification by the Members.
2. This Convention shall in any case remain in force in its actual form and content for those Members which have ratified it but have not ratified the revising Convention.

Article 16

The English and French versions of the text of this Convention are equally authoritative.

References

Baland, Jean-Marie and James A. Robinson (2000) 'Is child labour inefficient?' *Journal of Political Economy* 108, 663–679

Bhukuth, Augendra. "Defining child labour: a controversial debate" *Development in Practice* (2008) 18, 385–394

Christiaan Grootaert and Harry Anthony Patrinos (1999). *The Policy Analysis of Child Labour: A Comparative Study.* Palgrave Macmillan

Mario Biggeri and Santosh Mehrotra (2007). *Asian Informal Workers: Global Risks, Local Protection.* Routledge

Humbert, Franziska. *The Challenge of Child Labour in International Law* (2009)

Humphries, Jane. *Childhood and Child Labour in the British Industrial Revolution* (2010)

7

Children's Right to Education

Education is an essential right, which permits each person to receive instruction and to blossom socially. The right to an education is vital for the economic, social and cultural development of all societies.

Education entails that its subjects acquire a variety of knowledge. It begins with the acquisition of elementary knowledge—that is to say, literacy—on the part of the youngest members of society. At this stage, children learn to read and write thanks to primary instruction and parental oversight.

This is an essential stage which will permit the child to pursue his/her education by integrating secondary and post-secondary instruction.

Education also consists of a form of learning that is necessary for the development of one's personality and identity, as well as his physical and intellectual capabilities. Education permits, notably, the transmission of common principles to new generations, and the conservation and perpetuation of social values. It also contributes to the flourishing of individuality through the enhancement of social and professional integration.

Education has as its ultimate objective the improvement of a person's quality of life. It offers to underprivileged adults and children a chance to escape from poverty. It is thus an essential tool for the economic, social and cultural development of all populations around the world.

Education is a human right which ought to be accessible to everyone, without any discrimination. All children must be able to go to school, and thereby benefit from the same opportunities to build a future. Additionally, educational instruction must be equally gratuitous so that children from disadvantaged environments will be able to enjoy their right to an education.

Beyond the question of accessibility, the right to an education also supposes that the objectives of learning will be attained. This means that all children have the right to benefit from a quality education adapted to their needs. Moreover, professors must be trained in techniques of teaching which combine pedagogy and play for the purpose of arousing children's interest.

It is the responsibility of countries to guarantee each child's right to an education. They must focus their efforts on primary instruction so as to make schools accessible and free for all children and thus enable them to learn to read and write.

Education as a Human Right

Education has been formally recognised as a human right since the adoption of the Universal Declaration of Human Rights in 1948. This has since been affirmed in numerous global human rights treaties, including the United Nations Educational, Scientific and Cultural Organisation (UNESCO) Convention against Discrimination in Education (1960), the International Covenant on Economic, Social and Cultural Rights (1966) and the Convention on the Elimination of All Forms of Discrimination against Women (1981). These treaties establish an entitlement to free, compulsory primary education for all children; an obligation to develop secondary education, supported by measures to render it accessible to all children, as well as equitable access to higher education; and a responsibility to provide basic education for individuals who have not completed primary education. Furthermore, they affirm that the aim of education is to promote personal development, strengthen respect for human rights and freedoms, enable individuals to participate effectively in a free society, and promote understanding, friendship and tolerance. The right to education has long been recognised as encompassing not only access to educational provision, but also the obligation to eliminate discrimination at all levels of the educational system, to set minimum standards and to improve quality. In addition, education is necessary for the fulfilment of any other civil, political, economic or social right.

The United Nations Convention on the Rights of the Child (1989) further strengthens and broadens the concept of the right to education, in particular through the obligation to consider in its implementation the Convention's four core principles: non-discrimination; the best interests of the child; the right to life, survival and development of the child to the maximum extent possible; and the right of children to express their views in all matters affecting them and for their views to be given due weight in accordance with their age and maturity. These underlying principles make clear a strong commitment to ensuring that children are recognised as active agents in their own learning and that education is designed to promote and respect their rights and needs. The Convention elaborates an understanding of the right to education in terms of universality, participation, respect and inclusion. This approach is exemplified both in the text itself and in its interpretation by the Committee on the Rights of the Child, the international body established to monitor governments' progress in implementing child rights.

The perspectives introduced in the Convention on the Rights of the Child are given below:

1. The right to education is to be achieved on the basis of equality of opportunity.
2. Measures must be taken to encourage regular school attendance and reduce dropout. It is not sufficient just to provide formal education. It is also necessary to remove such barriers as poverty and discrimination and to provide education of sufficient quality, in a manner that ensures children can benefit from it.
3. Discipline must be administered in a manner consistent both with the child's dignity and with the right to protection from all forms of violence, thus sustaining respect for the child in the educational environment.
4. The aims of education are defined in terms of the potential of each child and the scope of the curriculum, clearly establishing that education should be a preparatory process for promoting and respecting human rights. This approach is elaborated in the General Comment on the aims of education, in which the Committee on the Rights of the Child stresses that article 29 requires the development of education that is child centred, child friendly and empowering, and that education goes

beyond formal schooling to embrace a broad range of life experiences through which positive development and learning occur.

5. In its General Comment on early childhood, the Committee on the Rights of the Child interprets the right to education as beginning at birth and encourages governments to take measures and provide programes to enhance parental capacities to promote their children's development.

Beyond the formal obligations undertaken by governments in ratifying these human rights treaties, a number of global conferences have affirmed the right to education. Although lacking the legally binding force of the treaties, these conferences have introduced an additional impetus for action, together with elaborated commitments and time frames for their attainment. The World Conference on Education for All (1990) set the goal of universal primary education for the year 2000, a goal not met but subsequently reaffirmed for 2015 at the World Education Forum in 2000. This Forum also committed to an expansion and improvement of early childhood care and education, the elimination of gender disparities in education and the improvement of quality in education.

In addition, the international community and leading development institutions have agreed to the Millennium Development Goals, expressed in the Millennium Declaration, which commit them to ensuring that all girls and boys complete a full course of primary education and that gender disparity is eliminated at all levels of education by 2015. More recently, the 'International Conference on the Right to Basic Education as a Fundamental Human Right and the Legal Framework for Its Financing' (Jakarta, Indonesia, 2–4 December 2005) adopted the Jakarta Declaration. This emphasises that the right to education is an internationally recognised right in its interrelationship with the right to development, and that the legal and constitutional protection of this right is indispensable to its full realisation.

Situation of Children's Right to Education Worldwide

Today, education remains an inaccessible right for millions of children around the world. More than 72 million children of primary education age are not in school and 759 million adults are illiterate and do not have the awareness necessary to improve both their living conditions and those of their children.

Causes of Lack of Education

Marginalisation and poverty

For many children who still do not have access to education, it is notably because of persisting inequality and marginalization.

In developing and developed countries alike, children do not have access to basic education because of inequalities that originate in sex, health and cultural identity (ethnic origin, language, religion). These children find themselves on the margins of the education system and do not benefit from learning that is vital to their intellectual and social development.

Factors linked to poverty such as unemployment, illness and the illiteracy of parents, multiply the risk of non-schooling and the drop-out rate of a child by 2.

Undeniably, many children from disadvantaged backgrounds are forced to abandon their education due to health problems related to malnutrition or in order to work and provide support for the family.

Financial deficit of developing countries

Universal primary education is a major issue and a sizeable problem for many states. Many emerging countries do not appropriate the financial resources necessary to create schools, provide schooling materials, nor recruit and train teachers. Funds pledged by the international community are generally not sufficient enough to allow countries to establish an education system for all children.

Equally, a lack of financial resources has an effect on the quality of teaching. Teachers do not benefit from basic teacher training and schools, of which there are not enough, have oversized classes.

This overflow leads to classes where many different educational levels are forced together which does not allow each individual child to benefit from an education adapted to their needs and abilities. As a result, the drop-out rate and education failure remains high.

Right to Education Worldwide

Most Affected Regions

As a result of poverty and marginalization, more than 72 million children around the world remain unschooled.

Sub-Saharan Africa is the most affected area with over 32 million children of primary school age remaining uneducated. Central and Eastern Asia, as well as the Pacific, are also severely affected by this problem with more than 27 million uneducated children.

Additionally, these regions must also solve continuing problems of educational poverty (a child in education for less than 4 years) and extreme educational poverty (a child in education for less than 2 years). .

Essentially this concerns Sub-Saharan Africa where more than half of children receive an education for less than 4 years. In certain countries, such as Somalia and Burkina Faso, more than 50% of children receive an education for a period less than 2 years. .

The lack of schooling and poor education have negative effects on the population and country. The children leave school without having acquired the basics, which greatly impedes the social and economic development of these countries.

Inequality between girls and boys: the education of girls in jeopardy

Today, it is girls who have the least access to education. They make up more than 54% of the non-schooled population in the world.

This problem occurs most frequently in Arab States, in central Asia and in Southern and Western Asia and is principally explained by the cultural and traditional privileged treatment given to males. Girls are destined to work in the family home, whereas boys are entitled to receive an education.

In sub-Saharan Africa, over 12 million girls are at risk of never receiving an education. In Yemen, it is more than 80% of girls who will never have the opportunity to go to school. Even more alarming, certain countries such as Afghanistan or Somalia make no effort to reduce the gap between girls and boys with regard to education.

Although many developing countries may congratulate themselves on dramatically reducing inequality between girls and boys in education, a lot of effort is still needed in order to achieve universal primary education.

Rights-based Approach to Education

Needs-based development approaches to education have, to date, failed to achieve the Education for All goals. Because it is inclusive and provides a common language for partnership, a rights-based approach although certainly not without tensions and challenges has the potential to contribute to the attainment of the goals of governments, parents and children. Girls' right to education, for example, can be achieved more effectively if measures are also implemented to address their rights to freedom from discrimination, protection from exploitative labor, physical violence and sexual abuse, and access to an adequate standard of living. Equally, the right to education is instrumental in the realisation of other rights. Research indicates, for example, that one additional year of schooling for 1,000 women helps prevent two maternal deaths.

A rights-based approach can contribute significant added value:

1. *It promotes social cohesion, integration and stability*: Human rights promote democracy and social progress. Even where children have access to school, a poor quality of education can contribute to disaffection. A rights-based approach to education, which emphasises quality, can encourage the development of school environments in which children know their views are valued. It includes a focus on respect for families and the values of the society in which they are living. It can also promote understanding of other cultures and peoples, contributing to intercultural dialogue and respect for the richness of cultural and linguistic diversity, and the right to participate in cultural life. In this way, it can serve to strengthen social cohesion.

2. *It builds respect for peace and non-violent conflict resolution*: A rights-based approach to education is founded on principles of peace and non-violent conflict resolution. In achieving this goal, schools and communities must create learning environments that eliminate all forms of physical, sexual or humiliating punishment by teachers and challenge all forms of bullying and aggression among students. In other words, they must promote and build a culture of non-violent conflict resolution. The lessons children learn from school-based experiences in this regard can have far-reaching consequences for the wider society.

3. *It contributes to positive social transformation*: A rights-based approach to education that embodies human rights education empowers children and other stakeholders and represents a major building block in efforts to achieve social transformation towards rights-respecting societies and social justice.

4. *It is more cost-effective and sustainable*: Treating children with dignity and respect and building inclusive, participatory and accountable

education systems that respond directly to the expressed concerns of all stakeholders will serve to improve educational outcomes. In too many schools, the failure to adapt to the needs of children, particularly working children, results in high levels of dropout and repeated grades. Children themselves cite violence and abuse, discriminatory attitudes, an irrelevant curriculum and poor teaching quality as major contributory factors in the inability to learn effectively and in subsequent dropout. In addition, health issues can diminish the ability of a child to commence and continue schooling, and for all children, especially girls, an inclusive education can reduce the risk of HIV infection. A rights-based approach is therefore not only cost-effective and economically beneficial but also more sustainable.

5. *It produces better outcomes for economic development*: A rights-based approach to education can be entirely consistent with the broader agenda of governments to produce an economically viable workforce. Measures to promote universal access to education and overcome discrimination against girls, children with disabilities, working children, children in rural communities, and minority and indigenous children will serve to widen the economic base of society, thus strengthening a country's economic capability.
6. *It builds capacity*: By focusing on capacity-building and empowerment, a rights-based approach to education harnesses and develops the capacities of governments to fulfil their obligations and of individuals to claim their rights and entitlements.

Applying a Rights-based Approach to Policy and Programming

The UN Statement of Common Understanding elaborates what is understood to be a rights-based approach to development cooperation and development programming. It emphasises that all programes of development cooperation, policies and technical assistance should further the realisation of human rights, and therefore that human rights principles and standards should guide all phases of the programming process. The following elements are necessary, specific and unique to a rights-based approach and can be used for policy and programming in the education sector:

1. Assessment and analysis identify the claims of human rights in education and the corresponding obligations of governments, as well as the immediate, underlying and structural causes of the non-realisation of rights.

2. Programes assess the capacity of individuals to claim their rights and of governments to fulfil their obligations. Strategies are then developed to build those capacities.
3. Programes monitor and evaluate both the outcomes and processes, guided by human rights standards and principles.
4. Programming is informed by the recommendations of international human rights bodies and mechanisms.

In addition, many elements of good programming practice are essential within a rights-based approach. Overall, then, the required steps are:

1. Situation assessment and analysis.
2. Assessing capacity for implementation.
3. Programe planning, design and implementation.
4. Monitoring and evaluation.

How 'Good Programming' can be Enhanced by a Human Rights-based Approach

1. *In good programming, it is recognised that people cannot be developed; they must develop themselves. Children, young people and other learners, including those who are poor, should be recognised as key actors in their own education and development rather than as passive beneficiaries of services and transfers of commodities.*

   In a rights-based approach to education, children and other learners, including those who are poor, are subjects of rights with 'claims to' education and 'claims from' duty bearers. Rights-based education programming should therefore develop the capacities of children, young people, their parents and other learners to claim their rights. Human rights education is an important instrument in empowering people to understand, claim and realise their rights.

2. *In good programming, participation is crucial, both as an end and a means. Participation does not mean that 'they' participate in 'our' education programe, but rather that we all participate in meeting the learning needs identified.*

   Participation, including children's and women's participation, is a human right enshrined in many conventions. In a rights-based approach to education, participation is both a necessary process and an outcome.

3. *In good programming, empowerment is important, but it is not a strategy. Empowerment may be an aspect of any strategy, such as advocacy, capacity-building or service delivery.*

   A rights-based approach, which implies dignity and respect for the individual, acknowledges that empowerment is both a necessary strategy and a goal. Emphasis is placed on promoting opportunities to obtain remedies for grievances through both formal and informal justice mechanisms.

4. *In good programming, monitoring of outcome and processes, as well as actual use of information for decision-making at all levels of education, is very important.*

   A rights-based approach implies accountability of those with duties or obligations in fulfilling, respecting and protecting the right to education.

5. *In good programming, stakeholder analysis is very useful for the development and evaluation of education programes because it identifies clear accountabilities in the community and society.*

   Most stakeholders in education are also duty bearers. An important step in a rights-based approach is to identify the key relations between claim-holders and duty bearers. This is similar to, but goes beyond, stakeholder analysis.

   The relationship between claims and duties implies clear accountabilities the commitments made under human rights treaties are entitlements, not promises or charity. Development assistance must be the result of those international obligations.

6. *In good programming, education programes should respond to basic needs of children and other people, with a focus on vulnerable groups. Local ownership is important, and development support from outside should always build on existing capabilities.*Poverty elimination and disparity reduction should be long-term goals in all education development efforts.

   Education programes should respond to need but must also take account of the rights of children, young people and other learners. Stakeholders in education should have an ownership of education programes as a right, rather than an option. The right to education is a means to reduce disparity and poverty. Education programming should therefore articulate the explicit linkages between proposed actions and their relationship to reducing disparities and eliminating poverty and injustice. This may involve both institutional and legal reform. Human rights standards provide tools and legitimacy for advocacy for change.

7. *In good programming, education programes should be developed on the basis of a situation analysis that identifies priority problems and their immediate, underlying and basic causes, which should be addressed either simultaneously or in sequence.*

   A rights-based approach to education requires that underlying causes of poverty and inequality be addressed. The indivisibility of human rights also emphasises simultaneous attention to causes at all levels.

8. *In good programming, setting goals is important, and the necessity for scaling up should be considered at the planning stage. Efforts should be made to ensure that positive changes are sustainable and sustained. This includes environmental sustainability.*

   The realisation of rights-based education requires both the achievement of desirable outcomes and achieving them through a process that reflects human rights values. A rights-based approach to education calls for simultaneous attention to outcomes and processes. A shift of focus is needed away from service delivery towards capacity development and advocacy.

Situation Assessment and Analysis

Whereas a development approach to situation analysis addresses risks, power, stakeholders, root causes and gender, a rights-based approach to programming is informed by reference to the full range of relevant human rights including any guidance provided by treaty bodies through General Comments and their concluding observations in relation to education. It also necessitates the following dimensions:

1. *Analysis of the legislative, policy and practice environment*: It is not sufficient that legislation is in place. Too often, legislation exists but is not implemented. Inadequate resources, lack of capacities in terms of the where withal to implement policy, lack of public demand and low levels of information, awareness and training render it ineffective, and there are no means of redress if the rights it introduces are not respected.

2. *A focus on primary responsibility of governments*: In education, governments bear the primary responsibility to, for example, provide

schools, train teachers, develop the curriculum, monitor standards, eliminate discrimination and promote equal opportunity of access. Other key players such as local authorities, schools, parents and communities also have responsibilities, although in some cases their capacities to fulfil these are necessarily dependent on the government meeting its primary responsibilities.

3. *Applying the four central principles of the Convention on the Rights of the Child*: Non-discrimination, best interests of the child, the right to life, survival and development, and the right to express views and have them given due weight must be a focus throughout the analysis.
4. *Analysis of rights violations and denials*: It is essential that this analysis includes the immediate, underlying and structural causes of violations and is extended to access to education, quality in education and respect for children's rights within education.
5. *A focus on the poorest and most vulnerable*: These groups are usually the most disempowered and at greatest risk of violation or denial of their rights.
6. *A participatory approach*: This enables the input of a range of stakeholders including parents, teachers, religious leaders, community groups and children into the analysis and provides opportunities to feed back on its conclusions.Children's perspectives are indispensable. Whenever possible, the views of girls and boys of different ages, in and out of school, with and without disabilities, and from different ethnic groups, geographic locations and socio-economic situations should be taken into account.
7. *Disaggregated data*: To ensure the visibility of all groups of children in relation to enrolment, attendance, completion, attainment in education and other pertinent factors, it is crucial that data are disaggregated by sex, disability, race, ethnic or social origin, economic status, religion, language, geographic location and other status.

Assessing Capacity for Implementation

A rights-based approach to education policy and programming places a particular focus on assessing the capacity of both rights holders to claim their rights and governments and public authorities to fulfil their obligations. The process should involve plans and activities to increase the capacity of individuals to support the implementation of education priorities.

Capacities of Rights Holders to Claim Rights

In order to claim rights, people need to know what their rights are and how they are being addressed, how decisions are made and by whom, and what mechanisms, if any, exist to seek redress in cases of violations. If teachers are persistently absent or fail to teach, parents and the community need to know that their children have the right to education and that they should join together to demand the resolution of such problems. They need opportunities for access to policymakers and the media. They may also need support in analysing how their rights are being denied and how to argue their case for change. Efforts also need to be made to build opportunities for children to claim their rights. There is a growing body of tools and strategies for promoting children's access to the media, policymakers and politicians, as well as evidence of the capacity for effective child advocacy. Empowering rights holders to claim their rights requires a range of strategies, including information, advocacy, capacity-building, parent networking, peer support and technical assistance.

Capacities of Government and Public Authorities to Fulfil Obligations

Assessment of the capacities of government and public authorities to meet their obligations with regard to educational rights is key. Obstacles to complying with responsibilities may derive from:

1. *Lack of resources*—financial (tax base or budget priorities) or human (skills and institutional capacity).
2. *Lack of authority*—legal, moral, spiritual or cultural.
3. *Lack of responsibility*—refusing to accept obligations and demonstrating no political commitment to doing so.
4. Lack of coordination between levels and sectors.
5. *Lack of knowledge*—for example, illiterate parents may not know that they have an obligation to send their children to school.

The analysis will indicate the strategies necessary to achieve change. For example, in order to assess parents' capacities to fulfil their obligation to send their children to school, States need to analyse the real costs associated with schooling. The absence of school fees may be insufficient to eliminate the economic burden on parents; school uniforms, equipment and transportation, as well as the loss of domestic support or the earnings of a child, need to be included in the analysis when developing policies aimed at universal education. In situations of crisis, conflict and transition, the obstacles are likely to be particularly acute. However, it is possible to build capacity and commitment to sustain or restore access to education even in war-torn environments.

Programe Planning, Design and Implementation

A rights-based approach to programming recognises that the process of development is as important as the outcome. Indeed, the process largely determines the type of outcome resulting from development activities. The principles that inform a rights-based approach outlined above should be taken into consideration in the planning, design and implementation of programes. Although not all are new to development practice participation and accountability, for example, are also characteristic of good programming the added value of a rights-based approach is that such principles acquire moral and political force. This is important, given that the people who may benefit the most from the application of these principles, i.e., poor and marginalised groups, are not generally in a position to claim their rights.

Taking a rights-based approach to education will necessitate that:

1. The programe engages with government in a constructive dialogue regarding its obligations, and how best it can fulfil these. This may require incentives and technical assistance, as well as capacity-building.
2. Claims holders are involved in the assessment, decision-making and implementation of education provision.
3. Evidence-based advocacy is used to increase the scale of impact through, for example, replication, legislative and policy change, and resource allocation.
4. Civil society is involved in programe design and implementation to promote government accountability.
5. Special attention is paid to the most marginalised and discriminated against groups. This approach involves going beyond addressing poorer communities to identify the most vulnerable people among the poor, for example, children with disabilities, children in low castes, internally displaced persons and children living with HIV. It then develops programming specifically to reach them.
6. All programe activities are explicitly linked to human rights standards. Such standards set minimum guarantees for poor and disadvantaged

groups. They also help identify where problems exist and what capacities and functions are required to address them. In the programming process, human rights standards can help define a comprehensive but targeted scope for development strategies that will yield more cost-effective results. They can also help to set results-based outcomes and outputs.

Monitoring and Evaluation

A rights-based approach to monitoring and evaluating education has implications, beyond those that would be addressed as good development practice, for both the process by which it is undertaken and the outcomes it seeks to measure. In terms of process, there is a need for greater transparency of information about education provision. In addition, children and their communities need to be actively engaged as partners and involved in design, analysis, sharing of information and documentation. Their involvement empowers them and improves the quality of the information. Such monitoring and evaluation frameworks will help capture both the qualitative and quantitative indicators in respect of realising the rights-based approach to education. In terms of outcomes, monitoring and evaluation needs to address:

1. Changes in the lives of children to measure whether their education rights are better realised or no longer violated.
2. Changes in legislation, policy, structures and practices and their impact on the realisation of educational rights.
3. Changes in relation to equity and non-discrimination in respect of access to education, the quality of that education and the experience of children within it. For example, have more marginalised children been reached and have discriminatory references in the curriculum been removed?
4. Opportunities for participation and active citisenship of children, as well as other stakeholders, in schools and in the wider development of education policy.
5. Changes in civil society and community capacity to support the rights-based approach for example, through advocacy for improved education, active support for local schools, and ensuring the equal right of girls and boys.

Addressing Tensions

A rights-based approach to programming is not a magic wand. It does not provide simple solutions to challenges that have proved intractable for many years. While providing a principled framework and a methodology for its application, it can also expose tensions, real or apparent, between different rights, among rights holders, and between rights and responsibilities.

Reconciling Conflicting Agendas for Education

In its General Comment on the aims of education, the Committee on the Rights of the Child emphasised that the overarching aim must be to promote, support and protect "the human dignity innate in every child and his or her equal and inalienable rights" while taking into account the child's developmental needs and diverse evolving capacities. This is to be achieved through the holistic development of the full potential of the child, including a respect for human rights, an enhanced sense of identity and affiliation, and socialisation with others and with the environment.

In practice, however, there are competing agendas for the aims of education systems. For governments, there are two major goals in funding education: to develop the economic workforce and potential future wealth; and to promote social cohesion, integration and a sense of national identity. Indeed, the development of mass education during the 20th century is recognised to have played an important role in promoting national integration and uniformity in both industrialised countries and the developing world. A rights-based understanding of education moves beyond the more traditional model of schooling, which has defined the education agenda very much from the perspective of the government by emphasising training, human capital investment, and containment of young people and their socialisation.

Parents, too, have demands of the education system. Most parents want it to equip their children for a successful life, and hence expect it to provide their children with the knowledge, skills and confidence that will help them gain employment and achieve economic success. They also look to schools to transmit their values, culture and language in other words, they seek in the education system the reinforcement and promotion of their own beliefs.

A third constituency with demands on education is, of course, the child, for whom the goal is acquiring the capacities through which to fulfil her or his aspirations. Education also provides the opportunity for emotional development and friendship outside the family. It is the route through which economically and socially marginalised children can escape poverty and participate fully in their communities. It also plays a vital role in safeguarding children from exploitative and hasardous labor and sexual exploitation, promoting human rights and democracy, and protecting the environment.

There are, then, significant and sometimes competing expectations of the education system from governments that are providing the legal and administrative framework and funding, from parents responsible for their children's upbringing and from children themselves as rights holders. Some expectations are common to all: economic success, reinforcement of values and social standing. However, the fact that governments are concerned with the wider society and parents with their individual child can and does create significant tensions in the education agenda. These tensions are acknowledged in international human rights law, which introduces the right of parents to educate their children according to their beliefs. It reflects the need to limit a government's power to impose its economic, political and religious agenda on children.

The UN Convention on the Rights of the Child introduces an additional perspective. It imposes limits not only on the state but also on parents. It insists that children's best interests must be a primary consideration in all matters affecting them, that their views must be given serious consideration and that the child's evolving capacities must be respected. In other words, the Convention affects the right of parents to freedom of choice in their child's education; parental rights to choose their children's education are not absolute and are seen to decline as children grow older. The rationale behind parental choice is not to legitimise a denial of their child's rights. Rather, it is to prevent any state monopoly of education and to protect educational pluralism. In the case of conflict between a parental choice and the best interests of the child, however, the child should always be the priority.

The right to education thus involves these three principal players: the state, the parent and the child. There is a triangular relationship between them, and in the development of rights-based education it is important to bear in mind that their differing objectives need to be reconciled. In addition, other actors with a significant contribution and responsibility include teachers, the local community, policymakers, the media and the private sector.

Balancing Rights and Responsibilities of Children

Human rights are not contingent on the exercise of responsibility. They are innate and universal. There is no requirement on the part of a child, for example, that she or he demonstrate a responsible attitude in order to 'earn' an entitlement to education. Nevertheless, there is a direct and complex relationship between rights and responsibilities, rooted in the reciprocal and mutual nature of human rights.

All children have a right to learn. This means they are entitled to an effective learning environment in multiple spaces, not just the school setting and at the primary level. It also implies that they have responsibilities to ensure their behavior does not deny that right to other children. All children are entitled to express their views and have them given due weight. This involves listening as well as talking. It requires that children play a part in the creation of constructive spaces that promote mutual respect. And as teachers have responsibilities for children's rights, so children, too, have responsibilities towards teachers. The same principles of mutual respect apply between children and adults. The right to protection from violence extends to both children and adults, and places a responsibility on children to avoid the use of aggression or physical violence. While teachers bear responsibility for preparing lessons, teaching, grading work, maintaining positive classroom discipline and creating opportunities for children to express views, so children carry responsibilities for undertaking their work, collaborating with other children, keeping the classroom in order and, so far as it is within their means, arriving regularly and on time.

One of the most effective means of promoting children's understanding of the reciprocal basis of rights is to create an environment where their own rights are respected. Through this experience, they develop the capacities to exercise responsibility.

Tensions in the Implementation of a Rights-based Approach

In a rights-based approach to education, founded on principles of universality and equity, there are inevitable tensions that arise in the process of implementation. Some of these are associated with limits on resources and can only be addressed through a commitment to progressive realisation. Some derive from insufficient understanding of the concept of rights or the potential strategies that can be adopted to resolve them.

Access and Quality

Where resources are scarce, the requirement to make education universally available can mean a reduction in the per capita funding for each child leading to higher teacher-student ratios, overcrowded classes, fewer materials and resources per class, and lower building standards thereby sacrificing quality for access. In these circumstances, access to education is an overriding concern, and it is not acceptable to discriminate between groups of children and offer preferential treatment to some on the basis of resources. Yet, whenever possible, efforts need to be made to increase the budgetary allocation to ensure there is access to quality education for all children. A tendency to discriminate must be guarded against, and donors may need to ensure that funding is dedicated to the provision of education without discrimination on any grounds.

Equity and Efficiency

The approaches necessary to make schooling available for all children may be less efficient and cost-effective. Although it may be more expensive to develop small satellite schools in villages, for example, this may be the only way of encouraging parents to allow young girls to attend. It may be more economically efficient to place all children who do not speak the national language in a separate school, but doing so may deny them the right to an education on an equal basis with other children. It is important to consult with children, parents and communities to explore what will work most effectively in their environment. This will help build a sense of ownership and collaboration in finding solutions that will best strengthen access to education.

Universality and Diversity

The respect for difference and the right to be different in regard to cultural, linguistic and religious identity needs to be reconciled with the universal right to education as part of a broader set of human rights. Approaches to education provision that ensure universal education for all need to be undertaken with due regard for local and regional differences, particularly in regard to language and culture. Failure to do so implies a failure to reach out to all communities.

Priorities and Trade-offs

Scarce resources can lead to trade-offs, such as the decision to invest in primary education at the cost of limiting access to secondary education, or to postpone the development of educational opportunities for children with disabilities. Realistically, it is not possible for all governments to fulfil their obligations to ensure the right to education for all children immediately. However, where financial and human resources are limited, the principle of progressive realisation requires governments to have a clear strategy and time frame for achieving the objective of universal access to primary and secondary education, and each action should be conducive to the full realisation of the right to education for all.

Outcomes and Process

Pressure to achieve such targets as the Millennium Development Goals may lead to strategies that are designed to produce immediate results but fail to invest in long-term social change to sustain a genuine commitment to and capacity for meaningful education. For example, an increased number of school places and teachers may lead to higher levels of enrolment, only to result in increased drop-out rates because no accommodation has been made to children's particular circumstances. Ensuring attendance, completion and reasonable attainment in school involves consultations with children and parents; policies to address poverty; the development of more relevant curricula; and respect for children's rights in school, including the abolition of physical and humiliating punishments.

Emergency Responses in the Short and Longer Term

In emergencies, the immediate focus is inevitably on survival and the provision of food, water, shelter and medical treatment. For children, however, the immediate re-introduction of education is not only a right but can also be a vital resource in restoring normality, overcoming psychosocial trauma, building capacities for survival and providing structure out of chaos. There are a growing number of positive examples of programes designed to provide immediate schooling in the aftermath of crises. Ensuring that a maximum number of children attend school under these difficult circumstances has to be balanced, however, with the parallel need to guarantee quality education in the short and longer term.

Teachers' and Children's Rights

It is sometimes argued by teachers that affording respect for the rights of children diminishes respect for their own rights. They may erroneously believe that prohibiting physical punishment or involving students in decisions diminishes their position or makes it more difficult to maintain discipline. This view derives from an assumption that rights represent a fixed quantity of entitlement and that giving more to one constituency necessarily deprives the other. It also derives from an authoritarian understanding of the teacher-child relationship. While respecting the rights of children does involve some transfer of power, this does not necessitate the loss of rights on the part of the teacher. In practice, without mutual respect, the pedagogic relationship is fragile. Creating a school environment in which children's rights are respected is more likely to enhance respect for the role of the teacher, although this outcome can only be achieved if teachers are appropriately supported and resourced.

Work and School

Controversy about the role of work in children's lives continues. There are tensions associated with the extent to which it, on the one hand, provides preparation for life, and on the other, impedes educational outcomes. There is no consensus as to whether there are forms of work that are acceptable and can be accommodated alongside the right to education or whether all child work should be prohibited during the years of compulsory schooling. The Convention on the Rights of the Child makes clear that children must be protected from all forms of work that are harmful to their development or that interfere with their education. International Labor Organisation (ILO) Convention 182 elaborates the worst forms of child labor and makes clear governments' obligations to protect all children from these areas of work. Governments need to introduce legislation and policies that guarantee these protections. It is also incumbent on governments to provide education that offers a viable alternative to employment in terms of its quality and relevance; to introduce policies that address the poverty and livelihood insecurity that force many children into work; and to make education sufficiently flexible and inclusive to allow those children to attend who have no choice but to work.

Rights-based Conceptual Framework for Education

The development of a human rights-based approach to education requires a framework that addresses the right of access to education, the right to quality education and respect for human rights in education. These dimensions are interdependent and interlinked, and a rights-based education necessitates the realisation of all three.

The right to education requires a commitment to ensuring universal access, including taking all necessary measures to reach the most marginalised children. But getting children into schools is not enough; it is no guarantee of an education that enables individuals to achieve their economic and social objectives and to acquire the skills, knowledge, values and attitudes that bring about responsible and active citisenship. A study by the Southern and Eastern African Consortium for Monitoring Educational Quality (1995–1998), for example, measures primary school students' reading literacy against standards established by national reading experts and sixth-grade teachers. In four out of seven countries, fewer than half of sixth grade students achieved minimum competence in reading. Poor achievement is also evident in a study conducted by the Programe d'Analyse des Systèmes Éducatifs de la CONFEMEN (PASEC) in six French-speaking African countries in 1996–2001: Achievement levels were "low" in French or mathematics for up to 43 percent of fifth grade pupils in all six countries, and more than 40 percent of students in Senegal struggled to put several numbers with two decimal points in order. Achieving a quality education is also a challenge in industrialised nations. Recent studies show that large numbers of students in rich countries do not acquire the basic skills to be competent in today's world.

To ensure quality education in line with the Dakar Framework for Action (2002) and the aims of education elaborated by the Committee on the Rights of the Child, attention must be paid to the relevance of the curriculum, the role of teachers, and the nature and ethos of the learning environment. A rights-based approach necessitates a commitment to recognising and respecting the human rights of children while they are in school including respect for their identity, agency and integrity. This will contribute to increased retention rates and also makes the process of education empowering, participatory, transparent and accountable. In addition, children will continue to be excluded from education unless measures are taken to address their rights to freedom from discrimination, to an adequate standard of living and to meaningful participation. A quality education cannot be achieved without regard to children's right to health and well-being. Children cannot achieve their optimum development when they are subjected to humiliating punishment or physical abuse.

This conceptual framework highlights the need for a holistic approach to education, reflecting the universality and indivisibility of all human rights. The following sections set out the central elements that therefore need to be addressed in each of the three dimensions mentioned above.

1. The right of access to education
   - Education throughout all stages of childhood and beyond
   - Availability and accessibility of education
   - Equality of opportunity
2. The right to quality education
   - A broad, relevant and inclusive curriculum
   - Rights-based learning and assessment
   - Child-friendly, safe and healthy environments
3. The right to respect in the learning environment
   - Respect for identity
   - Respect for participation rights
   - Respect for integrity

The Right of Access to Education

Obligations to Ensure the Right of Access to Education

1. Provide free and compulsory primary education.
2. Develop forms of secondary education that are available and accessible to everyone, and introduce measures to provide free education and financial assistance in cases of need.
3. Provide higher education that is accessible on the basis of capacity by every appropriate means.
4. Provide accessible educational and vocational information and guidance.
5. Introduce measures to encourage regular attendance and reduce dropout rates.
6. Provide education on the basis of equal opportunity.
7. Ensure respect for the right to education without discrimination of any kind on any grounds.

8. Ensure an inclusive education system at all levels.
9. Provide reasonable accommodation and support measures to ensure that children with disabilities have effective access to and receive education in a manner conducive to achieving the fullest possible social integration.
10. Ensure an adequate standard of living for physical, mental, spiritual, moral and social development.
11. Provide protection and assistance to ensure respect for the rights of children who are refugees or seeking asylum.
12. Provide protection from economic exploitation and work that interferes with education.

The right of access to education comprises three elements: the provision of education throughout all stages of childhood and beyond, consistent with the Education for All goals; the provision of sufficient, accessible school places or learning opportunities; and equality of opportunity.

Education throughout All Stages of Childhood and Beyond

Learning is a lifelong process. A rights-based approach to education seeks to build opportunities for children to achieve their optimum capacities throughout their childhood and beyond. It requires a life-cycle approach, investing in learning and ensuring effective transitions at each stage of the child's life.

Although the Convention on the Rights of the Child does not impose explicit obligations to provide early childhood education, the Committee on the Rights of the Child interprets the right to education as beginning at birth and as closely linked to the child's right to maximum development. It calls on governments to ensure that young children have access to programes of health care and education designed to promote their well-being, and stresses that the right to optimum development implies the right to education during early childhood, with systematic and quality family involvement.

Quality education during the early years plays a vital part in promoting readiness for school and is also the best guarantee of promoting sustainable economic and social development, and attaining the Millennium Development Goals and the Education for All and A World Fit for Children goals. A study of children in Nepal shows that more than 95 percent of children who had attended a non-formal preschool facility enrolled in primary school, where they also performed better than those who had not attended. Around 80 percent of the first group passed grade one, compared to around 60 percent of the group without preschool experience.

While human rights law affirms that every child is entitled to free, compulsory primary education, obligations in respect of secondary education are less emphatic. The duty is to encourage its development and make it available and accessible to every child, and free where possible. The weaker formulation does not reflect a lesser commitment to secondary education, but rather a recognition that it is currently beyond the resources of many countries to make it free and compulsory. Since these conventions were drafted, there has been an increasing recognition of the fundamental importance of secondary education.

Moreover, development does not cease at age 18. Education can and should take place throughout life consistent with the third goal of Education for All, which calls for meeting the learning needs of all young people and adults through access to learning and life skills programes. Governments should support the achievement of a strong base for lifelong learning, through education directed towards responsible autonomy, self-directed learning and preparation for full citisenship.

Availability and Accessibility of Education

States have obligations to establish the legislative and policy framework, together with sufficient resources, to fulfil the right to education for every child. Each child must therefore be provided with an available school place or learning opportunity, together with appropriately qualified teachers and adequate and appropriate resources and equipment. The level of provision of primary education must be consistent with the numbers of children entitled to receive it.

All learning environments must be both physically and economically accessible for every child, including the most marginalised. It is important to recognise that a school that is accessible to one child may not be accessible to another. Schools must be within safe physical reach or accessible through technology (for example, access to a 'distance learning' programe). They must also be affordable to all.

Equality of Opportunity

Every child has an equal right to attend school. Making schools accessible and available is an important first step in fulfilling this right but not sufficient to ensure its realisation. Equality of opportunity can only be achieved by removing barriers in the community and in schools.

Even where schools exist, economic, social and cultural factors including gender, disability, AIDS, household poverty, ethnicity, minority status, orphanhood and child labor often interlink to keep children out of school. Governments have obligations to develop legislation, policies and support services to remove barriers in the family and community that impede children's access to school.

Schools can directly or indirectly impede the access of some children, for example, through reflecting a male-dominated culture, pervading patterns of violence and sexual abuse or prevailing societal norms, such as caste bias. Negative teacher attitudes towards girls, biases in the curriculum, lack of female teachers and role models, and lack of adequate access to hygiene and sanitation can also inhibit enrolment and contribute to poor attainment and high dropout levels. Schools may refuse to accept children with disabilities or AIDS. Inflexibility in school systems may exclude many working children. Governments should take action to ensure the provision of education that is both inclusive and non-discriminatory and that is adapted to ensure the equal opportunity of every child to attend.

The Right to Quality Education

Obligations to Ensure the Right to Quality Education

1. Develop children's personalities, talents, and mental and physical abilities to their fullest potential.
2. Promote respect for human rights and fundamental freedoms, and prepare children for a responsible life in a spirit of peace, tolerance, equality and friendship.
3. Promote respect for the child's, his or her parents' and others' cultural identity, language and values.
4. Promote respect for the natural environment.
5. Ensure the child's access to information from a diversity of sources.
6. Ensure that the best interests of children are a primary consideration.
7. Promote respect for the evolving capacities of children in the exercise of their rights.

8. Respect the right of children to rest, leisure, play, recreation, and participation in arts and culture.

The Dakar Framework for Action commits nations to the provision of primary education of good quality and to improving all aspects of educational quality. Although there is no single definition of 'quality', most attempts to define it incorporate two fundamental perspectives. First, cognitive development is a primary objective of education, with the effectiveness of education measured against its success in achieving this objective. Second, education must promote creative and emotional development, supporting the objectives of peace, citisenship and security, fostering equality and passing global and local cultural values down to future generations.

These perspectives have been integrated into the aims of education set out in the Convention on the Rights of the Child, which formulates a philosophy of respect for children as individuals, recognising each child as "unique in characteristics, interests, abilities and needs." It sets out a framework of obligations to provide education that promotes children's optimum development. Article 29 implies "the need for education to be child-centred, child-friendly and empowering, and it highlights the need for educational processes to be based on the very principles it enunciates." Every child has a right to an education that empowers him or her by developing life skills, learning and other capacities, self-esteem and self-confidence. The provision of a quality education demands attention to the content of the curriculum, the nature of the teaching and the quality of the learning environment. It implies a need for the creation of flexible, effective and respectful learning environments that are responsive to the needs of all children.

Inclusive Curriculum

Common guidance is provided in all the key human rights treaties for the development of the curriculum, indicating an underlying global consensus on the content and scope necessary for a rights-based education.

The curriculum must enable every child to acquire the core academic curriculum and basic cognitive skills, together with essential life skills that equip children to face life challenges, make well-balanced decisions and develop a healthy lifestyle, good social relationships, critical thinking and the capacity for non-violent conflict resolution. It must develop respect for human rights and fundamental freedoms, and promote respect for different cultures and values and for the natural environment. The Committee on the Rights of the Child stipulates that the curriculum, both in early childhood provision and in school, "must be of direct relevance to the child's social, cultural, environmental and economic context, and to his or her present and future needs and take full account of the child's evolving capacities"

The curriculum must be inclusive and tailored to the needs of children in different or difficult circumstances. All teaching and learning materials should be free from gender stereotypes and from harmful or negative representations of any ethnic or indigenous groups. To enable all children with disabilities to fulfil their potential, provision must be made to enable them to, for example, learn Braille, orientation or sign language.

Rights-based Learning and Assessment

The way in which children are provided with the opportunity to learn is as important as what they learn. Traditional models of schooling that silence children and perceive them as passive recipients are not consistent with a rights-based approach to learning.

There should be respect for the agency of children and young people, who should be recognised as active contributors to their own learning, rather than passive recipients of education. There should also be respect for the evolving and differing capacities of children, together with recognition that children do not acquire skills and knowledge at fixed or predetermined ages. Teaching and learning must involve a variety of interactive methodologies to create stimulating and participatory environments. Rather than simply transmitting knowledge, educators involved in creating or strengthening learning opportunities should facilitate participatory learning. Learning environments should be child friendly and conducive to the optimum development of children's capacities.

Assessment of learning achievement is vital. Testing enables schools to identify learning needs and develop targeted initiatives to provide support to individual children. Analysis of results enables governments to assess whether they are achieving their educational objectives and to adjust policy and resources accordingly. Dissemination of results is a necessary aspect of accountability and transparency in education and facilitates discussions on the quality of education. At the same time, a commitment to realising children's rights to their optimum capacities implies the need for sensitive and constructive methods of appraising and monitoring children's' work that take account of their differing abilities and do not discriminate against those with particular learning needs.

A Child-friendly, Safe and Healthy Environment

The obligation to give primacy to the best interests of children and to ensure their optimum development requires that learning environments are welcoming, gender sensitive, healthy, safe and protective. Although situations of extreme poverty, emergency and conflict may often impede this, children should never be expected to attend schools where the environment is detrimental to their health and well-being. Schools should take measures to contribute towards children's health and well-being, taking into account the differing needs of children. This will necessitate measures to ensure that obstacles to health and safety are removed—for example, consideration as to the location of schools, travel to and from school, factors that might cause illness or accidents in the classroom or playgrounds, and appropriate facilities for girls. It also requires the proactive provision of facilities, services and policies to promote the health and safety of children and the active participation of the local community. A healthy environment also needs to provide safe and stimulating opportunities for play and recreation.

Right to Respect in the Learning Environment

Obligations to Respect Children's Rights in the Learning Environment

1. Respect every child equally without discrimination on any grounds.
2. Teach respect for human rights and fundamental freedoms, for difference and for life in a society where there is understanding, peace, tolerance, equality and friendship.
3. Give primary consideration to the best interests of the child.
4. Respect the evolving capacities of the child.
5. Respect the right of children to express their views on all matters of concern to them and have those views given due weight in accordance with children's age and maturity.
6. Recognise the right to freedom of expression, religion, conscience, thought and assembly.
7. Respect the privacy of children.

8. Take all appropriate measures to ensure that school discipline is administered in a manner consistent with the child's dignity and all other rights in the Convention on the Rights of the Child.
9. Protect children from all forms of physical violence, injury or abuse, neglect or negligence, maltreatment or exploitation, including sexual abuse.

Human rights are inalienable. In other words, they are inherent in each human being. Accordingly, they must be respected in all learning environments. The right to education must be understood as incorporating respect for children's identity, their right to express their views on all matters of concern to them, and their physical and personal integrity.

Respect for Identity

UNESCO's Convention against Discrimination in Education (1960) protects the educational rights of national minorities. Depending on the educational policy of each State, it establishes the right to use or be taught in one's own language, provided this does not exclude minorities from understanding the language and culture of the community as a whole and that it is not provided at a lower standard than the one generally provided. The Convention on the Protection and Promotion of Diversity in Cultural Expressions (2005) introduces obligations to respect cultural diversity, including through educational programes.In addition, article 30 of the Convention on the Rights of the Child stresses the right of children to enjoy their own culture, practice their own religion and use their own language. International human rights law also requires States to respect the freedom of parents to decide the kind of education they would like for their child. Governments are entitled to determine which religion, if any, should be taught in schools, as well as the medium of instruction for schools. And finally, the Convention on the Rights of the Child, in its recognition of the right of children to express their views on all matters of concern to them and to have those views given due weight, introduces a further dimension to the issue of choice and freedom in education provision.

There is no simple solution to these tensions, nor any one correct approach. Whatever approach is adopted, however, governments have obligations to ensure that children do not experience discrimination, that respect is afforded to their culture and religion, and that every effort is made to prevent social exclusion and educational disadvantage as a consequence of speaking a minority language. In determining the most appropriate system for addressing respect for identity, a rights-based approach requires that children, families and communities are consulted and involved. And if relevant obligations are not being fulfilled, mechanisms should be in place to challenge schools, education authorities and the government.

Respect for Participation Rights

Article 12 of the Convention on the Rights of the Child establishes that children are entitled to express their views on all matters of concern to them and to have these given due weight in accordance with their age and maturity. This principle of participation is affirmed by other rights to freedom of expression, religion and association. These rights apply to all aspects of their education and have profound implications for the status of children throughout the education system. Participation rights do not simply extend to the pedagogic relationships in the classroom but also across the school and in the development of legislation and policy. The Committee on the Rights of the Child has frequently recommended that governments take steps to encourage greater participation by children in schools. Children can also play an important role in advocating for the realisation of their rights. Governments need to introduce legislation and policy to establish and support these rights at all levels in the education system

Respect for Integrity

The Convention demands not only that children are protected from all forms of violence but also that school discipline is administered in a manner consistent with the child's dignity. However, frequent and severe violence, including emotional abuse and humiliation in school, remains widespread in countries throughout the world. The Committee on the Rights of the Child has consistently argued that such punishments constitute a violation of the rights of the child and a denial of children's integrity. Much violence is also perpetrated by children against children and children against teachers, and it is equally important to challenge such behavior.

Physical and other forms of humiliating and abusive treatment are not only a violation of the child's right to protection from violence, but also highly counterproductive to learning. Children cite violence as a significant factor contributing to school dropout. Furthermore, it diminishes self-esteem and promotes the message that violence is acceptable. Many factors contribute to the continued use of violence towards children in schools, including:

1. Social and legal acceptance of violence against children.
2. Lack of adequate training for teachers, resulting in poor classroom management and a consequent breakdown of discipline.
3. Lack of knowledge of the benefits associated with positive discipline and how to promote it.
4. A failure to understand the harmful impact of physical punishment.
5. Lack of understanding of the different ways in which children learn, and the fact that children will differ in their development and their capacities to understand.

Action must be taken to address all these barriers and to achieve rights-respecting educational environments in which all forms of physical and humiliating punishments are prohibited and a commitment to non-violent conflict resolution is promoted.

Implementation of the International Laws

The right to education is law in Article 26 of the Universal Declaration of Human Rights and Articles 200 and 14 of the International Covenant on Economic, Social and Cultural Rights.

The right to education has been reaffirmed in the 1960 UNESCO Convention against Discrimination in Education and the 1981 Convention on the Elimination of All Forms of Discrimination Against Women.

In Europe, Article 2 of the first Protocol of 20 March 1952 to the European Convention on Human Rights states that the right to education is recognized as a human right and is understood to establish an entitlement to education. According to the International Covenant on Economic, Social and Cultural Rights, the right to education includes the right to free, compulsory primary education for all, an obligation to develop secondary education accessible to all in particular by the progressive introduction of free secondary education, as well as an obligation to develop equitable access to higher education in particular by the progressive introduction of free higher education. The right to education also includes a responsibility to provide basic education for individuals who have not completed primary education. In addition to these access to education provisions, the right to education encompasses also the obligation to eliminate discrimination at all levels of the educational system, to set minimum standards and to improve quality. The European Court of Human Rights in Strasbourg has applied this norm for example in the Belgian linguistic case. Article 10 of the European Social Charter guarantees the right to vocational education.

Education narrowly refers to formal institutional instructions. Generally, international instruments use the term in this sense and the right to education, as protected by international human rights instruments, refers primarily to education in a narrow sense. The 1960 UNESCO Convention against Discrimination in Education defines education in Article 1(2) as: "all types and levels of education, (including) access to education, the standard and quality of education, and the conditions under which it is given."

In a wider sense education may describe "all activities by which a human group transmits to its descendants a body of knowledge and skills and a moral code which enable the group to subsist". In this sense education refers to the transmission to a subsequent generation of those skills needed to perform tasks of daily living, and further passing on the social, cultural, spiritual and philosophical values of the particular community. The wider meaning of education has been recognised in Article 1(a) of UNESCO's 1974 Recommendation concerning Education for International Understanding, Co-operation and Peace and Education relating to Human Rights and Fundamental Freedoms. The article states that education implies:

"the entire process of social life by means of which individuals and social groups learn to develop consciously within, and for the benefit of, the national and international communities, the whole of their personal capabilities, attitudes, aptitudes and knowledge."

The European Court of Human Rights has defined education in a narrow sense as "teaching or instructions... in particular to the transmission of knowledge and to intellectual development" and in a wider sense as "the whole process whereby, in any society, adults endeavour to transmit their beliefs, culture and other values to the young."

Implementation

International law does not protect the right to pre-primary education and international documents generally omit references to education at this level. The Universal Declaration of Human Rights states that everyone has the right to education, hence the right applies to all individuals, although children are understood as the main beneficiaries.

The rights to education are separated into three levels:

1. Primary (Elemental or Fundamental) Education. This shall be compulsory and free for any child regardless of their nationality, gender, place of birth, or any other discrimination. Upon ratifying the International Covenant on Economic, Social and Cultural Rights States must provide free primary education within two years.
2. Secondary (or Elementary, Technical and Professional in the UDHR) Education must be generally available and accessible.
3. Higher Education (at the University Level) should be provided according to capacity. That is, anyone who meets the necessary education standards should be able to go to university.

Both secondary and higher education shall be made accessible "by every appropriate means, and in particular by the progressive introduction of free education".

The realisation of the right to education on a national level may be achieved through compulsory education, or more specifically free compulsory primary education, as stated in both the Universal Declaration of Human Rights and the International Covenant on Economic, Social and Cultural Rights.

Assessment of Fulfilment

The fulfilment of the right to education can be assessed using the 4 As framework, which asserts that for education to be a meaningful right it must be available, accessible, acceptable and adaptable. The 4 As framework was developed by the former UN Special Rapporteur on the Right to Education, Katarina Tomasevski, but is not necessarily the standard used in every international human rights instrument and hence not a generic guide to how the right to education is treated under national law.

The 4 As framework proposes that governments, as the prime duty-bearer, has to respect, protect and fulfil the right to education by making education available, accessible, acceptable and adaptable. The framework also places duties on other stakeholders in the education process: the child, which as the privileged subject of the right to education has the duty to comply with compulsory education requirements, the parents as the 'first educators', and professional educators, namely teachers.

The 4 As have been further elaborated as follows:

1. *Availability* – funded by governments, education is universal, free and compulsory. There should be proper infrastructure and facilities in place with adequate books and materials for students. Buildings should meet both safety and sanitation standards, such as having clean drinking water. Active recruitment, proper training and appropriate retention methods should ensure that enough qualified staff is available at each school.
2 *Accessibility* – all children should have equal access to school services regardless of gender, race, religion, ethnicity or socio-economic status. Efforts should be made to ensure the inclusion of marginalized groups including children of refugees, the homeless or those with disabilities. There should be no forms of segregation or denial of access to any students. This includes ensuring that proper laws are in place against any child labour or exploitation to prevent children from obtaining primary or secondary education. Schools must be within a reasonable distance for children within the community, otherwise transportation should be provided to students, particularly those that might live in rural areas, to ensure ways to school are safe and convenient. Education should be affordable to all, with textbooks, supplies and uniforms provided to students at no additional costs.
3. *Acceptability* – the quality of education provided should be free of discrimination, relevant and culturally appropriate for all students. Students should not be expected to conform to any specific religious or ideological views. Methods of teaching should be objective and unbiased and material available should reflect a wide array of ideas and beliefs. Health and safety should be emphasized within schools including the elimination of any forms of corporal punishment. Professionalism of staff and teachers should be maintained.
4. *Adaptability* – educational programs should be flexible and able to adjust according to societal changes and the needs of the community. Observance of religious or cultural holidays should be respected by schools in order to accommodate students, along with providing adequate care to those students with disabilities.

A number of international NGOs and charities work to realise the right to education using a rights-based approach to development.

References

Arts, K, Popvoski, V, *et al.* (2006) *International Criminal Accountability and the Rights of Children.* "From Peace to Justice Series". London: Cambridge University Press.

Bandman, B. (1999) *Children's Right to Freedom, Care, and Enlightenment.* Routledge. p 67.

Beiter, Klaus Dieter (2005). *The Protection of the Right to Education by International Law.* Martinus Nijhoff Publishers. pp. 226–227.

Calkins, C.F. (1972) "Reviewed Work: Children's Rights: Toward the Liberation of the Child by Paul Adams", *Peabody Journal of Education. 49*(4). p. 327.

"Right to education – What is it? Education and the 4 As". Right to Education project. Retrieved 2009-02-21.

8

Children's Rights to Health

Health is vitally important for every human being in the world. What ever our differences may be, health is our most important commodity. A person in bad health cannot really live life to the fullest.

Health is the state of physical, mental and social well-being and does not only mean an absence of illness or disease. The right to health is closely linked to other fundamental human rights, most notably access to potable water and adequate hygiene.

All children have the right to timely access to appropriate health services. This requires the establishment of a system to protect health, including access to essential medicine.

The realization of the right to health implies that each country will put in place health services that are available in any circumstance, accessible to everyone, of good quality and satisfactory (meaning they conform to medical ethics and are respectful of our biological and cultural differences.) However, this does not mean that the country must guarantee good health to everyone.

Prevention plays an essential role in maintaining public health, particularly children's health. Health education and vaccinations prevent the spread of infectious disease.

Vaccinations are efficient because they are fairly inexpensive and they protect children against the risk of death and handicaps caused by the most common children's diseases (tuberculosis, diphtheria, tetanus, leprosy, polio, whooping cough, measles.) In the long term, these vaccinations can even lead to the end of these diseases in a given country.

Vaccinating children, as well as awareness campaigns, can lead to a significant reduction in health risks. Additionally, spreading basic information about hygiene, nutritional needs, etc., as well as the circulation of simple illustrations reminding people of the fundamental rules are very efficient actions for informing populations and improving healthy behavior.

Additionally, it is important to inform the population about the harmful effects that child marriage or Female genital mutilation have on children's health.

For children, the right to health is vital because they are vulnerable beings, more at risk to illness and health complications. When children are spared from disease, they can grow into healthy adults, and in this way, contribute to the development of dynamic and productive societies.

Children require extra attention in order to enjoy the best possible health. This allows them to develop properly during their childhood and teenage years.

At every step of their physical and mental development, children have specific needs and different health risks. Additionally, a newborn is more vulnerable and more exposed to certain diseases than a young child or teenager (i.e. infectious disease, malnutrition.)

On the other hand, a teenager, due to his or her habits and behavior, are exposed to other kinds of risks (sexual health, mental health, alcohol and drug use etc.)

Generally, a child who benefits from appropriate health care will enjoy a better state of health during the stages of childhood and can become a healthy adult.

The right to children's health also includes pre and postnatal care for mothers. A newborn will have a much lower chance of survival if the mother dies due to complications from pregnancy or childbirth.

Health Access Inequalities

As we speak, the right to healthcare still isn't a reality for millions of children around the globe, and more particularly in developing countries. Every year, over 13 million children under the age of 5 years die from illnesses which could have been avoided or treated.

The poor populations are most affected.

The poor populations are most at risk of food shortage, lack of drinking water, and of a proper sanitation system.

Therefore, these populations, and especially their children, are most likely to become ill.

Infectious diseases are all the more frequent and serious with children suffering from malnutrition and/or having no access to drinking water. Sub-Saharan Africa and South Asia are the most affected by this issue. In these regions, five countries; India, Nigeria, Democratic Republic of Congo, Pakistan and Ethiopia account for over half of children's deaths worldwide. This represents over 6 million child deaths.

Healthcare and medicine are prohibitive for millions of people.

In many countries the populations do not benefit from health coverage. Thus, they do not have access to healthcare that remains beyond their means. Some must save up for years before being able to see a doctor or a specialist.

Additionally, the large pharmaceutical companies because of their medicines' extreme prices compound the precarious situation of the populations at risk. These are the people most in need of the medicine.

As we write, over 1/3 of the world population does not have access to the medicines essential to their health and survival because of the high prices.

Problem of healthcare access in developing countries

The failure of the healthcare system

In developing countries, vaccination levels are very low. In 2009, 24 million children from the poorest countries did not have access to the basic vaccines. Yet, the vaccination of these children could decrease the death rate of children linked to infectious diseases by 45%.

In addition, these countries usually don't have enough staff and healthcare equipment to offer healthcare access to the most in need. The countries of Sub-Saharan Africa and South East Asia only count 1 doctor for over 2000 inhabitants; this is 6 times less than in developed countries. Additionally, care cannot be given to everyone and many children die because of a lack of health coverage or having waited too long before undergoing examination or vital care.

Low health coverage for mothers and children

In poor regions, pregnancies and deliveries are often very risky for the mother's and the children's health.

Very few of them benefit from regular check-ups during their pregnancy and have no information on their health status and that of their unborn child. Any complication during the pregnancy, which could have been detected and treated with regular check-ups, can lead to the death of the mother and/or the child.

As we write, there are still 40% of mothers who give birth without any medical assistance. Furthermore, many die leaving behind a new-born who will be 10 times more at risk of dying before his fifth birthday.

Right to Nutrition

There is a long history of concern with the right to food, or, more broadly, the right to adequate nutrition, in international law. The Universal Declaration of Human Rights of 1948 provides that "everyone has the right to a standard of living adequate for the health and well-being of himself and his family, including food... " Article 11 of the International Covenant on Economic, Social, and Cultural Rights recognizes "the fundamental right of everyone to be free from hunger." Article 24 of the Convention on the Rights of the Child says that "States Parties recognize the right of the child to the enjoyment of the highest attainable standard of health" and shall take appropriate measures "to combat disease and malnutrition" through the provision of adequate nutritious foods, clean drinking water, and health care.

However, historically the idea of the right to adequate nutrition has not been taken seriously. There have been many nutrition programmes within countries and internationally, but they have been provided as a matter of charity, not entitlement. There has not been any legal recourse for those who fail to receive service. The right has not been effectively implemented.

The idea of the right to nutrition, in some form, should be more acceptable if it focuses on children. Very poor countries might limit their commitment only to severely malnourished children under five years of age, while others might assure that services would be provided for both moderately and severely malnourished children up to the age of 16. The important point is to establish the principle that vulnerable children are entitled to adequate nutrition as a matter of right. Implementing children's right to adequate nutrition does not necessarily mean creating new programmes; it means assuring that they get the nutrition services to which they are entitled.Increasing food production, nutrition education, feeding programmes, and all the other conventional approaches have important roles to play in ending hunger in the world, but so far they have not been adequate. Perhaps it would be useful to work more directly with the social/legal/political tools of entitlements, rights, responsibility, and accountability to get the job done.

There are different types of malnutrition, including protein-energy malnutrition and specific micronutrient deficiencies such as those due to inadequate vitamin A, iodine, iron, or other particular nutrients. Malnutrition may result not only from improper diet but also from ill health and inadequate or improper care. The most widespread form of malnutrition among children is protein-energy malnutrition. Apart from its most serious clinical manifestations (kwashiorkor and nutritional marasmus), protein-energy malnutrition can be gauged by measuring the heights and weights of children and comparing them with the heights and weights of well-nourished children. With these data, indicators can be derived for wasting (low weight for height), stunting (low height for age), and underweight (low weight for age). It is widely accepted that if a child's weight is more than two standard deviations below the reference for his or her age, that child should be described as malnourished. In recent decades the proportion of children in developing countries who are malnourished has declined, but the absolute number has gone up. At least 184 million children are underweight. More than half of these children are in South Asia. There are now more children on earth suffering from malnutrition than ever before in history. Malnutrition is a major factor in the massive morbidity and mortality of children throughout the world.

Throughout the 1980s and early 1990s more than 12 million children died before their fifth birthdays each year, many from a combination of malnutrition and disease.

When he was Director-General of the Food and Agriculture Organization of the United Nations (FAO), Addeke Boerma said that "if human beings have a right to life at all, they have a right to food". More recently, Richard Jolly, Deputy Executive Director of UNICEF, said: "Freedom from hunger is a basic human right. It is unacceptable that 150 million children under five should be suffering from serious malnutrition in a world that has the capacity to prevent it". Certainly widespread malnutrition and the massive mortality of children associated with it is unacceptable. But what about the idea that freedom from hunger is a basic human right? Is it true? Can it be implemented? The right to adequate nutrition (or right to food) concept has a long history. In 1948 the Universal Declaration of Human Rights asserted in article 25(1) that "everyone has the right to a standard of living adequate for the health and well-being of himself and his family, including food..."

Table 1. Regional prevalence and numbers of underweight preschool children (0-60 months of age) in developing countries, 1975-1990

Region	1975	1980	1985	1990
Sub-Saharan Africa	18.5	19.9	24.1	28.2
Near East/North Africa	5.2	5.0	5.0	4.8
South Asia	90.6	89.9	100.1	101.2
South-East Asia	24.3	22.8	21.7	19.9
China	20.8	20.5	21.1	23.6
Middle America/Caribbean	3.4	3.1	2.8	3.0
South America	4.8	3.1	2.9	2.8
Global total	168	164	178	184
Total	402	434	493	536

On 14 March 1963, a Special Assembly on Man's Right to Freedom from Hunger met in Rome and "issued an historic Manifesto calling on the governments and people of the world to unite in the struggle against man's common enemy—hunger." The manifesto described the character and scope of hunger in the world, and asserted that "freedom from hunger is man's first fundamental right". A variety of action programmes such as increasing agricultural productivity and improving trade relations were suggested and moral concerns were expressed, but the idea that "freedom from hunger is man's first fundamental right" was not elaborated.

The International Covenant on Economic, Social, and Cultural Rights was adopted by the United Nations General Assembly in 1966 and came into force in 1976. Article 11 says that "The States Parties to the present Covenant recognize the right of everyone to an adequate standard of living for himself and his family, including adequate food, clothing, and housing," and also recognize "the fundamental right of everyone to be free from hunger."

In 1974 the World Food Conference issued a Universal Declaration on the Eradication of Hunger and Malnutrition. It asserted that "Every man, woman and child has the inalienable right to he free from hunger and malnutrition in order to develop fully and maintain their physical and mental faculties." That declaration was endorsed by the United Nations General Assembly in Resolution 3348 (XXIX) of 17 December 1974.

In September 1976 both the United States Senate and House passed right to food resolutions. It was the sense of the Congress that every person throughout the world has a right to a nutritionally adequate diet, and the United States should increase its development assistance until it reached 1% of the US gross national product.

In November 1984 the World Food Assembly, comprised primarily of representatives of non-governmental organizations, met in Rome. Its purpose was to call attention to the fact that the promise made at the 1974 World Food Congress that "within a decade no child will go to bed hungry" had not been fulfilled. Its final statement asserted that "the hungry millions are being denied the most basic human right - the right to food."

In 1991 the House Select Committee on Hunger chaired by Congressman Tony Hall, through House Resolution (H.R. 2258) advocating the Freedom from Want Act, urged the United States to propose a United Nations Convention on the Right to Food.

In the Convention on the Rights of the Child, which came into force in 1990, two articles address the issue of nutrition. Article 24 says that "States Parties recognize the right of the child to the enjoyment of the highest attainable standard of health" and shall take appropriate measures "to combat disease and malnutrition" through the provision of adequate nutritious foods, clean drinking water, and health care. Article 27 says that States Parties "shall in case of need provide material assistance and support programmes, particularly with regard to nutrition, clothing, and housing."

The rights idea was voiced frequently at the International Conference on Nutrition, organized by the Food and Agriculture Organization of the United Nations and the World Health Organization and held in Rome in December 1992. In the conference's concluding World Declaration on Nutrition the nations of the world agreed that "access to nutritionally adequate and safe food is a right of each individual." Yet there was nothing in the accompanying Plan of Action for Nutrition to elaborate that right, nothing providing for clear entitlements with effective accountability.

The idea of the right to food appears in many different contexts in international law. Most are not binding. In some cases, as in the International Covenant on Economic, Social, and Cultural Rights, the obligations are technically binding on the States Parties. However, because the obligations lack specificity and because there are no effective mechanisms for implementation and accountability, they are not binding in practice. With regard to food or other issues, "the main problem in regard to social and economic rights has been to define the obligations corresponding to the rights.... The obligations remain vague until the present. In the absence of effective international supervision, they have not been made clearer through case law".

Several nations have articulated nutrition rights in some form in their laws. Cuba's constitution assures that "no child be left without schooling, food and clothing." The Italian, Spanish, and Greek constitutions assure a right to health. In many countries there is language referring to other sorts of assurances, such as the right to social security (as in the Netherlands and Spain) that can be interpreted as implying nutrition rights. In most cases, however, the assurances are vague and have not been enforced through the courts. There is practically no elaboration in detailed statutes of distinct nutrition rights, and no legal enforcement.

Although there have been many expressions of concern, and many laudable anti-hunger programmes at local, national, and global levels, the idea of the right has not yet been implemented. As Ved Nanda put it, "no framework presently exists for the realization of the right to food, nationally or internationally ".

Many groups vulnerable to malnutrition should be protected—mothers, the elderly, the handicapped, unborn children, refugees, people in armed conflict situations, and so on. The idea of the right to nutrition, in some form, will be far more acceptable if it focuses on children. There are several reasons for this.

First, no one can doubt the powerlessness of small children. Not even the most callous politician could tell a three-year-old that if she wants to eat she should go out and work.

Second, it can be argued that saving a child's life is more valuable than saving an older person's life simply because there are more life-years saved. Similarly, the benefits from an improvement in the quality of life accrue over many more life-years for a child than they would for an older person.

Third, there are well-developed means for assessing the nutrition status of children on an inexpensive and objective basis, using anthropometric techniques. There is a strong consensus among nutrition professionals on the interpretation of these data. Techniques for measuring malnutrition in other groups are not as well developed.

Fourth, anthropometric data collected around the world show unambiguously that children's malnutrition is a massive problem.

Fifth, graphic news coverage of the suffering in places like Ethiopia and Somalia and constant calls for donations keep the issue in the public's consciousness.

Sixth, political work for children can be based on creating alliances among the many organizations concerned with children and the many organizations concerned with nutrition. Hungry children already have a well-established constituency.

Seventh, the Convention on the Rights of the Child and the World Summit for Children of September 1990 have created new appreciation of the rights of children.

Eighth, both the World Summit for Children and the Declaration and Plan of Action on Nutrition agreed upon in Rome in December 1992 call upon participating states to prepare National Plans of Action, on children in one case and on nutrition in the other case. The obligation to prepare these two plans gives states new opportunities for examining the nutrition needs of children.

All these reasons together lead to the judgement that obtaining recognition of effective nutrition rights may be more politically feasible for children than for others. We can begin with children, and later go on to address the needs of other vulnerable groups as well.

Before setting out the ways in which children's right to nutrition can be meaningfully established in the law, it will be useful to have a systematic framework for understanding our responsibilities to children.

Our principal obligation toward children is to promote their development, understood as empowerment or increasing self-reliance. The task is to help increase children's capacity to define, analyse, and act on their own problems.

Who is responsible for children? The question is not whose fault is it that children suffer so much (who caused the problems?) but who should take action to remedy the problems. Many different social agencies may have some role in looking after children, but what should be the interrelationships among them? What should be the roles of churches, fraternal societies, local and national governments, and other agencies in dealing with the hunger problem? Most children have two vigorous advocates from the moment they are born, and even before they are born. Their parents devote enormous resources to serving their interests. These are not sacrifices. The best parents do not support their children out of a sense of obligation or as investments. They support their children as extensions of themselves, as part of their wholeness.

In many cases, however, that bond is broken or is never created. Fathers disappear. Many mothers disappear as well. In some cities hundreds of children are abandoned each month in the hospitals in which they are born. Bands of children live in the streets by their wits, preyed upon by others. Often children end up alone as a result of warfare or other political crises. Many children are abandoned because they are physically or mentally handicapped. Often parents become so disabled by drugs or alcohol that they cannot care for their children.

Often children who cannot be cared for by their biological parents are looked after by others. In many cultures children belong not only to their biological parents but to the community as a whole. The responsibility and the joy of raising children are widely shared.

In many places, especially in "developed" countries, that option is no longer available because of the collapse of the idea of community. Many of us live in nice neighbourhoods in well-ordered societies, but the sense of community of love and responsibility and commitment to one another—has vanished. In such cases the remaining hope of the abandoned child is the government, the modern substitute for community. We look to government to provide human services that the local community no longer provides.

As children mature the first priority is to help them become responsible for themselves. So long as they are not mature, however, children ought to get their nurturance from their parents. Failing that, they ought to get it from their local communities. Failing that, they ought to get it from the local governments. Failing that, it should come from their national governments. Failing that, they ought to get it from the international community. The responsibility hierarchy looks like this:

child

family

community

local government

state government

national government

international non-governmental organizations

international governmental organizations

We can picture this as a set of nested circles, with the child in the centre of the nest, surrounded, supported, and nurtured by family, community, government, and, ultimately, international organizations.

This is straightforward. The idea that needs to be added is that in cases of failure, agents more distant from the child should not simply substitute for those closer to the child. Instead, those who are more distant should try to work through and strengthen those who are closer to help them become more capable of fulfilling their responsibilities toward children. To the extent possible, local communities should not take children away from inadequate parents but should help parents in their parenting role. State governments should not replace local governments, but should support local governments in their work with children. The international community should help national governments in their work with children. The same reasoning should apply to care for the physically disabled and the mentally ill.

The international community is the last resort, the outer ring of responsibility in looking after the welfare of children. The very outermost ring includes international governmental organizations (IGOs) such as UNICEF, the Food and Agriculture Organization of the United Nations, the World Health Organization, and the United Nations Committee on Human Rights. Just inside that ring are the international non-governmental organizations (INGOs). In the pattern of concentric rings of responsibility, the international bodies' task is not to deliver services to children directly but, to the extent possible, to empower agencies in the inner rings.

The first Millennium Development Goal calls for the eradication of extreme poverty and hunger, and its achievement is crucial for national progress and development. Failing to achieve this goal jeopardises the achievement of other MDGs, including goals to achieve universal primary education (MDG 2), reduce child mortality (MDG 4) and improve maternal health (MDG 5).

One of the indicators used to assess progress towards MDG 1 is the prevalence of children under 5 years old who are underweight, or whose weight is less than it should be for their age. To have adequate and regular weight gain, children need enough good-quality food, they need to stay healthy and they need sufficient care from their families and communities.

To a great extent, achieving the MDG target on underweight depends on the effective implementation of large-scale nutrition and health programes that will provide appropriate food, health and care for all children in a country.

Since the MDGs were adopted in 2000, knowledge of the causes and consequences of undernutrition has greatly improved. Recent evidence makes it clear that in children under 5 years of age, the period of greatest vulnerability to nutritional deficiencies is very early in life: the period beginning with the woman's pregnancy and continuing until the child is 2 years old. During this period, nutritional deficiencies have a significant adverse impact on child survival and growth.

Chronic undernutrition in early childhood also results in diminished cognitive and physical development, which puts children at a disadvantage for the rest of their lives. They may perform poorly in school, and as adults they may be less productive, earn less and face a higher risk of disease than adults who were not undernourished as children.

For girls, chronic undernutrition in early life, either before birth or during early childhood, can later lead to their babies being born with low birthweight, which can lead again to under nutrition as these babies grow older. Thus a vicious cycle of undernutrition repeats itself, generation after generation.

Where undernutrition is widespread, these negative consequences for individuals translate into negative consequences for countries. Knowing whether children are at risk of nutritional deficiencies, and taking appropriate actions to prevent and treat such deficiencies, is therefore imperative.

Whether a child has experienced chronic nutritional deficiencies and frequent bouts of illness in early life is best indicated by the infant's growth in length and the child's growth in height. Day-to-day nutritional deficiencies over a period of time lead to diminished, or stunted, growth. Once children are stunted, it is difficult for them to catch up in height later on, especially if they are living in conditions that prevail in many developing countries.

Whereas a deficit in height (stunting) is difficult to correct, a deficit in weight (underweight) can be recouped if nutrition and health improve later in childhood. The weight of a child at 4–5 years old, when it is adequate for the child's age, can therefore mask deficiencies that occurred during pregnancy or infancy, and growth and development that have been compromised.

Governments, donors and partners that consider only underweight prevalence are overlooking a significant portion of the persistent problem of undernutrition. The high stunting burden in many countries should be an issue of great concern. Today, there is a much better understanding of the programe strategies and approaches to improve nutrition, based on sound evidence and improved health and nutrition data.

It describes, for example, how cost-effective nutrition interventions such as vitamin A supplementation reach the vast majority of children even in the least developed countries; that great progress has been made to improve infant feeding in many African countries; and that the treatment of severe acute malnutrition has expanded rapidly.

The large burden of undernutrition, and its influence on poverty reduction as well as the achievement of many of the MDGs, itself constitutes a call for action. The fact that even more children may become undernourished in some countries due to such recent events as the rapid increase in food prices and the financial crisis brings acute focus to the issue.

Causes of Undernutrition

Poverty, inequity, low maternal education and women's social status are among the underlying factors that need to be taken into consideration and addressed in order to reduce undernutrition in a sustained manner.

Poverty

The relationship between poverty and nutrition is two-sided: Economic growth, when it contributes to lowering the prevalence of poverty and food insecurity, can also lead to reduced undernutrition, albeit at a slow pace. Nutrition is one of the key elements for human capital formation, which in turn represents one of the fundamental drivers of economic growth.But economic growth does not necessarily translate to better and equitable outcomes for all individuals in society, and the nutritional status of a population does not always depend on national development, prosperity or economic growth.

The relationship between stunting and wealth varies significantly across countries. In India and Nigeria, children in the richest households are at a distinct advantage compared to children in other households. This contrasts with Ethiopia, where stunting is widespread even among children living in the wealthiest households, the prevalence of stunting is high, at 40 percent and in Egypt, where stunting prevalence is remarkably similar in all wealth quintiles. Children in rural areas in the developing world are almost twice as likely to be underweight as children in urban areas.

Gender and Social Norms

An analysis of nutrition indicators at the global level reveals negligible differences between boys and girls under 5 years old. Similarly, programe coverage and practice data that are disaggregated by sex reveal no significant differences on the basis of gender. But further disaggregation of data from some countries indicates there might be differences in the feeding and care of girls compared to boys, presumably stemming from power relations and social norms that perpetuate discriminatory attitudes and practices. Data in some countries point to the possible effects, such as Bangladeshi boys being significantly taller relative to their age than girls. In sub-Saharan Africa, on the other hand, boys are more likely to be stunted than girls.

Maternal Education

Significant disparity in nutritional status also exists in terms of mothers' education and literacy. A number of studies and analyses have found a significant association between low maternal literacy and poor nutrition status of young children. An analysis of survey data from 17 developing countries, for example, confirms a positive association between maternal education and nutritional status in children 3–23 months old, although a large part of these associations is the result of education's strong link to household economics. A study in Pakistan revealed that the majority of infants with signs of undernutrition had mothers with virtually no schooling. The study also observed that the introduction of complementary foods for infants at an appropriate age (6 months) improved when mothers were educated.

Women's Social Status

In many developing countries, the low status of women is considered to be one of the primary determinants of undernutrition across the life cycle. Women's low status can result in their own health outcomes being compromised, which in turn can lead to lower infant birthweight and may affect the quality of infant care and nutrition. A study in India showed that women with higher autonomy (indicated by access to money and freedom to choose to go to the market) were significantly less likely to have a stunted child when compared with their peers who had less autonomy.

Challenges of Undernutrition

The level of child and maternal undernutrition remains unacceptable throughout the world, with 90 percent of the developing world's chronically undernourished (stunted) children living in Asia and Africa. Detrimental and often undetected until severe, undernutrition undermines the survival, growth and development of children and women, and it diminishes the strength and capacity of nations.

Brought about by a combined lack of quality food, frequent attacks of infectious disease and deficient care, undernutrition continues to be widely prevalent in both developing and industrialised countries, to different degrees and in different forms. Nutritional deficiencies are particularly harmful while a woman is pregnant and during a child's first two years of life. During this period, they pose a significant threat to mothers and to children's survival, growth and development, which in turn negatively affects children's ability to learn in school, and to work and prosper as adults.

Undernutrition greatly impedes countries' socio-economic development and potential to reduce poverty. Many of the Millennium Development Goals (MDGs) particularly MDG 1 (eradicate extreme poverty and hunger), MDG 4 (reduce child mortality) and MDG 5 (improve maternal health) will not be reached unless the nutrition of women and children is prioritised in national development programes and strategies. With persistently high levels of undernutrition in the developing world, vital opportunities to save millions of lives are being lost, and many more children are not growing and thriving to their full potential.

In terms of numbers, the bulk of the world's undernutrition problem is localised. Twenty-four countries account for more than 80 percent of the global burden of chronic undernutrition, as measured by stunting (low height for age). Although India does not have the highest prevalence of stunted children, due to its large population it has the greatest number of stunted children.

Stunting remains a problem of greater magnitude than underweight or wasting, and it more accurately reflects nutritional deficiencies and illness that occur during the most critical periods for growth and development in early life. Most countries have stunting rates that are much higher than their underweight rates, and in some countries, more than half of children under 5 years old are stunted.

Nutrition remains a low priority on the national development agendas of many countries, despite clear evidence of the consequences of nutritional deprivation in the short and long term. The reasons are multiple.

Nutrition problems are often unnoticed until they reach a severe level. But mild and moderate undernutrition are highly prevalent and carry consequences of enormous magnitude: growth impediment, impaired learning ability and, later in life, low work productivity. None of these conditions is as visible as the diseases from which the undernourished child dies. Children may appear to be healthy even when they face grave risks associated with undernutrition. Not recognising the urgency, policymakers may not understand how improved nutrition relates to national economic and social goals.

In many countries, nutrition has no clear institutional home; it is often addressed in part by various ministries or departments, an arrangement that can hinder effective planning and management of programes.

In some of the countries with the highest levels of undernutrition, governments are faced with multiple challenges—poverty, economic crisis, conflict, disaster, inequity all of them urgent, and all of them competing for attention. Undernutrition often does not feature prominently among these problems, unless it becomes very severe and widespread.

Some leaders may not consider nutrition to be politically expedient because it requires investment over the long term and the results are not always immediately visible. Furthermore, the interests of donor agencies with limited budgetary allocations for aid in general are often focused elsewhere.

In the past, nutrition strategies were not always effective and comprehensive, programes were insufficient in scale and human resources were woefully inadequate, partly due to insufficient coordination and collaboration between international institutions and agencies working in nutrition. But cost-effective programming strategies and interventions that can make a significant difference in the health and lives of children and women are available today. These interventions urgently require scaling up, a task that will entail the collective planning and resources of developing country governments at all levels and of the international development community as a whole.

Undernutrition can be greatly reduced through the delivery of simple interventions at key stages of the life cycle for the mother, before she becomes pregnant, during pregnancy and while breast-feeding; for the child, in infancy and early childhood. Effectively scaled up, these interventions will improve maternal nutrition, increase the proportion of infants who are exclusively breast-fed up to 6 months of age, improve continued breast-feeding rates, enhance complementary feeding and micronutrient intake of children between 6 and 24 months old, and reduce the severity of infectious diseases and child mortality.

Undernutrition is a violation of child rights. The Convention on the Rights of the Child emphasises children's right to the highest attainable standard of health and places responsibility on the State to combat malnutrition. It also requires that nutritious food is provided to children and that all segments of society are supported in the use of basic knowledge of child nutrition (article 24). Nutrition must be placed high on national and international agendas if this right is to be fulfilled.

Importance of Nutrition

Children who are undernourished, not optimally breast-fed or suffering from micronutrient deficiencies have substantially lower chances of survival than children who are well nourished. They are much more likely to suffer from a serious infection and to die from common childhood illnesses such as diarrhoea, measles, pneumonia and malaria, as well as HIV and AIDS.

According to the most recent estimates, maternal and child undernutrition contributes to more than one third of child deaths. Undernourished children who survive may become locked in a cycle of recurring illness and faltering growth, with irreversible damage to their development and cognitive abilities.

Every level of undernutrition increases the risk of a child's dying. While children suffering from severe acute malnutrition are more than nine times more likely to die than children who are not undernourished, a large number of deaths also occurs among moderately and mildly undernourished children who may otherwise appear healthy. Compared to children who are severely undernourished, children who are moderately or mildly undernourished have a lower risk of dying, but there are many more of the latter.

Undernutrition in children can manifest itself in several ways, and it is most commonly assessed through the measurement of weight and height. A child can be too short for his or her age (stunted), have low weight for his or her height (wasted), or have low weight for his or her age (underweight). A child who is underweight can also be stunted or wasted or both.

Each of these indicators captures a certain aspect of the problem. Weight is known to be a sensitive indicator of acute deficiencies, whereas height captures more chronic exposure to deficiencies and infections. Wasting is used as a way to identify severe acute malnutrition.

Inadequate nutrition may also manifest itself in overweight and obesity, commonly assessed through the body mass index.

Micronutrient malnutrition, caused by deficiencies in vitamins and minerals, can manifest itself through such conditions as fatigue, pallor associated with anaemia (iron deficiency), reduced learning ability (mainly iron and iodine deficiency), goitre (iodine deficiency), reduced immunity, and night blindness (severe vitamin A deficiency).

Low birthweight is related to maternal undernutrition; it contributes to infections and asphyxia, which together account for 60 percent of neonatal deaths. An infant born weighing between 1,500 and 2,000 grams is eight times more likely to die than an infant born with an adequate weight of at least 2,500 grams. Low birthweight causes an estimated 3.3 percent of overall child deaths.

Thus, the achievement of Millennium Development Goal 4 to reduce the under-five mortality rate by two thirds between 1990 and 2015 will not be possible without urgent, accelerated and concerted action to improve maternal and child nutrition.

Food and Nutrition

Undernutrition is not just about the lack of food. An individual's nutritional status is influenced by three broad categories of factors—food, care and health and adequate nutrition requires the presence of all three.

Poor infant and young child feeding and care, along with illnesses such as diarrhoea, pneumonia, malaria, and HIV and AIDS, often exacerbated by intestinal parasites, are immediate causes of undernutrition. Underlying and more basic causes include poverty, illiteracy, social norms and behavior.

Maternal nutrition and health greatly influence child nutritional status. A woman's low weight for height or anaemia during pregnancy can lead to low birthweight and continued undernutrition in her children. At the same time, maternal undernutrition increases the risk of maternal death during childbirth.

Household food security, often influenced by such factors as poverty, drought and other emergencies, has an important role in determining the state of child and maternal nutrition in many countries.

Optimal infant and young child feeding initiation of breast-feeding within one hour of birth, exclusive breast-feeding for the first six months of the child's life and continued breast-feeding until the child is at least 2 years old, together with age-appropriate, nutritionally adequate and safe complementary foods can have a major impact on child survival, with the potential to prevent an estimated 19 percent of all under-5 deaths in the developing world, more than any other preventive intervention. In the conditions that normally exist in developing countries, breast-fed children are at least 6 times more likely to survive in the early months than non-breast-fed children; in the first six months of life they are 6 times less likely to die from diarrhoea and 2.4 times less likely to die from acute respiratory infection.

Vitamin A is critical for the body's immune system; supplementation of this micronutrient can reduce the risk of child mortality from all causes by about 23 percent. The provision of high-dose vitamin A supplements twice a year to all children 6–59 months old in countries with high child mortality rates is one of the most cost-effective interventions. Since supplementation can reduce the prevalence of diarrhoea in children by 27 percent because it shortens the duration and reduces the severity of a diarrhoea episode.

Impacts of Nutrition Interventions

The period of children's most rapid physical growth and development is also the period of their greatest vulnerability. Significant brain formation and development takes place beginning from the time the child is in the womb. Adequate nutrition providing the right amount of carbohydrates, protein, fats, and vitamins and minerals is essential during the antenatal and early childhood period.

Maternal undernutrition, particularly low body mass index, which can cause fetal growth retardation, and non-optimal infant and young child feeding are the main causes of faltering growth and undernutrition in children under 2 years old. These conditions can have a lifelong negative impact on brain structure and function.

Stunting is an important predictor of child development; it is associated with reduced school outcome. Compared to children who are not stunted, stunted children often enrol later, complete fewer grades and perform less well in school. In turn, this underperformance leads to reduced productivity and income-earning capacity in adult life.Iodine and iron deficiency can also undermine children's school performance. Studies show that children from communities that are iodine deficient can lose 13.5 IQ points on average compared with children from communities that are non-deficient, and the intelligence quotients of children suffering iron deficiency in early infancy were lower than those of their peers who were not deficient. Iron deficiency makes children tired, slow and listless, so they do not perform well in school.

Iron-deficiency anaemia is highly prevalent among women in developing-country settings and increases the risk of maternal death. It causes weakness and fatigue, and reduces their physical ability to work. Adults suffering from anaemia are reported to be less productive than adults who are not anaemic.

Early childhood is also a critical period for a child's cognitive development. Particularly in settings where ill health and undernutrition are common, it is important to stimulate the child's cognitive development during the first two years through interaction and play. Nutrition and child development interventions have a synergistic effect on growth and development outcomes.

Nutrition in early childhood has a lasting impact on health and well-being in adulthood. Children with deficient growth before age 2 are at an increased risk of chronic disease as adults if they gain weight rapidly in later stages of childhood. For chronic conditions such as cardiovascular disease and diabetes, a worst-case scenario is a baby of low birthweight who is stunted and underweight in infancy and then gains weight rapidly in childhood and adult life. This scenario is not uncommon in countries where underweight rates have been reduced but stunting remains relatively high.

Undernutrition has dominated discussions on nutritional status in developing countries, but overweight among both children and adults has emerged in many countries as a public health issue, especially in countries undergoing a so-called 'nutrition transition'. Overweight is caused in these countries mainly by poverty and by poor infant and young child feeding practices; the 'transition' refers to changes in traditional diets, with increased consumption of high-calorie, high-fat and processed foods.

Height at 2 years of age is clearly associated with enhanced productivity and human capital in adulthood, so early nutrition is also an important contributor to economic development. There is evidence that improving growth through adequate complementary feeding can have a significant effect on adult wages. An evaluation of one programe in Latin America that provided good-quality complementary food to infant and young boys found their wages in adulthood increased by 46 percent compared to peers who did not participate in the programe.

Status of Child Nutrition

Stunting

Stunting affects approximately 195 million children under 5 years old in the developing world, or about one in three. Africa and Asia have high stunting rates—40 percent and 36 percent, respectively—and more than 90 percent of the world's stunted children live on these two continents.

Of the 10 countries that contribute most to the global burden of stunting among children, 6 are in Asia. These countries all have relatively large populations: Bangladesh, China, India, Indonesia, Pakistan and the Philippines.

Due to the high prevalence of stunting (48 percent) in combination with a large population, India alone has an estimated 61 million stunted children, accounting for more than 3 out of every 10 stunted children in the developing world.

More than half the children under 5 years old are stunted in nine countries, including Guatemala, whose stunting rate of 54 percent rivals that of some of the highest-prevalence countries in Africa and Asia. Of countries with available data, Afghanistan and Yemen have the highest stunting rates: 59 percent and 58 percent, respectively.

A nation's average rate of stunting may mask disparities. For example, an analysis of disparities in Honduras indicates that children living in the poorest households or whose mothers are uneducated have almost a 50 percent chance of being stunted, whereas on average, throughout the country 29 percent of children are stunted.

Reducing Stunting in Peru

The stunting rate in Peru is high, particularly among those who are poor. One reason for the continued high prevalence of stunting is the perception that undernutrition is primarily a food security issue. But in some regions of the country, more holistic, community-based efforts to improve basic health practices have led to an improvement in stunting levels among young children.

In 1999, the programe 'A Good Start in Life' was initiated in five regions four in the Andean highlands and one in the Amason region as a collaboration between the Ministry of Health, the United States Agency for International Development and UNICEF. Efforts focused on reaching pregnant and lactating women. Methods included such community-based interventions as antenatal care, promotion of adequate food intake during pregnancy and lactation, promotion of exclusive breast-feeding of infants under 6 months of age and improved complementary feeding from six months, growth promotion, control of iron and vitamin A deficiency, promotion of iodised salt, and personal and family hygiene.

Programe teams were led by local governments, which worked with communities, health facility staff and local non-governmental organisations. The programe emphasised strengthening the capacity and skills of female counsellors and rural health promoters. By 2004, it covered the inhabitants of 223 poor, rural communities, including approximately 75,000 children under 3 years old, and 35,000 pregnant and lactating women.

A comparison between 2000 and 2004 shows that in the communities covered by the programe the stunting rate for children under 3 years old declined from 54 percent to 37 percent, while anaemia rates dropped from

76 percent to 52 percent. The total cost of the programe was estimated to be US$116.50 per child per year. A Good Start in Life' inspired the design and implementation of a national programe, which has since been associated with reduced stunting rates.

Since 1990, stunting prevalence in the developing world has declined from 40 percent to 29 percent, a relative reduction of 28 percent. Progress has been particularly notable in Asia, where prevalence dropped from 44 percent around 1990 to 30 percent around 2008. This reduction is influenced by marked declines in China.

The decline in Africa has been modest, from 38 percent around 1990 to 34 percent around 2008. Moreover, due to population growth, the overall number of African children under 5 years old who are stunted has increased, from an estimated 43 million in 1990 to 52 million in 2008.

Stunting rates have declined significantly in a number of countries including Bangladesh, Eritrea, Mauritania and Viet Nam—underscoring that marked improvements can be achieved. In countries where the burden of stunting is high, there is an urgent need to accelerate integrated programes addressing nutrition during the mother's pregnancy and before the child reaches 2 years of age.

Underweight

Today, an estimated 129 million children under 5 years old in the developing world are underweight nearly one in four. Ten percent of children in the developing world are severely underweight. The prevalence of underweight among children is higher in Asia than in Africa, with rates of 27 percent and 21 percent, respectively. In 17 countries, underweight prevalence among children under 5 years old is greater than 30 percent. The rates are highest in Bangladesh, India, Timor-Leste and Yemen, with more than 40 percent of children underweight.

Some countries have low underweight prevalence but unacceptably high stunting rates. For example, in Albania, Egypt, Iraq, Mongolia, Peru and Swaziland, stunting rates are more than 25 percent although underweight prevalence is 6 percent or less. For national development and public health, it is important to reduce both stunting and underweight.

Progress towards the reduction of underweight prevalence has been limited in Africa, with 28 percent of children under 5 years old being underweight around 1990, compared with 25 percent around 2008. Progress has been slightly better in Asia, with 37 percent underweight prevalence around 1990 and 31 percent around 2008. Countries with underweight prevalence of 6 percent or less and stunting rates of more than 25 percent.

Wasting

Children who suffer from wasting face a markedly increased risk of death. According to the latest available data, 13 percent of children under 5 years old in the developing world are wasted, and 5 percent are severely wasted (an estimated 26 million children).

A number of African and Asian countries have wasting rates that exceed 15 percent, including Bangladesh (17 percent), India (20 percent) and the Sudan (16 percent). The country with the highest prevalence of wasting in the world is Timor-Leste, where 25 percent of children under 5 years old are wasted (8 percent severely).

Out of 134 countries with available data, 32 have wasting prevalence of 10 percent or more among children under 5 years old. At such elevated levels, wasting is considered a public health emergency requiring immediate intervention, in the form of emergency feeding programes.

Ten countries account for 60 percent of children in the developing world who suffer from wasting. The top eight countries all have wasting prevalence of 10 percent or higher. More than one third of the developing world's children who are wasted live in India.

The burden of severe wasting is particularly high—6 percent or more in countries with large populations; Indonesia, Nigeria, Pakistan and the Sudan, in addition to India, all have high rates of wasting.

Overweight

Although being overweight is a problem most often associated with industrialised countries, some developing countries and countries in transition also have high prevalence of overweight children. In Georgia, Guinea-Bissau, Iraq, Kazakhstan, Sao Tome and Principe, and the Syrian Arab Republic, for example, 15 percent or more of children under 5 years old are overweight.

Some countries are experiencing a 'double burden' of malnutrition, having high rates of both stunting and overweight. In Guinea-Bissau and Malawi, for example, more than 10 percent of children are overweight, while around half are stunted.

Micronutrient Deficiencies

Vitamin and mineral deficiencies are highly prevalent throughout the developing world. The status of vitamin A, iron and iodine deficiencies are highlighted below, but other deficiencies such as zinc and folate are also common.

Vitamin A deficiency remains a significant public health challenge across Africa and Asia and in some countries of South America. An estimated 33 percent (190 million) of preschool-age children and 15 percent (19 million) of pregnant women do not have enough vitamin A in their daily diet, and can be classified as vitamin A deficient. The highest prevalence and numbers are found in Africa and some parts of Asia, where more than 40 percent of preschool-age children are estimated to be vitamin A deficient.

Iron deficiency affects about 25 percent of the world's population, most of them children of preschool-age and women. It causes anaemia, and the highest proportions of preschool-age children suffering from anaemia are in Africa (68 percent).

Iodine deficiency, unlike many other nutrition problems, affects both developed and developing countries. Although most people are now protected through the consumption of iodised salt, the proportion of the population affected by iodine deficiency is highest in Europe (52 percent). Africa is also affected, with 42 percent of the population assessed as deficient.

Interventions to Improve Nutrition

Infant and Young Child Feeding

Optimal infant and young child feeding entails the initiation of breast-feeding within one hour of birth; exclusive breast-feeding for the first six months of the child's life; and continued breast-feeding for two years or more, together with safe, age-appropriate feeding of solid, semi-solid and soft foods starting at 6 months of age.

While infant feeding practices need to be strengthened overall, increasing the rates of early initiation of breast-feeding and of exclusive breast-feeding is critical to improving child survival and development. Less than 40 percent of all infants in the developing world receive the benefits of immediate initiation of breast-feeding. Similarly, just 37 percent of children under 6 months of age are exclusively breast-fed. Less than 60 percent of children 6–9 months old receive solid, semi-solid or soft foods while being breast-fed. In addition, the quality of the food received is often inadequate, providing insufficient protein, fat or micronutrients for optimal growth and development.

Exclusive Breast-feeding

In the developing world, less than 40 percent of infants under 6 months old receive the benefits of exclusive breast-feeding. The rate is particularly low in Africa, where less than one third of infants under 6 months old are exclusively breast-fed.

Over the past 10–15 years exclusive breast-feeding rates have increased in many countries of Africa and Asia. In the developing world as a whole, however, progress has been modest, from 33 percent around 1995 to 37 percent around 2008.

Evidence from a variety of countries indicates that marked improvements in exclusive breast-feeding are possible if supported by effective regulatory frameworks and guidelines, and when comprehensive programmatic approaches are at scale.

Exclusive breast-feeding rates are very low and stunting prevalence is high in several countries that have experienced emergencies and longer-term challenges, such as Chad, Côte d'Ivoire, Djibouti and the Niger. In these countries, urgent actions are needed to promote and support exclusive breast-feeding in order to reduce the rate of infectious diseases and ensure optimal infant nutrition.

Integrated Approaches to Improving Infant Feeding in Kenya

The exclusive breast-feeding rate for children under 6 months old in Kenya remained static at around 13 percent from 1993 to 2003. But after the Government, supported by UNICEF, established a comprehensive infant and young child feeding (IYCF) programe in 2007, a substantial increase in the rate of exclusive breast-feeding for this age group took place, according to preliminary data from 2008.

The programe in Kenya is based on the comprehensive, multi-level approach to improving exclusive breast-feeding rates that had proved successful in a number of countries in sub-Saharan Africa and elsewhere. An assessment of people's knowledge, attitudes and practices towards infant and young child feeding guided programe development and laid the foundation for communication and advocacy addressing the challenges to infant feeding in the context of HIV.

Government, non-governmental organisations, and bilateral and multilateral stakeholders then developed a comprehensive IYCF strategy addressing action at the national level, including policy and legislation, at the health-services level and at the community level. Guidelines and training materials were created for use in national capacity and service development, including in maternity facilities, during various maternal and child health contacts, and within communities.

In 2008, the first full year of the programe's implementation, 25 percent of all health and nutrition service providers and community health workers in most provinces were trained in integrated IYCF counselling. Infant feeding practices in 60 percent of the country's public hospitals were assessed based on Baby-Friendly Hospital Initiative standards. Communication messages on the benefits of exclusive breast-feeding were broadcast nationwide. The package of services delivered as part of the response to emergency situations emphasised IYCF

Improved support for infant and young child feeding reached 73 percent of women attending antenatal care or services to prevent mother-to-child transmission (PMTCT) of HIV in 2008, or an estimated 1.1 million out of the 1.5 million pregnant and lactating women in Kenya. The approach has not only strengthened the crucial infant feeding aspect of PMTCT, it also extended IYCF counselling and communication to the general population.

Non-governmental organisations and the United States President's Emergency Plan for AIDS Relief (PEPFAR) partners implemented the initial phase of IYCF activities; the package of ICYF activities is now being expanded as part of the PEPFAR programe. Within the next two to three years, high coverage of the various activities is anticipated in all provinces.

Early Initiation of Breast-feeding

Only 39 percent of newborns in the developing world are put to the breast within one hour of birth. The rate is especially low in Asia, at 31 percent. There is growing evidence of the benefits to mother and child of early initiation of breast-feeding, preferably within the first hour after birth. Early initiation of breast-feeding contributes to reducing overall neonatal mortality. It ensures that skin-to-skin contact is made early on, an important factor in preventing hypothermia and establishing the bond between mother and child.

Early initiation of breast-feeding also reduces a mother's risk of post-partum haemorrhage, one of the leading causes of maternal mortality. Colostrum, the milk produced by the mother during the first post-partum days, provides protective antibodies and essential nutrients, acting as a first immunisation for newborns, strengthening their immune system and reducing the chances of death in the neonatal period. In a subset of countries with available data, the low proportions of early initiation of breast-feeding contrast with substantially higher proportions of infants who are delivered by a skilled health professional and of infants whose mothers received antenatal care at least once from a skilled health professional. This gap constitutes a lost opportunity and highlights the critical need to improve the content and quality of counselling by healthcare providers.

Complementary Feeding

In the developing world, 58 percent of infants aged 6–9 months old receive complementary foods while continuing to be breast-fed. These data do not reflect the quality of the complementary foods received. Meeting minimum standards of dietary quality is a challenge in many developing-country settings, especially in areas where household food security is poor, and it has often not been given enough emphasis. Children may not receive complementary foods at the right age (often either too early or too late), are not fed frequently enough during the day, or the quality of the food may be inadequate. New programming options are now available to meet this challenge.

Complementary feeding is the most effective intervention that can significantly reduce stunting during the first two years of life. A comprehensive programe approach to improving complementary feeding includes counselling for caregivers on feeding and care practices and on the optimal use of locally available foods, improving access to quality foods for poor families through social protection schemes and safety nets, and the provision of micronutrients and fortified food supplements when needed.

Percentage of infants who were put to the breast within one hour of birth; percentage of births attended by a skilled health professional; and percentage of pregnant mothers with at least one antenatal care visit with a skilled health professional

1. Early initiation of breast-feeding
2. Skilled attendant at delivery

3. Antenatal care with a skilled professional

Recently adopted new indicators for infant and young child feeding (especially the 'minimum acceptable diet' indicator reflecting both frequency of feeding and dietary diversity) emphasise the importance of quality of food and allow for better assessment of complementary feeding practices.

Vitamin A Supplementation

Vitamin A is essential for a well-functioning immune system; its deficiency increases the risk of mortality significantly. In 2008, 71 percent of all children 6–59 months old in developing countries were fully protected against vitamin A deficiency with two doses of vitamin A. Coverage of 85 percent for the least developed countries highlights the success of programes in reaching the most vulnerable populations.

In 2008, 22 out of 34 least developed countries with data had surpassed the 80 percent target of full coverage of vitamin A supplementation. Service provided through integrated child health events has helped to ensure high coverage in a large number of these countries, where weak health systems would otherwise not have reached children. In 2008, integrated child health events were the most effective platform for delivery of vitamin A supplements, resulting in more than 80 percent coverage on average. Nearly three quarters of the 20 countries with the highest number of deaths among children under 5 years old achieved more than 80 percent full coverage of vitamin A supplementation.

Vitamin A deficiency is widespread throughout India, but particularly so in rural India, where up to 62 percent of preschool-age children are deficient, according to the latest estimates. Moreover, the high prevalence of wasting (20 percent), stunting (48 percent) and anaemia (70 percent) in children under 5 years old indicates widespread nutritional deprivation.

India's national policy recommends that all children 9-59 months old be given preventive vitamin A supplementation twice yearly to reduce the risk of blindness, infection, undernutrition and death associated with vitamin A deficiency, particularly among the most vulnerable children. Many states in India have put the fight against vitamin A deficiency on a 'war footing', and Bihar State, one of the poorest in India is at the forefront of this battle.

The Government of Bihar, in partnership with UNICEF, the Micronutrient Initiative and others, supports a strategy to increase coverage of vitamin A supplementation beyond the levels achieved through routine contact with the health system. The goal is to reach out to all children, beginning with children in socially excluded groups, scheduled castes and minority groups in which undernutrition and mortality rates are significantly higher than among children outside these groups.

District planning has been a crucial tool. More than 11,000 health centres and 80,000 anganwadis, or child development centres, that serve as core distribution sites for vitamin A supplementation in Bihar have been mapped out, and more than 3,400 temporary sites have been organised to deliver vitamin A supplements within small, isolated communities. Frontline health and nutrition workers and community volunteers in the 38 districts of Bihar have been trained to administer preventive vitamin A syrup to children and to counsel mothers on how to improve the vitamin A content of their children's diet.

The latest coverage data indicate that in the first semester of 2009, Bihar's vitamin A supplementation programe reached 13.4 million children 9-59 months old, protecting 95 percent of children in this age group against the devastating consequences of vitamin A deficiency.

The Government of Bihar is demonstrating that it is feasible to undertake inclusive programming for child nutrition and to reach children who are traditionally excluded from services when efforts are made to understand who these children are and where they live and when political decisions are made to assign the human and programe resources needed to reach them

Vitamin A supplementation coverage rates show dramatic increases in a relatively short period of time. In Africa, full coverage of vitamin A supplementation has increased fivefold since 2000, due largely to the introduction of biannual child health days, the main platform for vitamin A supplement distribution in many African countries. Importantly, coverage more than doubled in the least developed countries, rising from 41 percent in 2000 to 88 percent in 2008, demonstrating that this life-saving intervention is reaching children in countries where it is most needed.

Some 72 percent of all households in developing countries now consume adequately iodised salt. About 73 percent of households in Asia and 60 percent in Africa consume adequately iodised salt. Africa's relatively high rate is largely due to high coverage in two populous countries—Nigeria (with 97 percent coverage) and the Democratic Republic of the Congo (79 percent) which masks the low coverage in many less populous countries of the region.

Universal Salt Iodisation

Iodine deficiency can be easily prevented by ensuring that salt consumed by households is adequately iodised. The most recent data indicate that 36 countries have reached the target of at least 90 percent of households using adequately iodised salt. This represents an increase from 21 countries in 2002, when the universal salt iodisation goal was endorsed at the United Nations General Assembly Special Session on Children. Despite this significant progress, about 41 million newborns a year remain unprotected from the enduring consequences of brain damage associated with iodine deficiency.

Increases in excess of 30 percentage points over the past decade have occurred in 19 countries where the current levels of household consumption of adequately iodised salt exceed 70 percent. These marked improvements are a product of a unique combination of innovative public policies, private-sector initiative and civic commitment. Thirteen of these countries have improved their coverage by more than 50 percentage points, indicating that the goal of universal salt iodisation can be attained even at the global level if efforts are similarly strengthened among countries that are lagging.

In the 1980s, iodine deficiency was a significant public health concern in Nigeria, with a total goitre rate of 67 percent in 1988. This left many children at risk of mental and cognitive impairment. To combat this public health problem, the Government, in collaboration with UNICEF, launched the Universal Salt Iodisation programe. This initiative is now managed by the National Agency for Food and Drug Administration and Control in collaboration with the Standards Organisation of Nigeria, the National Planning Commission and the Ministry of Health.

At the time the Universal Salt Iodisation programe started in 1993, only 40 percent of households consumed adequately iodised salt. The programe has achieved tremendous success, with 97 percent of households now consuming adequately iodised salt and with factories producing 90-100 percent iodised salt. The goitre rate has plummeted, to about 6 percent in 2007

By 2007, Nigeria became the first country in Africa to receive recognition by the Network for Sustained Elimination of Iodine Deficiency.

Nigeria's success in eliminating iodine deficiency disorder can be attributed to the commitment of the Government and the salt industry, effective legislation and strong enforcement.

Fortification of Staple Foods and Condiments

Along with the iodisation of salt, adding such vitamins and minerals as iron, zinc, vitamin A and folic acid to staple foods, complementary foods and condiments is a cost-effective way to improve the vitamin and mineral intake of the overall population, including women of reproductive age and children. As of March 2009, roughly 30 percent of the world's wheat flour produced in large roller mills was fortified, while 57 countries had legislation or decrees mandating fortification of one or more types of flour with either iron or folic acid. Although many foods, such as fats, oils and margarine, have been fortified for years in some countries, this approach has not yet been scaled up in many lower-income countries. Through increased efforts by various partnerships and alliances, it is expected that food fortification will continue to gain momentum.

Multiple Micronutrient Supplementation/home Fortification

Among products recently developed to provide iron and other vitamins and minerals to young children and women of reproductive age, multiple micronutrient powders (MNPs) are considered particularly promising; studies have found they may reduce anaemia in young children by as much as 45 percent. MNP sachets contain a blend of vitamins and minerals in powdered form that can be sprinkled onto home-prepared foods, enabling families without access to commercially fortified foods to add micronutrients directly to their diets. There is emerging evidence that MNPs can contribute to improving complementary feeding practices if programes are designed with that goal in mind.

Multi-micronutrients for Mongolian Children

In recent years, multiple micronutrient powders that can improve vitamin and mineral intake among infants over 6 months old and young children have become available globally to address what appeared to be an intractable, widespread public health problem of iron-deficiency anaemia. The powders can contain 5-15 vitamins and minerals (such as iron, and vitamins A and D), are relatively tasteless, and are safe, easy to use and acceptable to caregivers. They cost about US$0.03 per sachet (one child typically gets 60-90 sachets per year), and there is sufficient commercial supply to meet programe needs.

Mongolia is among the many countries that are introducing and scaling up the use of MNPs as part of an integrated approach to improve young child feeding and reduce stunting and anaemia. The Mongolian effort, part of a comprehensive national nutrition strategy to tackle chronic undernutrition, is also a way to address the nutritional fallout from the economic instability and chronic food shortages that have plagued the country in the past few years.

The country's approach builds on an experience of distributing MNPs to children 6-36 months old to reduce anaemia and vitamin D deficiency. At the onset of that distribution, in 2001, the baseline prevalence of anaemia was around 42 percent. Children received MNPs via a community distribution model and also had biweekly visits by community workers supported by the Ministry of Health.

One year into the programe, 13,000 children, or more than 80 percent of those targeted, had received multi-micronutrient powders, and anaemia was reduced to half of baseline levels. With technical and financial support from the Asian Development Bank, Mongolia plans to expand the programe to reach some 15,000 children 6-24 months old (or 22 percent of all children in this age range) by targeting provinces based on poverty levels, geographical access and health indicators.

References

Brennan, S. and Noggle, R. (1997) "The Moral Status of Children: Children's Rights, Parent's Rights, and Family Justice," *Social Theory and Practice. 23.*

Cutting, E. (1999) "Giving Parents a Voice: A Children's Rights Issue,"*Rightlines. 2* ERIC #ED428855.

Freeman, M. (2000) "The Future of Children's Rights," *Children & Society. 14*(4) p 277-93.

Lansdown, G. "Children's welfare and children's rights," in Hendrick, H. (2005) *Child Welfare And Social Policy: An Essential Reader.* The Policy Press. p. 117

Rodham, H. (1973). "Children Under the Law". Harvard Educational Review 43: 487–514.

9

Children's Right to Life

The right to life is a universally recognized right for all human beings. It is a fundamental right which governs all other existing rights. In its absence, all other fundamental rights have no reason to exist.

For children, the right to life is the chance to be able to live and have the possibility to grow, to develop and become adults. This right comprises two essential aspects: the right to have one's life protected from birth and the right to be able to survive and develop appropriately.

The right to life is an inherent right for each and every person. From his or her birth, the individual is considered a living being who must be protected. In effect, the human character implies that the dignity of the person must be respected, something which proceeds, above all, from the protection of one's right to live. Thus, from birth, all children have the right to have their life protected.

The right to life means also the right not to be killed. It is the formal interdiction against intentionally causing the death of a person. For children, this right implies, on the one hand, that countries will not subject children to the death penalty, and equally that countries will effectively protect the lives of children by actively fighting against and condemning acts of infanticide.

The child's right to life also proceeds through the necessity of assuring that children have the possibility to grow and develop under favorable conditions. It is then necessary for children to be able to benefit from appropriate healthcare, a balanced diet, and a quality education, as well as being able to live in a healthy environment.

It is the role of countries, beyond the responsibility of parents, to ensure that children have the possibility to develop in a healthy and normal fashion, under all circumstances (peace, war, natural catastrophe. . .). They must guarantee a protection that is suitable for all children, regardless of their social or ethnic origins.

Situation of Children's Right to Life

Children's right to life, to survival and to development is a fundamental right acknowledged by all international treaties relating to Human Rights and the Rights of the Child. However, every day children are losing their lives.

Childrens' right to life is not effectively guaranteed in many countries. Millions of children are killed every year with impunity for the perpetrator.

There are two issues at the center of the international community concerns, sex-selective infanticides and the death penalty against juvenile offenders.

Sex-selective Infanticides

In certain countries, essentially India, China and Japan, boys are given preference over girls because of tradition and religion. In those societies, men play a prominent part since they are the only ones who can inherit family property and pass the family name down. Conversely, the birth of a girl is considered too heavy a financial burden, so parents wish they had sons in order to ensure family survival and continuity.

The preference for boys, consequently, generates worrying behaviors. Parents intentionally eliminate unborn baby girls through abortions and even already born girls.

Sex-selective abortion and infanticide are forbidden practices across the whole world. However, they are still common practice today. Due to the proliferation of those practices; today, one can estimate that there is a deficiency of more than one million women in Asia. This results in a real sex-ratio imbalance in the world.

Death Penalty for Minors

All international treaties strictly prohibit the death penalty for children under

18. This sentence is a cruel and disproportionate punishment against children.

Children cannot be treated the same way as adults because of their immaturity and vulnerability. Their lack of sound judgement and their difficulty in distinguishing between what is good and what is bad explains why their deeds cannot be judged with the same severity as adults.

Today, five countries in the world still inflict the death penalty on minors. They are Iran, Saudi Arabia, Pakistan, Sudan and Yemen. These countries receive close scrutiny by the international community, who aim to eliminate this sentence.

Difficulty in Guaranteeing Children's Right to Life and Development

Every year, about 10 million children under 5 die of diseases that could have been avoided or treated.

By guaranteeing these children a right to survival and an adequate development, countries could prevent the death of millions of children in the world. Guaranteeing this right is not always that easy for certain countries. The right to survival and development is closely linked to a country's level of economic development.

In countries which have not yet achieved a sufficient level of economic development, people's quality of life is generally below the poverty line.

As a result, many children are not fortunate enough to enjoy an environment favorable to their development. For these countries, it is often difficult to provide basic services that ensure the supervision and protection of children.

In these countries, millions of children do not go to school and have to work from an early age, which hinders both their development and self-fulfilment.

Even worse, millions of children in the world suffer from malnutrition, the lack of drinking water, and the lack of adequate sewage treatment. These children die of diseases that could have been avoided such as pneumonia, diarrhea or malaria.

In developed countries, people's quality of life is already sufficiently high. Most children already have access to all the rights that make their development possible and to the oversight and protection services offered in these countries. These children are allowed to grow up, develop and flourish in favorable conditions.

Female Foeticide

It has been six long decades since India gained independence but many Indians are still trapped in age-old traditional beliefs. Here, 'old beliefs' imply the mindset of people who still find themselves in the trap of girl-boy inequality. The 'liberal' Indian society has failed to transform the other orthodox India. No doubt India is advancing at a fast pace in the field of science and technology, and also in aping of the western culture, but if we look at the grass root level, the picture is not so rosy; it is rather a dark, especially when it comes to how we treat the fairer sex.

The status of females in India aptly symbolizes India's status of being a developing nation – miles away from becoming a developed state. Of course, India deserves to be in this list because here, in this 21st century, the girl child continues to be murdered before she is born. Female foeticide is still prevalent in the Indian society, in fact, it has been a practice for hundreds of years.

Narrow-minded people do not mind murdering their unborn daughters for the fear of giving huge amounts of dowry at the time of her marriage. Such people, whenever they discover they are going to have a girl child (through illegal sex selection tests), get the foetus aborted. Else they would continue to reproduce till they get a male heir. When price rise is already taking a toll on the standard of living, is it necessary to go in for more than two children irrespective of their gender?

Many families put pressure on women to give birth to boy so that he can take family's name forward, light the funeral pyre and be the bread earner of the family. But these days, are girls less competent than boys? Just look at the results of Board exams or any other competitive exams, girls mostly outshine boys. Women empowerment has led to inundation of females excelling in the corporate world, engineering and medical professions.

Sadly, there have been numerous incidents of the foetus being found lying in farms, floating in rivers, wrapped up in jute bags etc. India's major social problem is the intentional killing of the girl child. The struggle for a girl child starts the day her existence is known in her mother's womb. The fear and struggle to survive swallow most of the girl's life even if she is 'allowed' to live in this cruel world.

In India, the girl child is considered a burden as huge amounts of money, gold and other items need to be given in the form of dowry when she gets married. Dowry is not the only reason for poor couple to abort their girl child. The ages old traditions, customs and beliefs of the Indian society are largely responsible for creating a negative mindset among the couples. More shocking is the fact that the sinful crime of female foeticide is not only common in rural areas where social discrimination against women, lack of proper education etc. can be considered as reasons behind carrying out such acts, but also the ultra modern, so-called 'educated' people living in urban areas and metropolitan cities who are a step ahead in killing the girl child in the womb.

The truth behind this crime has been brought into light several times by the print and electronic media. But, it has failed to melt the hearts and minds of those who remain unaffected by the consequences of the grave sin they are committing.

The matter was discussed in length and breadth in the inaugural episode of the show 'Satyamave Jayate' anchored by Bollywood actor Aamir Khan. The show has once again ignited the spirited discussion on the female foeticide in the country. That episode had mothers from different parts of rural and urban India talking about the pressure and the problems they faced for delivering a girl child. Although the show is doing really well and has already garnered positive reviews from the audiences, we will have to wait and see whether the impact will remain even after the programme stops beaming into our drawing rooms every Sunday. The emotional connect which the show has successfully created should be strong enough to stop the killing of the girl child before being born.

If we look at the figures of sex ratio in India, according to the 2011 Census, the number of girls stands at 940 which is a marginal increase from 933 in 2001. Not surprisingly, Haryana has the lowest sex ratio among the states while Kerala remains at the top with the highest sex ratio. In the national capital Delhi, the statistics stand at 821 girls against 1000 boys in 2001 compared to 866 in 2011.

According to the statistics, nearly 10 million female foetuses have been aborted in the country over the past two decades. Of the 12 million girls born in India, one million do not see their first birthdays.

As a result, human trafficking has become common in various states of India where teenage girls are being sold for cheap money by poor families.

The girls are treated as sex objects and more than half of such cases go unreported.

The United Nations' World Population Fund indicated that India has one of the highest sex imbalances in the world. Not surprisingly, demographers warn that there will be a shortage of brides in the next 20 years because of the adverse juvenile sex ratio, combined with an overall decline in fertility.

With the advent of technology, ultrasound techniques gained widespread use in India during the 1990s. It resulted in the foetal sex determination and sex selective abortion by medical professionals. Recently, incidences of female foeticide were reported from Beed district in Maharashtra where women used to come to a doctor's clinic to get their female child aborted for Rs 2000. Just think for a moment about the doctor's connivance in this illegal act. Doctors, whose aim is to save the lives of people, happily kill the foetus for a meagre two thousand bucks! And more heart wrenching is the fact that the aborted foetuses were very often fed to dogs.

The above mentioned case is not the only one of such heart wrenching heinous crimes. There are thousands of such clinics where illegal activities are carried out on a daily basis and in some cases, in connivance with politicians and police men.

The life transition from a female foetus to a school going girl to a caring woman is never an easy task for the fairer sex. She has to face challenges at every step of her life. Daily, there is news related to rape, sexual harassment, molestation, verbal abuse, torture, exploitation. She has to fight against gender indiscrimination, inequality, and hundreds of social norms are tagged with her the day she puts her steps outside her home.

In most of the cases, women abort their female child involuntarily when they succumb to family pressures. The in-laws' illogical demand/ desire for a boy preference makes the life of women hell. Sometimes, she is left by her husband if she is unable to give birth to a child and worse happens when she conceives a girl child.

Ironically, it all happens in a country where the girl is seen as an incarnation of Goddess 'Laxmi'. True, many families are out of bounds in joy when a girl child is born in their family. They think she will bring luck, harmony, happiness and peace in their family. They even touch her feet to seek her blessings. Many childless couples even adopt a girl child irrespective of the worries of her future.

In such a grim scenario, it's really difficult to digest the harsh reality of the differences between a boy and a girl. India has a deeply rooted patriarchal attitude to which even the doctors and the women, who in spite of being the victims, unthinkingly subscribe. There is an urgent need of undoing the historical and traditional wrongs of a gendered society; only then the hope of abolition of female infanticide and boy preference can positively adjust the figures in favour of the girl child in future. The skewed sex ratio has to find a balance in order to maintain the progress of the country.

Sex-selective Infanticide

Infanticide is the intentional killing of infants. Neonaticide, killing within 24 hours of a child's birth, is most commonly done by the mother whereas infanticide of a child more than one day old is slightly more likely to be committed by the father.

In many past societies, certain forms of infanticide were considered permissible. In some countries, female infanticide is more common than the killing of male offspring, due to sex-selective infanticide.

The practice of infanticide has taken many forms. Child sacrifice to supernatural figures or forces, such as the one practiced in ancient Carthage, may be only the most notorious example in the ancient world. Anthropologist Laila Williamson notes that "Infanticide has been practiced on every continent and by people on every level of cultural complexity, from hunter gatherers to high civilizations, including our own ancestors. Rather than being an exception, then, it has been the rule." A frequent method of infanticide in ancient Europe and Asia was simply to abandon the infant, leaving it to die by exposure (i.e. hypothermia, hunger, thirst, or animal attack). Infant abandonment still occurs in modern societies. In at least one island in Oceania, infanticide was carried out until the 20th century by suffocating the infant, while in pre-Columbian Mesoamerica and in the Inca Empire it was carried out by sacrifice.

Historical Practices

Many Neolithic groups routinely resorted to infanticide in order to control their numbers so that their lands could support them. Joseph Birdsell believed that infanticide rates in prehistoric times were between 15% and 50% of the total number of births, while Laila Williamson estimated a lower rate ranging from 15% to 20%. Both anthropologists believed that these high rates of infanticide persisted until the development of agriculture during the Neolithic Revolution. Comparative anthropologists have calculated that 50% of female newborn babies were killed by their parents during the Paleolithic era. Decapitated skeletons of hominid children have been found with evidence of cannibalism. The children were not necessarily actively killed, but neglect and intentional malnourishment may also have occurred, as proposed by Vicente Lull as an explanation for an apparent surplus of men and the below average height of women in prehistoric Menorca.

Archaeologists have uncovered physical evidence of child sacrifice at several locations. Some of the best attested examples are the diverse rites which were part of the religious practices in Mesoamerica and the Inca Empire.

Three thousand bones of young children, with evidence of sacrificial rituals, have been found in Sardinia. Infants were offered to the Babylonian goddess Ishtar. Pelasgians offered a sacrifice of every tenth child during difficult times. Syrians sacrificed children to Jupiter and Juno. Many remains of children have been found in Gezer excavations with signs of sacrifice. Child skeletons with the marks of sacrifice have been found also in Egypt dating 950-720 BCE. In Carthage "[child] sacrifice in the ancient world reached its infamous zenith." Besides the Carthaginians, other Phoenicians, and the Canaanites, Moabites and Sepharvites offered their first-born as a sacrifice to their gods.

In Egyptian households, at all social levels, children of both sexes were valued and there is no evidence of infanticide. The religion of the Ancient Egyptians forbade infanticide and during the Greco-Roman period they rescued abandoned babies from manure heaps, a common method of infanticide by Greeks or Romans, and were allowed to either adopt them as foundlings or raise them as slaves, often giving them names such as "copro -" to memorialise their rescue. Strabo considered it a peculiarity of the Egyptians that every child must be reared. Diodorus indicates infanticide was a punishable offence. Egypt was heavily dependent on the annual flooding of the Nile to irrigate the land and in years of low inundation severe famine could occur with breakdowns in social order resulting, notably between 930-1070 AD and 1180-1350 AD. Instances of cannibalism are recorded during these periods but it is unknown if this happened during the pharaonic era of Ancient Egypt. Beatrix Midant-Reynes describes human sacrifice as having occurred at Abydos in the early dynastic period (c. 3150-2850 BCE), while Jan Assmann asserts there is no clear evidence of human sacrifice ever happening in Ancient Egypt.

According to Shelby Brown, Carthaginians, descendants of the Phoenicians, sacrificed infants to their gods. Charred bones of hundreds of infants have been found in Carthaginian archaeological sites. One such area harbored as many as 20,000 burial urns. Skeptics suggest that the bodies of children found in Carthaginian and Phoenician cemeteries were merely the cremated remains of children that died naturally.

Plutarch (ca. 46–120 AD) mentions the practice, as do Tertullian, Orosius, Diodorus Siculus and Philo. The Hebrew Bible also mentions what appears to be child sacrifice practiced at a place called the Tophet (from the Hebrew taph or toph, to burn) by the Canaanites. Writing in the 3rd century BCE, Kleitarchos, one of the historians of Alexander the Great, described that the infants rolled into the flaming pit. Diodorus Siculus wrote that babies were roasted to death inside the burning pit of the god Baal Hamon, a bronze statue.

The historical Greeks considered the practice of adult and child sacrifice barbarous. However, exposure of newborns was widely practiced in ancient Greece. In Greece the decision to expose a child was typically the father's, although in Sparta the decision was made by a group of elders. Exposure was the preferred method of disposal, as that act in itself was not murder; moreover, the exposed child technically had a chance of being rescued by the gods or any passersby. This very situation was a recurring motif in Greek mythology. To notify the neighbors of a birth of a child, a woolen strip was hung over the front door - this indicated a female baby. An olive branch indicated a boy had been born. Families did not always keep their new child. After a woman had a baby, she would show it to her husband. If the husband accepted it, it would live, but if he refused it, it would die. Babies would often be rejected if they were illegitimate, unhealthy or deformed, the wrong sex (female for example), or too great a burden on the family. These babies would not be directly killed, but put in a clay pot or jar and deserted outside the front door or on the roadway. In ancient Greek religion, this practice took the responsibility away from the parents because the child would die of natural causes, for example hunger, asphyxiation or exposure to the elements.The practice was prevalent in ancient Rome, as well. Philo was the first philosopher to speak out against it.

Infanticide became a capital offense in Roman law in 374 AD, but offenders were rarely if ever prosecuted.

According to mythological legend, Romulus and Remus, twin infant sons of the war god, Mars, survived near-infanticide after being tossed into the Tiber River. According to the mythology, they were raised by wolves and later founded the city of Rome.

Judaism prohibits infanticide, and has for some time, dating back to at least early Common Era. Roman historians wrote about the ideas and customs of other peoples, which often diverged from their own. Tacitus recorded that the Jews "regard it as a crime to kill any late-born children." Josephus, whose works give an important insight into 1st-century Judaism, wrote that God "forbids women to cause abortion of what is begotten, or to destroy it afterward."

In his book Germania, Tacitus wrote that the ancient Germanic tribes enforced a similar prohibition. He found such mores remarkable and commented: "[The Germani] hold it shameful to kill any unwanted child." Modern scholarship differs. John Boswell believed that in ancient Germanic tribes unwanted children were exposed, usually in the forest. "It was the custom of the [Teutonic] pagans, that if they wanted to kill a son or daughter, they would be killed before they had been given any food." Usually children born out of wedlock were disposed that way.In his highly influential Pre-historic Times, John Lubbock described burnt bones indicating the practice of child sacrifice in pagan Britain.

The last canto, Marjatan poika (Son of Marjatta), of Finnish national epic Kalevala describes an assumed infanticide. Väinämöinen orders the infant bastard son of Marjatta to be drowned in marsh.

The Íslendingabók, a main source for the early history of Iceland, recounts that on the Conversion of Iceland to Christianity in 1000 it was provided - in order to make the transition more palatable to Pagans - that "(...)the old laws allowing exposure of newborn children will remain in force". However, this provision - like other concessions made at the time to the Pagans - was abolished some years later.

Christianity rejects infanticide. The Teachings of the Apostles or Didache said "You shall not kill that which is born." The Epistle of Barnabas stated an identical command. Apologists Tertullian, Athenagoras, Minucius Felix, Justin Martyr and Lactantius also maintained that exposing a baby to death was a wicked act. In 318 AD, Constantine I considered infanticide a crime, and in 374 AD, Valentinian I mandated the rearing all children (exposing babies, especially girls, was still common). The Council of Constantinople declared that infanticide was homicide, and in 589 AD, the Third Council of Toledo took measures against the Spanish custom of killing their own children. There is one debated example of child killing in Old Testament, Jephthah's Vow. Biblical scholars disagree as to whether Jephthah's daughter was actually sacrificed, or merely dedicated to a life of chaste service.

Whereas theologians and clerics preached sparing their lives, newborn abandonment continued as registered in both the literature record and in legal documents. According to William L. Langer, exposure in the Middle Ages "was practiced on gigantic scale with absolute impunity, noticed by writers with most frigid indifference". At the end of the 12th century, notes Richard Trexler, Roman women threw their newborns into the Tiber river in daylight.

Unlike other European regions, in the Middle Ages the German mother had the right to expose the newborn. In Gotland, Sweden, children were also sacrificed.

In the High Middle Ages, abandoning unwanted children finally eclipsed infanticide. Unwanted children were left at the door of church or abbey, and the clergy was assumed to take care of their upbringing. This practice also gave rise to the first orphanages.

The pre-Islamic Arabian society practiced infanticide as a form of "post-partum birth control". Regarding the prevalence of this practice, we know it was "common enough among the pre-Islamic Arabs to be assigned a specific term, wa?d". Infanticide was practiced either out of destitution (thus practiced on males and females alike), or as sacrifices to gods, or as "disappointment and fear of social disgrace felt by a father upon the birth of a daughter".

Some authors believe that there is little evidence that infanticide was prevalent in pre-Islamic Arabia or early Muslim history, except for the case of the Tamim tribe, who practiced it during severe famine. Others state that "female infanticide was common all over Arabia during this period of time" (pre-Islamic Arabia), especially by burying alive a female newborn.

Infanticide is explicitly prohibited by the Qur'an. "And do not kill your children for fear of poverty; We give them sustenance and yourselves too; surely to kill them is a great wrong."

The Qur'an rejected the practice of infanticide. Together with polytheism and homicide, infanticide was regarded as a grave sin (6:151 and 60:12). Infanticide is also implicitly denounced in the story of Pharaoh's slaughter of the male children of Israelites (2:49; 7:127; 7:141; 14:6; 28:4 ;40:25).

Infanticide may have been practiced as human sacrifice, as part of the pagan cult of Perun. Ibn Fadlan describes sacrificial practices at the time of his trip to Kiev Rus (present day Ukraine) in 921-922 CE, and describes an incident of a woman voluntarily sacrificing her life as part of a funeral rite for a prominent leader, but makes no mention of infanticide. The Primary Chronicle, one of the most important literary sources before the 12th century, indicates that human sacrifice to idols may have been introduced by Vladimir the Great in 980 CE. The same Vladimir the Great formally converted Kiev Rus into Christianity just 8 years later, but pagan cults continued to be practiced clandestinely in remote areas as late as the 13th century.

In Kamchatka, babies were killed and thrown to the dogs. American explorer George Kennan noted that among the Koryaks, a Mongoloid people of north-eastern Siberia, infanticide was still common in the 19th century. One of the twins was always sacrificed.

Marco Polo, the famed explorer, saw newborns exposed in Manzi. China's society practiced sex selective infanticide. Philosopher Han Fei Tzu, a member of the ruling aristocracy of the 3rd century BCE, who developed a school of law, wrote: "As to children, a father and mother when they produce a boy congratulate one another, but when they produce a girl they put it to death." Among the Hakka people, and in Yunnan, Anhui, Sichuan, Jiangxi and Fujian a method of killing the baby was to put her into a bucket of cold water, which was called "baby water".

Infanticide was known in China as early as the 3rd century BCE, and, by the time of the Song Dynasty (960-1279 CE), it was widespread in some provinces. Buddhist belief in transmigration allowed poor residents of the country to kill their newborn children if they felt unable to care for them, hoping that they would be reborn in better circumstances. Furthermore, the Chinese did not consider newborn children fully "human", and saw "life" beginning at some point after the sixth month after birth.

Contemporary writers from the Song Dynasty note that, in Hubei and Fujian provinces, residents would only keep three sons and two daughters (among poor farmers, two sons and one daughter), and kill all babies beyond that number at birth. Initially the sex of the child was only one factor to consider. By the time of the Ming Dynasty, however (1368–1644), male infanticide was becoming increasingly uncommon. The prevalence of female infanticide remained high much longer. The magnitude of this practice is subject to some dispute; however, one commonly quoted estimate is that, by late Qing, between one fifth and one quarter of all newborn girls, across the entire social spectrum, were victims of infanticide. If one includes excess mortality among female children under 10 (ascribed to gender-differential neglect), the share of victims rises to one third.

Female infanticide of newborn girls was systematic in feudatory Rajputs in South Asia for illegitimate female children during the Middle Ages. According to Firishta, as soon as the illegitimate female child was born she was held "in one hand, and a knife in the other, that any person who wanted a wife might take her now, otherwise she was immediately put to death". The practice of female infanticide was also common among the Kutch, Kehtri, Nagar, Bengal, Miazed, Kalowries in India inhabitants, and also among the Sindh in British India. It was not uncommon that parents threw a child to the sharks in the Ganges River as a sacrificial offering. The British colonists were unable to outlaw the custom until the beginnings of the 19th century.

In Africa some children were killed because of fear that they were an evil omen or because they were considered unlucky. Twins were usually put to death in Arebo; as well as by the Nama Hottentots of South West Africa; in the Lake Victoria Nyanza region; by the Tswana in Portuguese East Africa; among the Ilso and Igbo people of Nigeria; and by the !Kung Bushmen of the Kalahari Desert. The Kikuyu, Kenya's most populous ethnic group, practiced ritual killing of twins. If a mother died in childbirth among the Ibo people of Nigeria, the newborn was buried alive. It suffered a similar fate if the father died.

In the Eastern Shoshone there was a scarcity of Indian women as a result of female infanticide. For the Maidu native Americans twins were so dangerous that they not only killed them, but the mother as well. In the region known today as southern Texas, the Mariame Indians practiced infanticide of females on a large scale. Wives had to be obtained from neighboring groups.

Bernal Díaz recounted that, after landing on the Veracruz coast, they came across a temple dedicated to Tezcatlipoca. "That day they had sacrificed two boys, cutting open their chests and offering their blood and hearts to that accursed idol". In The Conquest of New Spain Díaz describes more child sacrifices in the towns before the Spaniards reached the large Aztec city Tenochtitlan.

The Tapirapé indigenous people of Brazil allowed no more than three children per woman. Furthermore, no more than two had to be of the same sex. If the rule was broken infanticide was practiced. The people in the Bororo tribe killed all the newborns that did not appear healthy enough. Infanticide is also documented in the case of the Korubo people in the Amazon.

While Capacocha was practiced in the Peruvian large cities, child sacrifice in the pre-Columbian tribes of the region is less documented. However, even today studies on the Aymara Indians reveal high incidences of mortality among the newborn, especially female deaths, suggesting infanticide. The Abipones, a small tribe of Guaycuran stock, of about 5,000 by the end of the 18th century in Paraguay, practiced systematic infanticide; with never more than two children being reared in one family. The machigenga killed their disabled children. Infanticide among the Chaco in Paraguay was estimated as high as 50% of all newborns in that tribe, who were usually buried. The infanticidal custom had such roots among the Ayoreo in Bolivia and Paraguay that it persisted until the late 20th century.

Infanticide in Modern Times

Infanticide has become less common in the Western world. The frequency has been estimated to be approximately 1 in 3000-5000 children of all ages and 2.1 per 100,000 newborns per year. It is thought that infanticide today continues at a much higher rate in areas of extremely high poverty and overpopulation, such as parts of China and India. Female infants, then and even now, are particularly vulnerable, a factor in sex-selective infanticide.

In spite of the fact that it is illegal, in Benin, West Africa, parents secretly continue with infanticidal customs.

There have been some accusations that infanticide occurs in the People's Republic of China due to the one-child policy. In the 1990s, a certain stretch of the Yangtze River was known to be a common site of infanticide by drowning, until government projects made access to it more difficult. Others assert that China has twenty-five million fewer girl children than expected, but this can partially be explained by sex selective abortion. The illegal use of ultrasound is widespread in China, and itinerant sonographers with plain vans in parking lots offer inexpensive sonographs to determine the sex of a fetus. Recent studies suggest that over 40 million girls and women are 'missing' in China.

The practice has continued in some rural areas of India. Infanticide is illegal in India. According to a recent report by the United Nations Children's Fund (UNICEF) up to 50 million girls and women are missing in India's population as a result of systematic sex discrimination. The UNICEF study has been criticized by the Indian Medical Association for utilizing outdated data and for deliberately demonizing Indians for the purposes of politics.

The People's Republic of China returns all illegal immigrants from North Korea which usually imprisons them in a short term facility. Women who are suspected of being impregnated by Chinese fathers are subjected to forced abortions; babies born alive are killed, sometimes by exposure or being buried alive.

Killings of newborn babies has been on the rise in Pakistan, corresponding to an increase in poverty across the country. More than 1,000 infants, mostly girls, have been killed or abandoned to die in Pakistan in 2009 according a Pakistani charity organization. Infanticide of girls in Pakistan is attributed to a patriarchal society where women are less valued than men.

The Edhi Foundation found 1,210 dead babies in 2010. Many more are abandoned and left at the doorsteps of mosques. As a result Edhi centers feature signs "Do not murder, lay them here.". Though female infanticide is punishable by life in prison, such crimes are rarely prosecuted.

In November 2008 it was reported that in Agibu and Amosa villages of Gimi region of Eastern Highlands province of Papua New Guinea where tribal fighting in the region of Gimi has been going on since 1986 (many of the clashes arising over claims of sorcery) women had agreed that if they stopped producing males, allowing only female babies to survive, their tribe's stock of boys would go down and there would be no men in the future to fight. They agreed to have all newborn male babies killed. It is not known how many male babies were killed by being smothered, but it had reportedly happened to all males over a 10-year period and probably was still happening.

In England and Wales there were typically 30 to 50 homicides per million children less than 1 year old between 1982 and 1996. The younger the infant, the higher the risk. The rate for children 1 to 5 years was around 10 per million children. The homicide rate of infants less than 1 year is significantly higher than for the general population.

The United States ranked eleventh for infants under 1 year killed, and fourth for those killed from 1 through 14 years (the latter case not necessarily involving filicide), circa 1983. In the U.S. over six hundred children were killed by their parents in 1983. In Canada 114 cases of child murder by a parent were reported during 1964-1968. The U.S. Centers for Disease Control's latest available data from 2007 show that U.S. infant mortality is 21% higher in male infants than female, but makes no suggestion that this is due to any pattern of preferential infanticide. Some of the cases that made news were those of Amy Grossberg and Brian Peterson, Genene Jones, Marybeth Tinning, Melissa Drexler, Dena Schlosser and Waneta Hoyt.

In the United States the infanticide rate during the first hour of life dropped from 1.41 per 100,000 during 1963 to 1972 to 0.44 per 100,000 for 1974 to 1983; the rates during the first month of life also declined, whereas those for older infants rose during this time. The legalization of abortion, which was completed in 1973, was the most important factor in the decline in neonatal mortality during the period from 1964 to 1977, according to a study by economists associated with the National Bureau of Economic Research.

Explanations for the Practice

There are various reasons for infanticide. Neonaticide typically has different patterns and causes than for killing of older infants. Traditional neonaticide is often related to economic necessity - inability to provide for the infant. In England and the United States, Older infants are typically killed for reasons related to child abuse, domestic violence or mental illness. For infants older than one day, younger infants are more at risk, and boys are more at risk than girls. Risk factors for the parent include: Family history of violence, violence in current relationship, history of abuse or neglect of children, and personality disorder and/or depression.

Economic Reasons

Many historians believe the reason to be primarily economic, with more children born than the family is prepared to support. In societies that are patrilineal and patrilocal, the family may choose to allow more sons to live and kill some daughters, as the former will support their birth family until they die, whereas the latter will leave economically and geographically to join their husband's family, possibly only after the payment of a burdensome dowry price. Thus the decision to bring up a boy is more economically rewarding to the parents. However, this does not explain why infanticide would occur equally among rich and poor, nor why it would be as frequent during decadent periods of the Roman Empire as during earlier, less affluent, periods. Before the appearance of effective contraception, infanticide was a common occurrence in ancient brothels. Unlike usual infanticide - where historically girls have been more likely to be killed - prostitutes in certain areas preferred to kill their male offspring.

Instances of infanticide in Britain in 18th and 19th century is often attributed to the economic position of the women, with juries committing pious perjury in many subsequent court cases. The knowledge of the difficulties faced in the 18th century by those women who attempted to keep their children can be seen as reason for juries to show compassion. If the woman chose to keep the child, society was not set up to ease the pressure placed upon the woman, legally, socially or economically.

Macfarlane argues in Illegitimacy and Illegitimates in Britain (1980) that English society greatly concerned itself with the burden that a bastard child places upon its communities and had gone to some lengths to ensure that the father of the child is identified in order to maintain its wellbeing. Assistance could be gained through maintenance payments from the father, however, this was capped 'at a miserable 2s and 6d a week'. If the father got into arrears with the payments he could only be asked 'to pay a maximum of 13 weeks arrears'.

Despite the accusations of some that women were getting a free hand-out there is evidence that many women were far from receiving adequate assistance from their parish. 'Within Leeds in 1822 ... relief was limited to 1s per week'. Sheffield required women to enter the workhouse, whereas Halifax gave no relief to the women who required it. The prospect of entering the workhouse was certainly something to be avoided. Lionel Rose quotes Dr Joseph Rogers in Massacre of the Innocents ... (1986). Dr Rogers, who was employed by a London workhouse in 1856 stated that conditions in the nursery were 'wretchedly damp and miserable ... [and] ... overcrowded with young mothers and their infants'.

The loss of social standing for a servant girl was a particular problem in respect of producing a bastard child as they relied upon a good character reference in order to maintain their job and more importantly, to get a new or better job. In a large number of trials for the crime of infanticide, it is the servant girl that stood accused. The disadvantage of being a servant girl is that they had to live to the social standards of their superiors or risk dismissal and no references. Whereas within other professions, such as in the factory, the relationship between employer and employee was much more anonymous and the mother would be better able to make other provisions, such as employing a minder. The result of the lack of basic social care in Britain in the 18th and 19th century is the numerous accounts in court records of women, particularly servant girls, standing trial for the murder of their child.

There may have been no specific offence of infanticide in England before about 1623 because infanticide was a matter for the by ecclesiastical courts, possibly because Infant mortality from natural causes was high (about 15% or one in six)

Thereafter the accusation of the suppression of bastard children by lewd mothers was a crime incurring the presumption of guilt

The Infanticide Acts is the name of several laws. That of 1922 made the killing of an infant child by its mother during the early months of life as a lesser crime than murder. The acts of 1938 and 1939 abolished the earlier act, but introduced the idea that Postpartum depression was legally to be regarded as a form of diminished responsibility.

Population control

Marvin Harris estimated that among Paleolithic hunters 23-50% of newborn children were killed. He argued that the goal was to preserve the 0.001% population growth of that time. He also wrote that female infanticide may be a form of population control. Population control is achieved not only by limiting the number of potential mothers; increased fighting among men for access to relatively scarce wives would also lead to a decline in population. For example, on the Melanesian island of Tikopia infanticide was used to keep a stable population in line with its resource base. Research by Marvin

Harris and William Divale supports this argument, it has been cited as an example of environmental determinism.

Customs and taboos

In 1888, Lieut. F. Elton reported that Ugi beach people in the Solomon Islands killed their infants at birth by burying them, and women were also said to practice abortion. They reported that it was too much trouble to raise a child, and instead preferred to buy one from the bush people. Larry S. Milner, author of Hardness of Heart/Hardness of Life, a treatise on infanticide, believes that superstition has always reigned supreme in tribal religion. In chapters 9 through 21 Milner explores diverse customs and taboos as possible causes of infanticide, from punishment and shame to poverty, famine, revenge, depression and insanity and superstitious omens.

Psychological Factors

Evolutionary psychology have proposed several theories for different forms of infanticide. Infanticide by stepfathers, as well as child abuse in general by stepfathers, has been explained by spending resources on not genetically related children reducing reproductive success. Infanticide is one of the few forms of violence more often done by women than men. Cross-cultural research have found that this is more likely to occur when the child has deformities or illnesses as well as when there are lacking resources due to factors such as poverty, other children requiring resources, and no male support. Such a child may have a low chance of reproductive success in which case it would decrease the mother's inclusive fitness, in particular since women generally have a greater parental investment than men, to spend resources on the child.

Early infanticidal childrearing

A minority of academics subscribe to an alternate school of thought, considering the practice as "early infanticidal childrearing". They attribute parental infanticidal wishes to massive projection or displacement of the parents' unconscious onto the child, because of intergenerational, ancestral abuse by their own parents. Clearly, an infanticidal parent may have multiple motivations, conflicts, emotions, and thoughts about their baby and their relationship with their baby, which are often colored both by their individual psychology, current relational context and attachment history, and, perhaps most saliently, their psychopathology. Almeida, Merminod, and Schechter suggest that parents with fantasies, projections, and delusions involving infanticide need to be taken seriously and assessed carefully, whenever possible, by an interdisciplinary team that includes infant mental health specialists or mental health practitioners who have experience in working with parents, children, and families.

Wider effects

In addition to debates over the morality of infanticide itself, there is some debate over the effects of infanticide on surviving children, and the effects of childrearing in societies that also sanction infanticide. Some argue that the practice of infanticide in any widespread form causes enormous psychological damage in children. Conversely, studying societies that practice infanticide Géza Róheim reported that even infanticidal mothers in New Guinea, who ate a child, did not affect the personality development of the surviving children; that "these are good mothers who eat their own children". Harris and Divale's work on the relationship between female infanticide and warfare suggests that there are, however, extensive negative effects.

Psychiatric disorders of childbirth

Postpartum psychosis is also a causative factor of infanticide. Stuart S. Asch, MD, a Professor of Psychiatry at Cornell University established the connections between some cases of infanticide and post-partum depression., The books, From Cradle to Grave, and The Death of Innocents, describe selected cases of maternal infanticide and the investigative research of Professor Asch working in concert with the New York City Medical Examiner's Office. Stanley Hopwood wrote that childbirth and lactation entail severe stress on the female sex, and that under certain circumstances attempts at infanticide and suicide are common. A study published in the American Journal of Psychiatry revealed that 44% of filicidal fathers had a diagnosis of psychosis. In addition to postpartum psychosis, dissociative psychopathology and sociopathy have also been found to be associated with neonaticide in some cases

Sex selection

Sex selection may be one of the contributing factors of infanticide. In the absence of sex-selective abortion, sex-selective infanticide can be deduced from very skewed birth statistics. The biologically normal sex ratio for humans at birth is approximately 105 males per 100 females; normal ratios hardly ranging beyond 102-108. When a society has an infant male to female ratio which is significantly higher or lower than the biological norm, sex selection can usually be inferred.

Current Law against Infanticide

In England and Wales, the Infanticide Act 1938 describes the offence of infanticide as one which would otherwise amount to murder (by his/her mother) if the victim was older than 12 months and the mother was not suffering from an imbalance of mind due to the effects of childbirth or lactation. Where a mother who has killed such an infant has been charged with murder rather than infanticide s.1(3) of the Act confirms that a jury has the power to find alternative verdicts of Manslaughter in English law or guilty but insane.

In 2009, Texas state representative Jessica Farrar proposed legislation that would define infanticide as a distinct and lesser crime than homicide. Under the terms of the proposed legislation, if jurors concluded that a mother's "judgment was impaired as a result of the effects of giving birth or the effects of lactation following the birth," they would be allowed to convict her of the crime of infanticide, rather than murder. The maximum penalty for infanciticide would be two years in prison. Farrar's introduction of this bill prompted liberal bioethics scholar Jacob M. Appel to call her "the bravest politician in America."

Prevention

Since infanticide, especially neonaticide, is often a response to an unwanted birth, preventing unwanted pregnancies through improved sex education and increased contraceptive access are advocated as ways of preventing infanticide. Increased use of contraceptives and access to safe legal abortions have greatly reduced neonaticide in many developed nations. Some say that where abortion is illegal, as in Pakistan, infanticide would decline if safer legal abortions were available.

Screening for psychiatric disorders or risk factors, and providing treatment or assistance to those at risk may help prevent infanticide. However in developed world significant proportions of neonaticides that are detected occur in young women who deny their pregnancy, and avoid outside contacts, so they may have limited contact with health care services.

In some areas baby hatches, safe places for a mother to anonymously leave an infant, are offered, in part to reduce the rate of infanticide. In other places, like the United States, safe-haven laws allow mothers to anonymously give infants to designated officials. Typically such babies are put up for adoption, or cared for in orphanages.

Granting women employment raises their status and autonomy. Having a gainful employment can raise the perceived worth of females. This can lead to an increase in the number of women getting an education and a decrease in the number of female infanticide. As a result, the infant mortality rate will decrease and economic development will increase.

Child Protection: The Role of UNICEF

UNICEF uses the term 'child protection' to refer to protection from violence, exploitation, abuse and neglect. Violations of the child's right to protection, in addition to being human rights violations, are also massive, under-recognized and underreported barriers to child survival and development. Children subjected to violence, exploitation, abuse and neglect are at risk of:

— shortened lives;

— poor physical and mental health;

— educational problems (including dropping out of school);

— poor parenting skills later in life;

— homelessness, vagrancy and displacement.

Conversely, successful protection increases a child's chances of growing up physically and mentally healthy, confident and self-respecting, and less likely to abuse or exploit others, including his or her own children.

Child protection is closely linked to other aspects of a child's well-being. An immunized child who is constantly beaten is not a healthy child; a school-going child taunted and abused for his or her ethnicity does not enjoy a good learning environment; and an adolescent sold into prostitution will not be empowered to participate in and contribute to society. Child protection is an integral part of the business of development.

Child protection is an issue for children in every country of the world:

— more than 1 million children worldwide are living in detention as a result of being in conflict with the law. In Central and Eastern Europe alone, about 1.5 million children were living in public care at the end of the 1990s;

— about 14 million children under 15 are estimated to have been orphaned as a result of AIDS alone;

— aproximately 246 million children work, with about 180 million engaged in the worst forms of child labour;

— an estimated 1.2 million children are trafficked every year;

— 2 million children are believed to be exploited through prostitution and pornography;

— at any given time over 300,000 child soldiers, some as young as eight, are exploited in armed conflicts in over 30 countries. More than 2 million children are estimated to have died as a direct result of armed conflicts during the 1990s;

— an estimated 100 million to 130 million women and girls alive today have undergone some form of genital mutilation/cutting;

— 40 million children below the age of 15 suffer from abuse and neglect, and require health and social care.

Building a Protective Environment for Children

Children are entitled to grow up in an environment that protects them. UNICEF identifies and responds to eight key aspects of a protective environment:

— *attitudes, traditions, customs, behaviour and practices*: In societies where attitudes or traditions facilitate abuse – for example, regarding sex with minors, the appropriateness of severe corporal punishment, the application of harmful traditional practices or differences in the perceived status and value of boys and girls – the environment will not be protective. In societies where all forms of violence against children are taboo, and where the rights of children are broadly respected by custom and tradition, children are more likely to be protected;

— *governmental commitment to fulfilling protection rights*: Government interest in,recognition of and commitment to child protection is an essential element for a protective environment;

— *open discussion of, and engagement, with child protection issues*: At the most immediate level, children need to be free to speak up about child protection concerns affecting them or other children. At the national level, both media attention and civil society engagement with the issue contribute to child protection. Partnerships among actors at all levels are essential for an effective and coordinated response;

— *legislation and enforcement*: An adequate legislative framework, its consistent implementation, accountability and a lack of impunity are essential elements of a protective environment;

— *capacity*: Health workers, teachers, police, social workers and many others who deal with children need to be equipped with the skills, knowledge, authority and motivation to identify and respond to child protection problems. The capacity of families and communities to protect their children is also essential. There are other broader types of capacity that relate to the protective environment, including the provision of education and safe areas for play;

— *children's life skills, knowledge and participation:* If children are unaware of their right not to be abused, or are not warned of the dangers of, for example, trafficking, they are more vulnerable to abuse. Children need information and knowledge to be equipped to protect themselves. Children also need to be provided with safe and protective channels for participation and self-expression;

— *monitoring and reporting:* A protective environment for children requires an effective monitoring system that records the incidence and nature of child protection abuses and allows for informed and strategic responses. Such systems can be more effective when they are participatory and locally based;

— *services for recovery and reintegration*: Child victims of any form of neglect, exploitation or abuse are entitled to care and non-discriminatory access to basic social services. These services must be provided in an environment that fosters the health, self-respect and dignity of the child.

Some elements of the protective environment will overlap. For example, governmental commitment may dictate whether services for victims of abuse are provided, or whether investment is made in monitoring mechanisms. Similarly, media attention can be a key factor in influencing attitudes.

UNICEF's Approach

In its work with partners, UNICEF seeks to strengthen the web of elements that make up a protective environment for the child. Prevention is the priority and we also support and advocate for mitigating the effects of abuse.

To achieve this, UNICEF employs a number of child protection strategies, including:

- national advocacy and initiating dialogue at all levels – from government to communities, families and children themselves;
- international advocacy, including the use of international human rights mechanisms;
- seeking societal behaviour change, challenging attitudes and traditions that can underpin child protection abuses and supporting those that are protective;
- strengthening capacity to assess and analyse protection issues;
- using law-based approaches, recognizing that legal standards are particularly important to child protection and that they need to be known, understood, accepted and enforced;
- working for and prioritizing child protection in and after conflict and instability;
- working with communities for child protection;
- ensuring access to services for recovery and reintegration for children who have suffered child protection abuses;
- promoting child participation and strengthening children's own resilience.

UNICEF seeks to mainstream protection throughout all its work. For example:

- in education, UNICEF promotes safe schools and discourages the use of corporal punishment;
- in its integrated approach to early childhood, UNICEF discourages violent forms of discipline and promotes early birth registration;
- in its work on HIV/AIDS, UNICEF tackles the stigma that is often attached to children affected by HIV/AIDS, and provides protection for vulnerable children who have been orphaned as a result of AIDS.

UNICEF in Action

In Angola, UNICEF has worked with NGOs to demobilize children through a programme for the reintegration of underage soldiers. Children returning from war received assistance to trace their relatives, and were transferred back to their home villages to be reunited. The programme also identified appropriate school and job training opportunities. Work in the communities was conducted by *catequistas*, trained local church members who provided psychosocial assistance. The group drew upon traditional beliefs and practices to aid local communities to accept former child soldiers and to facilitate their reintegration. UNICEF continues to be involved in current efforts to demobilize child soldiers and reunite them with their families.

In Bangladesh, UNICEF supported a major communications campaign on child rights addressing a number of protection issues including domestic child labour and violence against children. This involved a focused media campaign with television, radio and print media inputs, linked with NGO interventions in these areas.

In East Asia, UNICEF supports projects aimed at increasing the status of and opportunities for women and adolescent girls, while ensuring their protection. Activities include forums for the exchange of materials and information-sharing through street drama, songs and other community-based approaches. Materials warn of the dangers of travelling abroad for employment and provide additional information on HIV/AIDS and other sexually transmitted infections. Projects also provide skills training for communitybased support groups, non-formal education programmes and cross-border initiatives.

In Indonesia, UNICEF facilitated a consultative process and provided technical support for the drafting of new and comprehensive legislation on children's issues. The new legislation was adopted by the Indonesian parliament in 2002.

In Romania, UNICEF has sought to prevent child abandonment through a project in eight maternity hospitals. It provided counselling and material support for 765 pregnant women and mothers in difficult circumstances in order to encourage them to keep their babies. Support for foster families and family-like homes has prevented some children from being institutionalized.

In Timor-Leste, UNICEF and its partners support NGO initiatives in psychosocial support and counselling, with a special focus on victims of violence and/or sexual abuse. A shelter for sexually abused women is also being established. UNICEF also supported a review of laws relating to juvenile justice and conducted training of police officers, judges and public defenders on relevant international standards. This led to a series of legal revisions.

In Thailand, UNICEF supported the Office of the National Commission on Women's Affairs in organizing a 'Youth Camp for Ending Violence against Children and Women'. The aim is to build up youth networks and strengthen the capacity of local agencies to provide protection against domestic violence to children and women. After the training, participants were appointed as youth volunteers to monitor violence against children, youth and women in their communities.

Internationally, UNICEF is the lead agency for the realization of the goals and targets of 'A World Fit for Children', the outcome document of the United Nations General Assembly Special Session on Children, held in New York in May 2002. This includes key provisions relating to child protection in all areas.

Partnerships

UNICEF's protection work begins with partnerships. UNICEF's partners include governments, NGOs, other UN agencies, religious organizations, professional associations, children and youth, and the media. One important partner is the United Nations Committee on the Rights of the Child, which regularly highlights the importance of child protection and provides detailed recommendations and guidance to governments on how to effectively protect children.

References

Arnold, Fred, Kishor, Sunita, & Roy, T. K. (2002). "Sex-Selective Abortions in India". *Population and Development Review* 28 (4): 759–785.

Milner, Larry S. (2000). *Hardness of Heart / Hardness of Life: The Stain of Human Infanticide*. Lanham/New York/Oxford: University Press of America.

Radbill, Samuel X. (1974). "A history of child abuse and infanticide". In Steinmetz, Suzanne K. and Murray A. Straus.*Violence in the Family*. NY: Dodd, Mead & Co.. pp. 173–179..

Williamson, Laila (1978). "Infanticide: an anthropological analysis". In Kohl, Marvin. *Infanticide and the Value of Life*. NY:Prometheus Books. pp. 61–75..

10

Convention on the Rights of the Child

The United Nations Convention on the Rights of the Child (commonly abbreviated as the CRC, CROC, or UNCRC) is a human rights treaty setting out the civil, political, economic, social, health and cultural rights of children. The Convention defines a child as any human being under the age of eighteen, unless the age of majority is attained earlier under a state's own domestic legislation.

Nations that ratify this convention are bound to it by international law. Compliance is monitored by the UN Committee on the Rights of the Child, which is composed of members from countries around the world. Once a year, the Committee submits a report to the Third Committee of the United Nations General Assembly, which also hears a statement from the CRC Chair, and the Assembly adopts a Resolution on the Rights of the Child.

Governments of countries that have ratified the Convention are required to report to, and appear before, the United Nations Committee on the Rights of the Child periodically to be examined on their progress with regards to the advancement of the implementation of the Convention and the status of child rights in their country. Their reports and the committee's written views and concerns are available on the committee's website.

The UN General Assembly adopted the Convention and opened it for signature on 20 November 1989 (the 30th anniversary of its Declaration of the Rights of the Child). It came into force on 2 September 1990, after it was ratified by the required number of nations. Currently, 193 countries are party to it, including every member of the United Nations except Somalia, South Sudan and the United States. Somalia's cabinet ministers had announced plans in late 2009 to ratify the treaty.

Two optional protocols were adopted on 25 May 2000. The First Optional Protocol restricts the involvement of children in military conflicts, and the Second Optional Protocol prohibits the sale of children, child prostitution and child pornography. Both protocols have been ratified by more than 140 states.

The Convention deals with the child-specific needs and rights. It requires that states act in the best interests of the child. This approach is different from the common law approach found in many countries that had previously treated children as possessions or chattels, ownership of which was sometimes argued over in family disputes.

In many jurisdictions, properly implementing the Convention requires an overhaul of child custody and guardianship laws, or, at the very least, a creative approach within the existing laws. The Convention acknowledges that every child has certain basic rights, including the right to life, his or her own name and identity, to be raised by his or her parents within a family or cultural grouping, and to have a relationship with both parents, even if they are separated.

The Convention obliges states to allow parents to exercise their parental responsibilities. The Convention also acknowledges that children have the right to express their opinions and to have those opinions heard and acted upon when appropriate, to be protected from abuse or exploitation, and to have their privacy protected, and it requires that their lives not be subject to excessive interference.

The Convention also obliges signatory states to provide separate legal representation for a child in any judicial dispute concerning their care and asks that the child's viewpoint be heard in such cases. The Convention forbids capital punishment for children.

In its General Comment 8 (2006) the Committee on the Rights of the Child stated that there was an "obligation of all States parties to move quickly to prohibit and eliminate all corporal punishment and all other cruel or degrading forms of punishment of children". Article 19 of the Convention states that State Parties must "take all appropriate legislative, administrative, social and educational measures to protect the child from all forms of physical or mental violence", but it makes no reference to corporal punishment, and the Committee's interpretation on this point has been explicitly rejected by several States Party to the Convention, including Australia, Canada and the United Kingdom.

As of November 2009, 193 countries have ratified, accepted, or acceded to it (some with stated reservations or interpretations) including every member of the United Nations except Somalia and the United States, as well as the new nation of South Sudan. Somalia had announced in late 2009 that it would eventually do so.

Two optional protocols were adopted by the UN General Assembly on 25 May 2000. The first, the Optional Protocol on the Involvement of Children in Armed Conflict, requires governments to ensure that children under the age of eighteen are not recruited compulsorily into their armed forces, and calls on governments to do everything feasible to ensure that members of their armed forces who are under eighteen years of age do not take part in hostilities. This protocol entered into force on 12 July 2002; currently, 150 states are party to the protocol and another 21 states have signed but not ratified it.

The second, the Optional Protocol on the Sale of Children, Child Prostitution and Child Pornography, requires states to prohibit the sale of children, child prostitution and child pornography. It entered into force on 18 January 2002; currently, 161 states are party to the protocol and another 14 states have signed but not ratified it.

A third, the Optional Protocol to the Convention on the Rights of the Child on a Communications Procedure, which would allow children or their representatives to file individual complaints for violation of the rights of children, was adopted in December 2011 and opened for signature on 28 February 2012. The protocol currently has 35 signatures and two ratifications: it will enter into force on the tenth ratification.

The fulltext of the Convention is given below.

Preamble

The States Parties to the present Convention,

Considering that, in accordance with the principles proclaimed in the Charter of the United Nations, recognition of the inherent dignity and of the equal and inalienable rights of all members of the human family is the foundation of freedom, justice and peace in the world,

Bearing in mind that the peoples of the United Nations have, in the Charter, reaffirmed their faith in fundamental human rights and in the dignity and worth of the human person, and have determined to promote social progress and better standards of life in larger freedom,

Recognising that the United Nations has, in the Universal Declaration of Human Rights and in the International Covenants on Human Rights, proclaimed and agreed that everyone is entitled to all the rights and freedoms set forth therein, without distinction of any kind, such as race, color, sex, language, religion, political or other opinion, national or social origin, property, birth or other status,

Recalling that, in the Universal Declaration of Human Rights, the United Nations has proclaimed that childhood is entitled to special care and assistance,

Convinced that the family, as the fundamental group of society and the natural environment for the growth and well-being of all its members and particularly children, should be afforded the necessary protection and assistance so that it can fully assume its responsibilities within the community,

Recognising that the child, for the full and harmonious development of his or her personality, should grow up in a family environment, in an atmosphere of happiness, love and understanding,

Considering that the child should be fully prepared to live an individual life in society, and brought up in the spirit of the ideals proclaimed in the Charter of the United Nations, and in particular in the spirit of peace, dignity, tolerance, freedom, equality and solidarity,

Bearing in mind that the need to extend particular care to the child has been stated in the Geneva Declaration of the Rights of the Child of 1924 and in the Declaration of the Rights of the Child adopted by the General Assembly on 20 November 1959 and recognised in the Universal Declaration of Human Rights, in the International Covenant on Civil and Political Rights (in particular in articles 23 and 24), in the International Covenant on Economic, Social and Cultural Rights (in particular in article 10) and in the statutes and relevant instruments of specialised agencies and international organisations concerned with the welfare of children,

Bearing in mind that, as indicated in the Declaration of the Rights of the Child, "the child, by reason of his physical and mental immaturity, needs special safeguards and care, including appropriate legal protection, before as well as after birth",

Recalling the provisions of the Declaration on Social and Legal Principles relating to the Protection and Welfare of Children, with Special Reference to Foster Placement and Adoption Nationally and Internationally; the United Nations Standard Minimum Rules for the Administration of Juvenile Justice (The Beijing Rules) ; and the Declaration on the Protection of Women and Children in Emergency and Armed Conflict, Recognising that, in all countries in the world, there are children living in exceptionally difficult conditions, and that such children need special consideration,

Taking due account of the importance of the traditions and cultural values of each people for the protection and harmonious development of the child, Recognising the importance of international co-operation for improving the living conditions of children in every country, in particular in the developing countries,

Have agreed as follows:

Part I

Article 1

For the purposes of the present Convention, a child means every human being below the age of eighteen years unless under the law applicable to the child, majority is attained earlier.

Article 2

1. States Parties shall respect and ensure the rights set forth in the present Convention to each child within their jurisdiction without discrimination of any kind, irrespective of the child's or his or her parent's or legal guardian's race, color, sex, language, religion, political or other opinion, national, ethnic or social origin, property, disability, birth or other status.
2. States Parties shall take all appropriate measures to ensure that the child is protected against all forms of discrimination or punishment on the basis of the status, activities, expressed opinions, or beliefs of the child's parents, legal guardians, or family members.

Article 3

1. In all actions concerning children, whether undertaken by public or

private social welfare institutions, courts of law, administrative authorities or legislative bodies, the best interests of the child shall be a primary consideration.

2. States Parties undertake to ensure the child such protection and care as is necessary for his or her well-being, taking into account the rights and duties of his or her parents, legal guardians, or other individuals legally responsible for him or her, and, to this end, shall take all appropriate legislative and administrative measures.
3. States Parties shall ensure that the institutions, services and facilities responsible for the care or protection of children shall conform with the standards established by competent authorities, particularly in the areas of safety, health, in the number and suitability of their staff, as well as competent supervision.

Article 4

States Parties shall undertake all appropriate legislative, administrative, and other measures for the implementation of the rights recognised in the present Convention. With regard to economic, social and cultural rights, States Parties shall undertake such measures to the maximum extent of their available resources and, where needed, within the framework of international co-operation.

Article 5

States Parties shall respect the responsibilities, rights and duties of parents or, where applicable, the members of the extended family or community as provided for by local custom, legal guardians or other persons legally responsible for the child, to provide, in a manner consistent with the evolving capacities of the child, appropriate direction and guidance in the exercise by the child of the rights recognised in the present Convention.

Article 6

1. States Parties recognise that every child has the inherent right to life. 2. States Parties shall ensure to the maximum extent possible the survival and development of the child.

Article 7

1. The child shall be registered immediately after birth and shall have the

right from birth to a name, the right to acquire a nationality and. as far as possible, the right to know and be cared for by his or her parents.

2. States Parties shall ensure the implementation of these rights in accordance with their national law and their obligations under the relevant international instruments in this field, in particular where the child would otherwise be stateless.

Article 8

1. States Parties undertake to respect the right of the child to preserve his or her identity, including nationality, name and family relations as recognised by law without unlawful interference.
2. Where a child is illegally deprived of some or all of the elements of his or her identity, States Parties shall provide appropriate assistance and protection, with a view to re-establishing speedily his or her identity.

Article 9

1. States Parties shall ensure that a child shall not be separated from his or her parents against their will, except when competent authorities subject to judicial review determine, in accordance with applicable law and procedures, that such separation is necessary for the best interests of the child. Such determination may be necessary in a particular case such as one involving abuse or neglect of the child by the parents, or one where the parents are living separately and a decision must be made as to the child's place of residence.
2. In any proceedings pursuant to paragraph 1 of the present article, all interested parties shall be given an opportunity to participate in the proceedings and make their views known.
3. States Parties shall respect the right of the child who is separated from one or both parents to maintain personal relations and direct contact with both parents on a regular basis, except if it is contrary to the child's best interests.
4. Where such separation results from any action initiated by a State Party, such as the detention, imprisonment, exile, deportation or death (including death arising from any cause while the person is in the custody of the State) of one or both parents or of the child, that State Party shall, upon request, provide the parents, the child or, if

appropriate, another member of the family with the essential information concerning the whereabouts of the absent member(s) of the family unless the provision of the information would be detrimental to the well-being of the child. States Parties shall further ensure that the submission of such a request shall of itself entail no adverse consequences for the person(s) concerned.

Article 10

1. In accordance with the obligation of States Parties under article 9, paragraph 1, applications by a child or his or her parents to enter or leave a State Party for the purpose of family reunification shall be dealt with by States Parties in a positive, humane and expeditious manner. States Parties shall further ensure that the submission of such a request shall entail no adverse consequences for the applicants and for the members of their family.
2. A child whose parents reside in different States shall have the right to maintain on a regular basis, save in exceptional circumstances personal relations and direct contacts with both parents. Towards that end and in accordance with the obligation of States Parties under article 9, paragraph 1, States Parties shall respect the right of the child and his or her parents to leave any country, including their own, and to enter their own country. The right to leave any country shall be subject only to such restrictions as are prescribed by law and which are necessary to protect the national security, public order (ordre public), public health or morals or the rights and freedoms of others and are consistent with the other rights recognised in the present Convention.

Article 11

1. States Parties shall take measures to combat the illicit transfer and non-return of children abroad.
2. To this end, States Parties shall promote the conclusion of bilateral or multilateral agreements or accession to existing agreements.

Article 12

1. States Parties shall assure to the child who is capable of forming his or her own views the right to express those views freely in all matters affecting the child, the views of the child being given due weight in accordance with the age and maturity of the child.

2. For this purpose, the child shall in particular be provided the opportunity to be heard in any judicial and administrative proceedings affecting the child, either directly, or through a representative or an appropriate body, in a manner consistent with the procedural rules of national law.

Article 13

1. The child shall have the right to freedom of expression; this right shall include freedom to seek, receive and impart information and ideas of all kinds, regardless of frontiers, either orally, in writing or in print, in the form of art, or through any other media of the child's choice.
2. The exercise of this right may be subject to certain restrictions, but these shall only be such as are provided by law and are necessary:
   (a) For respect of the rights or reputations of others; or
   (b) For the protection of national security or of public order (ordre public), or of public health or morals.

Article 14

1. States Parties shall respect the right of the child to freedom of thought, conscience and religion.
2. States Parties shall respect the rights and duties of the parents and, when applicable, legal guardians, to provide direction to the child in the exercise of his or her right in a manner consistent with the evolving capacities of the child.
3. Freedom to manifest one's religion or beliefs may be subject only to such limitations as are prescribed by law and are necessary to protect public safety, order, health or morals, or the fundamental rights and freedoms of others.

Article 15

1. States Parties recognise the rights of the child to freedom of association and to freedom of peaceful assembly.
2. No restrictions may be placed on the exercise of these rights other than those imposed in conformity with the law and which are necessary in a democratic society in the interests of national security or public safety, public order (ordre public), the protection of public health or morals or the protection of the rights and freedoms of others.

Article 16

1. No child shall be subjected to arbitrary or unlawful interference with his or her privacy, family, home or correspondence, nor to unlawful attacks on his or her honour and reputation.
2. The child has the right to the protection of the law against such interference or attacks.

Article 17

States Parties recognise the important function performed by the mass media and shall ensure that the child has access to information and material from a diversity of national and international sources, especially those aimed at the promotion of his or her social, spiritual and moral well-being and physical and mental health.

To this end, States Parties shall:

(a) Encourage the mass media to disseminate information and material of social and cultural benefit to the child and in accordance with the spirit of article 29;

(b) Encourage international co-operation in the production, exchange and dissemination of such information and material from a diversity of cultural, national and international sources;

(c) Encourage the production and dissemination of children's books;

(d) Encourage the mass media to have particular regard to the linguistic needs of the child who belongs to a minority group or who is indigenous;

(e) Encourage the development of appropriate guidelines for the protection of the child from information and material injurious to his or her well-being, bearing in mind the provisions of articles 13 and 18.

Article 18

1. States Parties shall use their best efforts to ensure recognition of the principle that both parents have common responsibilities for the upbringing and development of the child. Parents or, as the case may be, legal guardians, have the primary responsibility for the upbringing and development of the child. The best interests of the child will be their basic concern.

2. For the purpose of guaranteeing and promoting the rights set forth in the present Convention, States Parties shall render appropriate assistance to parents and legal guardians in the performance of their child-rearing responsibilities and shall ensure the development of institutions, facilities and services for the care of children.
3. States Parties shall take all appropriate measures to ensure that children of working parents have the right to benefit from child-care services and facilities for which they are eligible.

Article 19

1. States Parties shall take all appropriate legislative, administrative, social and educational measures to protect the child from all forms of physical or mental violence, injury or abuse, neglect or negligent treatment, maltreatment or exploitation, including sexual abuse, while in the care of parent(s), legal guardian(s) or any other person who has the care of the child.
2. Such protective measures should, as appropriate, include effective procedures for the establishment of social programes to provide necessary support for the child and for those who have the care of the child, as well as for other forms of prevention and for identification, reporting, referral, investigation, treatment and follow-up of instances of child maltreatment described heretofore, and, as appropriate, for judicial involvement.

Article 20

1. A child temporarily or permanently deprived of his or her family environment, or in whose own best interests cannot be allowed to remain in that environment, shall be entitled to special protection and assistance provided by the State.
2. States Parties shall in accordance with their national laws ensure alternative care for such a child.
3. Such care could include, inter alia, foster placement, kafalah of Islamic law, adoption or if necessary placement in suitable institutions for the care of children. When considering solutions, due regard shall be paid to the desirability of continuity in a child's upbringing and to the child's ethnic, religious, cultural and linguistic background.

Article 21

States Parties that recognise and/or permit the system of adoption shall ensure that the best interests of the child shall be the paramount consideration and they shall:

(a) Ensure that the adoption of a child is authorised only by competent authorities who determine, in accordance with applicable law and procedures and on the basis of all pertinent and reliable information, that the adoption is permissible in view of the child's status concerning parents, relatives and legal guardians and that, if required, the persons concerned have given their informed consent to the adoption on the basis of such counselling as may be necessary;

(b) Recognise that inter-country adoption may be considered as an alternative means of child's care, if the child cannot be placed in a foster or an adoptive family or cannot in any suitable manner be cared for in the child's country of origin;

(c) Ensure that the child concerned by inter-country adoption enjoys safeguards and standards equivalent to those existing in the case of national adoption;

(d) Take all appropriate measures to ensure that, in inter-country adoption, the placement does not result in improper financial gain for those involved in it;

(e) Promote, where appropriate, the objectives of the present article by concluding bilateral or multilateral arrangements or agreements, and endeavour, within this framework, to ensure that the placement of the child in another country is carried out by competent authorities or organs.

Article 22

1. States Parties shall take appropriate measures to ensure that a child who is seeking refugee status or who is considered a refugee in accordance with applicable international or domestic law and procedures shall, whether unaccompanied or accompanied by his or her parents or by any other person, receive appropriate protection and humanitarian assistance in the enjoyment of applicable rights set forth in the present Convention and in other international human rights or humanitarian instruments to which the said States are Parties.

2. For this purpose, States Parties shall provide, as they consider appropriate, cooperation in any efforts by the United Nations and other competent intergovernmental organisations or non-governmental organisations cooperating with the United Nations to protect and assist such a child and to trace the parents or other members of the family of any refugee child in order to obtain information necessary for reunification with his or her family. In cases where no parents or other members of the family can be found, the child shall be accorded the same protection as any other child permanently or temporarily deprived of his or her family environment for any reason, as set forth in the present Convention.

Article 23

1. States Parties recognise that a mentally or physically disabled child should enjoy a full and decent life, in conditions which ensure dignity, promote self-reliance and facilitate the child's active participation in the community.
2. States Parties recognise the right of the disabled child to special care and shall encourage and ensure the extension, subject to available resources, to the eligible child and those responsible for his or her care, of assistance for which application is made and which is appropriate to the child's condition and to the circumstances of the parents or others caring for the child.
3. Recognising the special needs of a disabled child, assistance extended in accordance with paragraph 2 of the present article shall be provided free of charge, whenever possible, taking into account the financial resources of the parents or others caring for the child, and shall be designed to ensure that the disabled child has effective access to and receives education, training, health care services, rehabilitation services, preparation for employment and recreation opportunities in a manner conducive to the child's achieving the fullest possible social integration and individual development, including his or her cultural and spiritual development
4. States Parties shall promote, in the spirit of international cooperation, the exchange of appropriate information in the field of preventive health care and of medical, psychological and functional treatment of disabled children, including dissemination of and access to information

concerning methods of rehabilitation, education and vocational services, with the aim of enabling States Parties to improve their capabilities and skills and to widen their experience in these areas. In this regard, particular account shall be taken of the needs of developing countries.

Article 24

1. States Parties recognise the right of the child to the enjoyment of the highest attainable standard of health and to facilities for the treatment of illness and rehabilitation of health. States Parties shall strive to ensure that no child is deprived of his or her right of access to such health care services.
2. States Parties shall pursue full implementation of this right and, in particular, shall take appropriate measures:
   (a) To diminish infant and child mortality;
   (b) To ensure the provision of necessary medical assistance and health care to all children with emphasis on the development of primary health care;
   (c) To combat disease and malnutrition, including within the framework of primary health care, through, inter alia, the application of readily available technology and through the provision of adequate nutritious foods and clean drinking-water, taking into consideration the dangers and risks of environmental pollution;
   (d) To ensure appropriate prenatal and postnatal health care for mothers;
   (e) To ensure that all segments of society, in particular parents and children, are informed, have access to education and are supported in the use of basic knowledge of child health and nutrition, the advantages of breast-feeding, hygiene and environmental sanitation and the prevention of accidents;
   (f) To develop preventive health care, guidance for parents and family planning education and services.
3. States Parties shall take all effective and appropriate measures with a view to abolishing traditional practices prejudicial to the health of children.

4. States Parties undertake to promote and encourage international cooperation with a view to achieving progressively the full realisation of the right recognised in the present article. In this regard, particular account shall be taken of the needs of developing countries.

Article 25

States Parties recognise the right of a child who has been placed by the competent authorities for the purposes of care, protection or treatment of his or her physical or mental health, to a periodic review of the treatment provided to the child and all other circumstances relevant to his or her placement.

Article 26

1. States Parties shall recognise for every child the right to benefit from social security, including social insurance, and shall take the necessary measures to achieve the full realisation of this right in accordance with their national law.
2. The benefits should, where appropriate, be granted, taking into account the resources and the circumstances of the child and persons having responsibility for the maintenance of the child, as well as any other consideration relevant to an application for benefits made by or on behalf of the child.

Article 27

1. States Parties recognise the right of every child to a standard of living adequate for the child's physical, mental, spiritual, moral and social development.
2. The parent(s) or others responsible for the child have the primary responsibility to secure, within their abilities and financial capacities, the conditions of living necessary for the child's development.
3. States Parties, in accordance with national conditions and within their means, shall take appropriate measures to assist parents and others responsible for the child to implement this right and shall in case of need provide material assistance and support programes, particularly with regard to nutrition, clothing and housing.
4. States Parties shall take all appropriate measures to secure the recovery of maintenance for the child from the parents or other persons having

financial responsibility for the child, both within the State Party and from abroad. In particular, where the person having financial responsibility for the child lives in a State different from that of the child, States Parties shall promote the accession to international agreements or the conclusion of such agreements, as well as the making of other appropriate arrangements.

Article 28

1. States Parties recognise the right of the child to education, and with a view to achieving this right progressively and on the basis of equal opportunity, they shall, in particular:
   (a) Make primary education compulsory and available free to all;
   (b) Encourage the development of different forms of secondary education, including general and vocational education, make them available and accessible to every child, and take appropriate measures such as the introduction of free education and offering financial assistance in case of need;
   (c) Make higher education accessible to all on the basis of capacity by every appropriate means;
   (d) Make educational and vocational information and guidance available and accessible to all children;
   (e) Take measures to encourage regular attendance at schools and the reduction of dropout rates.
2. States Parties shall take all appropriate measures to ensure that school discipline is administered in a manner consistent with the child's human dignity and in conformity with the present Convention.
3. States Parties shall promote and encourage international cooperation in matters relating to education, in particular with a view to contributing to the elimination of ignorance and illiteracy throughout the world and facilitating access to scientific and technical knowledge and modern teaching methods. In this regard, particular account shall be taken of the needs of developing countries.

Article 29

1. States Parties agree that the education of the child shall be directed to:

(a) The development of the child's personality, talents and mental and physical abilities to their fullest potential;

(b) The development of respect for human rights and fundamental freedoms, and for the principles enshrined in the Charter of the United Nations;

(c) The development of respect for the child's parents, his or her own cultural identity, language and values, for the national values of the country in which the child is living, the country from which he or she may originate, and for civilisations different from his or her own;

(d) The preparation of the child for responsible life in a free society, in the spirit of understanding, peace, tolerance, equality of sexes, and friendship among all peoples, ethnic, national and religious groups and persons of indigenous origin;

(e) The development of respect for the natural environment.

2. No part of the present article or article 28 shall be construed so as to interfere with the liberty of individuals and bodies to establish and direct educational institutions, subject always to the observance of the principle set forth in paragraph 1 of the present article and to the requirements that the education given in such institutions shall conform to such minimum standards as may be laid down by the State.

Article 30

In those States in which ethnic, religious or linguistic minorities or persons of indigenous origin exist, a child belonging to such a minority or who is indigenous shall not be denied the right, in community with other members of his or her group, to enjoy his or her own culture, to profess and practise his or her own religion, or to use his or her own language.

Article 31

1. States Parties recognise the right of the child to rest and leisure, to engage in play and recreational activities appropriate to the age of the child and to participate freely in cultural life and the arts.

2. States Parties shall respect and promote the right of the child to participate fully in cultural and artistic life and shall encourage the provision of appropriate and equal opportunities for cultural, artistic, recreational and leisure activity.

Article 32

1. States Parties recognise the right of the child to be protected from economic exploitation and from performing any work that is likely to be hasardous or to interfere with the child's education, or to be harmful to the child's health or physical, mental, spiritual, moral or social development.
2. States Parties shall take legislative, administrative, social and educational measures to ensure the implementation of the present article. To this end, and having regard to the relevant provisions of other international instruments, States Parties shall in particular:
   (a) Provide for a minimum age or minimum ages for admission to employment;
   (b) Provide for appropriate regulation of the hours and conditions of employment;
   (c) Provide for appropriate penalties or other sanctions to ensure the effective enforcement of the present article.

Article 33

States Parties shall take all appropriate measures, including legislative, administrative, social and educational measures, to protect children from the illicit use of narcotic drugs and psychotropic substances as defined in the relevant international treaties, and to prevent the use of children in the illicit production and trafficking of such substances.

Article 34

States Parties undertake to protect the child from all forms of sexual exploitation and sexual abuse. For these purposes, States Parties shall in particular take all appropriate national, bilateral and multilateral measures to prevent:

(a) The inducement or coercion of a child to engage in any unlawful sexual activity;

(b) The exploitative use of children in prostitution or other unlawful sexual practices;

(c) The exploitative use of children in pornographic performances and materials.

Article 35

States Parties shall take all appropriate national, bilateral and multilateral measures to prevent the abduction of, the sale of or traffic in children for any purpose or in any form.

Article 36

States Parties shall protect the child against all other forms of exploitation prejudicial to any aspects of the child's welfare.

Article 37

States Parties shall ensure that:

(a) No child shall be subjected to torture or other cruel, inhuman or degrading treatment or punishment. Neither capital punishment nor life imprisonment without possibility of release shall be imposed for offences committed by persons below eighteen years of age;

(b) No child shall be deprived of his or her liberty unlawfully or arbitrarily. The arrest, detention or imprisonment of a child shall be in conformity with the law and shall be used only as a measure of last resort and for the shortest appropriate period of time;

(c) Every child deprived of liberty shall be treated with humanity and respect for the inherent dignity of the human person, and in a manner which takes into account the needs of persons of his or her age. In particular, every child deprived of liberty shall be separated from adults unless it is considered in the child's best interest not to do so and shall have the right to maintain contact with his or her family through correspondence and visits, save in exceptional circumstances;

(d) Every child deprived of his or her liberty shall have the right to prompt access to legal and other appropriate assistance, as well as the right to challenge the legality of the deprivation of his or her liberty before a court or other competent, independent and impartial authority, and to a prompt decision on any such action.

Article 38

1. States Parties undertake to respect and to ensure respect for rules of international humanitarian law applicable to them in armed conflicts which are relevant to the child.

2. States Parties shall take all feasible measures to ensure that persons who have not attained the age of fifteen years do not take a direct part in hostilities.
3. States Parties shall refrain from recruiting any person who has not attained the age of fifteen years into their armed forces. In recruiting among those persons who have attained the age of fifteen years but who have not attained the age of eighteen years, States Parties shall endeavour to give priority to those who are oldest.
4. In accordance with their obligations under international humanitarian law to protect the civilian population in armed conflicts, States Parties shall take all feasible measures to ensure protection and care of children who are affected by an armed conflict.

Article 39

States Parties shall take all appropriate measures to promote physical and psychological recovery and social reintegration of a child victim of: any form of neglect, exploitation, or abuse; torture or any other form of cruel, inhuman or degrading treatment or punishment; or armed conflicts. Such recovery and reintegration shall take place in an environment which fosters the health, self-respect and dignity of the child.

Article 40

1. States Parties recognise the right of every child alleged as, accused of, or recognised as having infringed the penal law to be treated in a manner consistent with the promotion of the child's sense of dignity and worth, which reinforces the child's respect for the human rights and fundamental freedoms of others and which takes into account the child's age and the desirability of promoting the child's reintegration and the child's assuming a constructive role in society.
2. To this end, and having regard to the relevant provisions of international instruments, States Parties shall, in particular, ensure that:
   (a) No child shall be alleged as, be accused of, or recognised as having infringed the penal law by reason of acts or omissions that were not prohibited by national or international law at the time they were committed;
   (b) Every child alleged as or accused of having infringed the penal law has at least the following guarantees:

(i) To be presumed innocent until proven guilty according to law;

(ii) To be informed promptly and directly of the charges against him or her, and, if appropriate, through his or her parents or legal guardians, and to have legal or other appropriate assistance in the preparation and presentation of his or her defence;

(iii) To have the matter determined without delay by a competent, independent and impartial authority or judicial body in a fair hearing according to law, in the presence of legal or other appropriate assistance and, unless it is considered not to be in the best interest of the child, in particular, taking into account his or her age or situation, his or her parents or legal guardians;

(iv) Not to be compelled to give testimony or to confess guilt; to examine or have examined adverse witnesses and to obtain the participation and examination of witnesses on his or her behalf under conditions of equality;

(v) If considered to have infringed the penal law, to have this decision and any measures imposed in consequence thereof reviewed by a higher competent, independent and impartial authority or judicial body according to law;

(vi) To have the free assistance of an interpreter if the child cannot understand or speak the language used;

(vii) To have his or her privacy fully respected at all stages of the proceedings.

3. States Parties shall seek to promote the establishment of laws, procedures, authorities and institutions specifically applicable to children alleged as, accused of, or recognised as having infringed the penal law, and, in particular:

(a) The establishment of a minimum age below which children shall be presumed not to have the capacity to infringe the penal law;

(b) Whenever appropriate and desirable, measures for dealing with such children without resorting to judicial proceedings, providing that human rights and legal safeguards are fully respected. 4. A variety of dispositions, such as care, guidance and supervision orders; counselling; probation; foster care; education and vocational training programes and other alternatives to institutional care shall be available to ensure that children are dealt with in a manner appropriate to their well-being and proportionate both to their circumstances and the offence.

Article 41

Nothing in the present Convention shall affect any provisions which are more conducive to the realisation of the rights of the child and which may be contained in:

(a) The law of a State party; or

(b) International law in force for that State.

Part II

Article 42

States Parties undertake to make the principles and provisions of the Convention widely known, by appropriate and active means, to adults and children alike.

Article 43

1. For the purpose of examining the progress made by States Parties in achieving the realisation of the obligations undertaken in the present Convention, there shall be established a Committee on the Rights of the Child, which shall carry out the functions hereinafter provided.
2. The Committee shall consist of ten experts of high moral standing and recognised competence in the field covered by this Convention. The members of the Committee shall be elected by States Parties from among their nationals and shall serve in their personal capacity, consideration being given to equitable geographical distribution, as well as to the principal legal systems.
3. The members of the Committee shall be elected by secret ballot from a list of persons nominated by States Parties. Each State Party may nominate one person from among its own nationals.
4. The initial election to the Committee shall be held no later than six months after the date of the entry into force of the present Convention and thereafter every second year. At least four months before the date

of each election, the Secretary-General of the United Nations shall address a letter to States Parties inviting them to submit their nominations within two months. The Secretary-General shall subsequently prepare a list in alphabetical order of all persons thus nominated, indicating States Parties which have nominated them, and shall submit it to the States Parties to the present Convention.

5. The elections shall be held at meetings of States Parties convened by the Secretary-General at United Nations Headquarters. At those meetings, for which two thirds of States Parties shall constitute a quorum, the persons elected to the Committee shall be those who obtain the largest number of votes and an absolute majority of the votes of the representatives of States Parties present and voting.

6. The members of the Committee shall be elected for a term of four years. They shall be eligible for re-election if renominated. The term of five of the members elected at the first election shall expire at the end of two years; immediately after the first election, the names of these five members shall be chosen by lot by the Chairman of the meeting.

7. If a member of the Committee dies or resigns or declares that for any other cause he or she can no longer perform the duties of the Committee, the State Party which nominated the member shall appoint another expert from among its nationals to serve for the remainder of the term, subject to the approval of the Committee.

8. The Committee shall establish its own rules of procedure.

9. The Committee shall elect its officers for a period of two years.

10. The meetings of the Committee shall normally be held at United Nations Headquarters or at any other convenient place as determined by the Committee. The Committee shall normally meet annually. The duration of the meetings of the Committee shall be determined, and reviewed, if necessary, by a meeting of the States Parties to the present Convention, subject to the approval of the General Assembly.

11. The Secretary-General of the United Nations shall provide the necessary staff and facilities for the effective performance of the functions of the Committee under the present Convention.

12. With the approval of the General Assembly, the members of the Committee established under the present Convention shall receive

emoluments from United Nations resources on such terms and conditions as the Assembly may decide.

Article 44

1. States Parties undertake to submit to the Committee, through the Secretary-General of the United Nations, reports on the measures they have adopted which give effect to the rights recognised herein and on the progress made on the enjoyment of those rights
   (a) Within two years of the entry into force of the Convention for the State Party concerned;
   (b) Thereafter every five years.
2. Reports made under the present article shall indicate factors and difficulties, if any, affecting the degree of fulfilment of the obligations under the present Convention. Reports shall also contain sufficient information to provide the Committee with a comprehensive understanding of the implementation of the Convention in the country concerned.
3. A State Party which has submitted a comprehensive initial report to the Committee need not, in its subsequent reports submitted in accordance with paragraph 1 (b) of the present article, repeat basic information previously provided.
4. The Committee may request from States Parties further information relevant to the implementation of the Convention.
5. The Committee shall submit to the General Assembly, through the Economic and Social Council, every two years, reports on its activities.
6. States Parties shall make their reports widely available to the public in their own countries.

Article 45

In order to foster the effective implementation of the Convention and to encourage international cooperation in the field covered by the Convention:

(a) The specialised agencies, the United Nations Children's Fund, and other United Nations organs shall be entitled to be represented at the consideration of the implementation of such provisions of the present Convention as fall within the scope of their mandate. The Committee may invite the specialised agencies, the United Nations Children's Fund and other competent bodies as it may consider appropriate to provide expert advice on the implementation of the Convention in areas falling within the scope of their respective mandates. The Committee may invite the specialised agencies, the United Nations Children's Fund, and other United Nations organs to submit reports on the implementation of the Convention in areas falling within the scope of their activities;

(b) The Committee shall transmit, as it may consider appropriate, to the specialised agencies, the United Nations Children's Fund and other competent bodies, any reports from States Parties that contain a request, or indicate a need, for technical advice or assistance, along with the Committee's observations and suggestions, if any, on these requests or indications;

(c) The Committee may recommend to the General Assembly to request the Secretary-General to undertake on its behalf studies on specific issues relating to the rights of the child;

(d) The Committee may make suggestions and general recommendations based on information received pursuant to articles 44 and 45 of the present Convention. Such suggestions and general recommendations shall be transmitted to any State Party concerned and reported to the General Assembly, together with comments, if any, from States Parties.

Part III

Article 46

The present Convention shall be open for signature by all States.

Article 47

The present Convention is subject to ratification. Instruments of ratification shall be deposited with the Secretary-General of the United Nations.

Article 48

The present Convention shall remain open for accession by any State. The instruments of accession shall be deposited with the Secretary-General of the United Nations.

Article 49

1. The present Convention shall enter into force on the thirtieth day following the date of deposit with the Secretary-General of the United Nations of the twentieth instrument of ratification or accession.
2. For each State ratifying or acceding to the Convention after the deposit of the twentieth instrument of ratification or accession, the Convention shall enter into force on the thirtieth day after the deposit by such State of its instrument of ratification or accession.

Article 50

1. Any State Party may propose an amendment and file it with the Secretary-General of the United Nations. The Secretary-General shall thereupon communicate the proposed amendment to States Parties, with a request that they indicate whether they favor a conference of States Parties for the purpose of considering and voting upon the proposals. In the event that, within four months from the date of such communication, at least one third of the States Parties favor such a conference, the Secretary-General shall convene the conference under the auspices of the United Nations. Any amendment adopted by a majority of States Parties present and voting at the conference shall be submitted to the General Assembly for approval.
2. An amendment adopted in accordance with paragraph 1 of the present article shall enter into force when it has been approved by the General Assembly of the United Nations and accepted by a two-thirds majority of States Parties.
3. When an amendment enters into force, it shall be binding on those States Parties which have accepted it, other States Parties still being bound by the provisions of the present Convention and any earlier amendments which they have accepted.

Article 51

1. The Secretary-General of the United Nations shall receive and circulate to all States the text of reservations made by States at the time of ratification or accession.
2. A reservation incompatible with the object and purpose of the present Convention shall not be permitted.

3. Reservations may be withdrawn at any time by notification to that effect addressed to the Secretary-General of the United Nations, who shall then inform all States. Such notification shall take effect on the date on which it is received by the Secretary-General

Article 52

A State Party may denounce the present Convention by written notification to the Secretary-General of the United Nations. Denunciation becomes effective one year after the date of receipt of the notification by the Secretary-General.

Article 53

The Secretary-General of the United Nations is designated as the depositary of the present Convention.

Article 54

The original of the present Convention, of which the Arabic, Chinese, English, French, Russian and Spanish texts are equally authentic, shall be deposited with the Secretary-General of the United Nations. IN WITNESS THEREOF the undersigned plenipotentiaries, being duly authorised thereto by their respective governments, have signed the present Convention.

Bibliography

Adair Dyer. "The Internationalization of Family Law". US Davis Law Review. Retrieved 2010-08-08.

Ahearn, D., Holzer, B. with Andrews, L. (2000) *Children's Rights Law: A Career Guide*. Harvard Law School. Retrieved 2/23/08.

Arnold, Fred, Kishor, Sunita, & Roy, T. K. (2002). "Sex-Selective Abortions in India". *Population and Development Review* 28 (4): 759–785.

Arts, K, Popvoski, V, *et al.* (2006) *International Criminal Accountability and the Rights of Children*. "From Peace to Justice Series". London: Cambridge University Press.

Baland, Jean-Marie and James A. Robinson (2000) 'Is child labour inefficient?' *Journal of Political Economy* 108, 663–679

Bales, Kevin (1999). *Disposable People: New Slavery in the Global Economy*. Berkeley, CA: University of California Press

Bandman, B. (1999) *Children's Right to Freedom, Care, and Enlightenment.* Routledge. p 67.

Beiter, Klaus Dieter (2005). *The Protection of the Right to Education by International Law*. Martinus Nijhoff Publishers. pp. 226–227.

Bhukuth, Augendra. "Defining child labour: a controversial debate" *Development in Practice* (2008) 18, 385–394

Brennan, S. and Noggle, R. (1997) "The Moral Status of Children: Children's Rights, Parent's Rights, and Family Justice," *Social Theory and Practice. 23.*

Calkins, C.F. (1972) "Reviewed Work: Children's Rights: Toward the Liberation of the Child by Paul Adams", *Peabody Journal of Education. 49*(4). p. 327.

Cherneva, Iveta. "Human Trafficking For Begging." Buffalo Human Rights Law Review 17 (2011): 25. LexisNexis Academic: Law Reviews.

Christiaan Grootaert and Harry Anthony Patrinos (1999). *The Policy Analysis of Child Labour: A Comparative Study.* Palgrave Macmillan

Covell, K. and Howe, R.B. (2001) *The Challenge of Children's Rights for Canada.* Wilfrid Laurier University Press. p 158.

Crosson-Tower, C. (2008). *Understanding Child Abuse and Neglect*. Boston, MA: Pearson Education.

Cutting, E. (1999) "Giving Parents a Voice: A Children's Rights Issue,"*Rightlines. 2* ERIC #ED428855.

D'Onofrio, Eve (2005), "Child Brides, Inegalitarianism, and the Fundamentalist Polygamous Family in the United States",*International Journal of Law, Policy and the Family* 19 (3): 373–394

Ernie Allen. "The kid is with a parent, how bad can it be?" The Crisis of Family Abductions. National Center for Missing and Exploited Children. Retrieved 2012-05-11.

Finkelhor, D. (19 February 2008). *Childhood Victimization: Violence, Crime, and Abuse in the Lives of Young People*. Oxford University Press. p. 244.

Franklin, B. (2001) *The new handbook of children's rights: comparative policy and practice.* Routledge. p 19.

Freeman, M. (2000) "The Future of Children's Rights," *Children & Society. 14*(4) p 277-93.

Goswami, Ruchira, 2010, "Child Marriage in India: Mapping the Trajectory of Legal Reform" http://sanhati.com/excerpted/2207/

"Hague Abduction Convention text". Hcch.net. Retrieved 2010-04-20.

Hoyano, L.; Keenan C. (2007). *Child Abuse: Law and Policy Across Boundaries*. Oxford University Press.

Humbert, Franziska. *The Challenge of Child Labour in International Law* (2009)

Humphries, Jane. *Childhood and Child Labour in the British Industrial Revolution* (2010)

I.L.O.. *Commercial Sexual Exploitation of Children and Adolescents: The I.L.O.'s Response*. Retrieved March 12, 2012.

Korbin, Jill E. (1983). *Child abuse and neglect: cross-cultural perspectives*. Berkeley, CA: University of California Press.

Lansdown, G. "Children's welfare and children's rights," in Hendrick, H. (2005) *Child Welfare And Social Policy: An Essential Reader.* The Policy Press. p. 117

Leto, Marisa (2000-04-01). "Whose best interest? International child abduction under the Hague Convention". Chicago Journal of International Law. Retrieved 2010-09-24.

Mario Biggeri and Santosh Mehrotra (2007). *Asian Informal Workers: Global Risks, Local Protection.* Routledge

Merle H. Weiner (2000). "International Child Abduction and the Escape from Domestic Violence". Fordham Law Review. Retrieved 2010-08-21.

Milner, Larry S. (2000). *Hardness of Heart / Hardness of Life: The Stain of Human Infanticide*. Lanham/New York/Oxford: University Press of America.

Nour, Nawal M. (2006), "Health Consequences of Child Marriage in Africa", *Emerging Infectious Diseases* 12(11): 1644–1649

Parental Child Abduction is Child Abuse. Nancy Faulkner, Ph.D. Presented to the United Nations Convention on Child Rights in Special Session, June 9, 1999

Raj, Anita, Niranjan Saggurti, Donta Balaiah, Jay G. Silverman, 2010, "Prevalence of Child Marriage and its Impact on the Fertility and Fertility Control Behaviors of Young Women in India" http://www.ncbi.nlm.nih.gov/pmc/articles/PMC2759702.

Radbill, Samuel X. (1974). "A history of child abuse and infanticide". In Steinmetz, Suzanne K. and Murray A. Straus.*Violence in the Family*. NY: Dodd, Mead & Co.. pp. 173–179.

"Right to education – What is it? Education and the 4 As". Right to Education project. Retrieved 2009-02-21.

Rodham, H. (1973). "Children Under the Law". Harvard Educational Review 43: 487–514.

Starr, RH (1975) *Children's Rights: Countering the Opposition.* Paper presented at the 83rd Annual Meeting of the American Psychological Association in Chicago, Illinois, Aug. 30-Sept.

Turton, Jackie (2008). *Child Abuse, Gender, and Society*. New York: Routledge. p. 161.

UNICEF, "Early marriage: A childhood interrupted" http://www.unicef.org/india/child_protection_1536.htm

United Nations (2000). *U.N. Protocol to Prevent, Suppress and Punish Trafficking in Persons, especially Women and Children.* Retrieved February 9, 2012.

Wheaton, Elizabeth M.; Edward J. Schauer, Thomas V. Galli (2010). "Economics of Human Trafficking". *International Migration* 48 (4). Retrieved April 12, 2012.

William M. Hilton (1997). "The Limitations on Art. 13(b) of The Convention on the Civil Aspects of International Child Abduction done at the Hague on 25 Oct 1980". Retrieved 2009-06-12.

Williamson, Laila (1978). "Infanticide: an anthropological analysis". In Kohl, Marvin. *Infanticide and the Value of Life.* NY:Prometheus Books. pp. 61–75..